JUNG AN

NATIVE AMERICAN MOON CYCLES

JUNG AND THE NATIVE AMERICAN MOON CYCLES

rhythms of influence

MICHAEL OWEN

NICOLAS-HAYS, INC.
Berwick, ME

First published in 2002 by
Nicolas-Hays, Inc.
P. O. Box 1126
Berwick, ME 03901-1126

Distributed to the trade by
Red Wheel/Weiser, LLC
P. O. Box 612
York Beach, ME 03910-0612
With offices at 368 Congress St., Boston, MA 02210
www.redwheelweiser.com

Library of Congress Cataloging-in-Publication Data
Owen, Michael.
Jung and the Native American moon cycles : rhythms of influence /Michael Owen
p. cm.
Includes bibliographical references and index.
ISBN 0-89254-059-1 (pbk.: alk. paper)
1. Jung, C. G. (Carl Gustav), 1875-1961. 2. Psychoanalysts—Switzerland—Biography.
3. Indians of North America—Region. I. Title.
BF109.J8 094 2002
150.19'54'092--dc21   20020338067

BJ
Cover and text design by Kathryn Sky-Peck
Typeset in 11/15 Berkeley

PRINTED IN THE UNITED STATES OF AMERICA
09 08 07 06 05 04 03 02
8   7   6   5   4   3   2   1

The paper used in this publication meets the minimum requirements of the
American National Standard for Information Sciences—Permanence of Paper for
Printed Library Materials Z39.48–1992 (R1997).

CONTENTS

BIG WEST MOON —
DEATH AND CHANGE, 77

ACKNOWLEDGMENTS

To the Grandmothers and Grandfather, the Sweet Dream Teachers, for finding a way between the worlds. To Harley Regan for his generous teaching many moons ago. To Lynley Hall for her way with the dream. To Therese McLachlan for her way with the animals. To Tui for its humor and way with the humans. To all these and many more, my heartfelt thanks.

This body of knowledge and tradition is Held and Kept by the inter-tribal Twisted Hair Medicine Society Council of Elders. They Keep and Hold this inter-tribal knowledge of the teachings and ceremonies of Turtle Island, and together with all First Nations of Turtle Island, they Keep and Hold the Heart Knowledge of Grandmother Earth. To them I offer my deep gratitude.

ABBREVIATIONS

CW *The Collected Works of C. G. Jung*, edited by Gerhard Adler, Michael Fordham, Herbert Read, and William McGuire, translated by R. F. C. Hull (Princeton: Princeton University Press, 1953-1978). Citations give volume and paragraph number.

Letters *C. G. Jung: Letters*, 2 vols., edited by Gerhard Adler and Aniela Jaffé (Princeton: Princeton University Press, 1973-1976). Citations give volume and page number.

MDR *Memories, Dreams, Reflections* by C. G. Jung, edited by Aniela Jaffé (New York: Vintage, 1989).

INTRODUCTION

*The Dreamer is the person responsible for the continued
existence of the People as a psychic (that is, tribal) entity.*
—PAULA GUNN ALLEN, *The Sacred Hoop*, p. 204

*The earliest origins of modern psychotherapy known to history lie in
archaic shamanism and in the practices of the medicine men of
primitive peoples . . . the figure of the shaman is characterized by
individual experience of the work of spirits
(which today we call the unconscious).*
—MARIE-LOUISE VON FRANZ, *C. G. Jung: His Myth in Our Time*, p. 99

INTRODU(TION

This is not a book on astrology nor is it a biography. It explores the relationship between the Moon Cycles, a Native American teaching, and the life of Carl Gustav Jung. The profound psychological insights of Jung and the equally profound medicine teachings of the Peoples of Turtle Island (North, South, and Central America) have a common root below ground. Indigenous traditions are the complementary, objective twin to the subjectivity of analytical psychology; both honor the worlds of matter and spirit, one extroverted, the other introverted. Both point to the same phenomena and each supplies what the other lacks.

Carl Jung lived several lives. He lived the life of dates, times, and places that were observed and shared by others; he lived the inner, symbolic life that was timeless and his alone to observe; he lived the life that he has written about; and he lived the life that others have written about. Each has its own reality. With that in mind, I have relied primarily on biographies written by those who knew Jung (Marie-Louise von Franz, Barbara Hannah, and Laurens van der Post) in order to remain true to Jung's individuality and his uniqueness. Many of the biographies by those who did not know him (for example, Paul Stern, Vincent Brome, Colin Wilson, Frank McLynn, and Richard Noll), although purporting to be more "objective," are disquieting in their emotional subjectivity.[1] But I have drawn from these biographies in their strength, which is the specifics of dates and places that Jung himself didn't care to record.

We can look at Jung's life in two ways. One is to view it as fact and reality: this happened and that happened. The other is to view it as a dream—dreamed by the Self—and in this regard we shall take Jung's autobiography, *Memories, Dreams, Reflections,* on its own terms, like a dream. Although there has been debate as to how much *Memories* is biography or autobiography, the debate itself probably reflects Jung's rightful ambivalence toward the pitfalls of autobiography.[2] We shall assume, however, that the unconscious, in some way, had a hand in its writing.

Jung lived the symbolic life and much of this he did not write about. In using the tincture of the Moon Cycles to "stain" the sections of Jung's life, perhaps we can reveal some of the hidden Patterns. To do this requires that we hold the tension between the dates and places in the outer world, and the imagination of the inner world that he so richly mapped. It also requires us to hold the center point between the demands of thinking, feeling, sensation, and intuition. None of these can have their requirements completely fulfilled. The approximation of dates and a symbolic attitude may trouble some readers' sensation and thinking functions, and the use of dates and literal events may slight the intuitive and feeling functions of others. The Moon Cycles, however, are a reflection of how the unconscious contains all the opposites, particularly in its relationship to time. On the one hand, the unconscious is timeless; dates, times, and places that are the stuff of daily life are irrelevant to it. On the other hand, it has an uncanny precision in its memory of anniversaries, emotionally significant events, and births and deaths (both symbolic and actual).

The Greek word *rhythmos* means recurring motion. The Moon Cycles teach us how the archetypal influences of the Medicine Wheel and the rhythms of birth and death affect us at different times in our lives. They are a four-dimensional Pattern that, of necessity, has been flattened into the two dimensions of words and diagrams. But like a dream they need to be seen, felt, thought of, and intuited by all the functions, particularly some feeling, some *sympatheia* for the rich tapestry that was Jung's life. Deprived of that, the Moon Cycles become a meaningless list of dates and events. In the final analysis, the meaning of the Moon Cycles is not in their content or application, useful or interesting though that may be, but as a reminder of the unseen, slower rhythms of our lives. We shall use them to understand Jung's life, and use Jung's life to understand the Moon Cycles. Such is the weaving.

I embarked on writing this book partly as an amplification of a dream of mine about the Moon Cycles, and partly from my professional interest in analytical psychology and my involvement over the years with indigenous peoples. Initially I had neither wished to dwell on, nor to avoid, the over-explored and controversial areas of Jung's life, particularly his relationships with women and his supposed anti-Semitism. However, I have devoted some space to these issues not from personal interest but from being led there by the Song of the Moon Cycles. Likewise, other paths opened up that I had not realized were there. As a result, the material that follows is only partly of my own choosing, the rest is where the Patterns led me.

Both Jung's writings and the language of Native traditions have a sense of the numinous that helps us establish a link with the unseen. Jung used many words in Greek or Latin that provided a connection to the unconscious and allowed a discrimination and feeling about certain matters that was not available in everyday English, so I have quoted Jung, and stayed close to his words, where appropriate in order not to intercede between Jung and the reader. The languages of the First Peoples of Turtle Island have a similar connection to spirit. Throughout this book, I have capitalized words that have a specific meaning or teaching attached to them. I hope this will provide some connection with the richness that lies beneath the language and beg the reader's indulgence for any seeming obscurity.

There is a commonality between indigenous peoples and it is tempting to look for similar elements across cultures and recombine them into a one-size-fits-all "core shamanism." In this process, however satisfying to the thinking function, we may extract the form, but we lose the particular feeling-tone and uniqueness of the tradition, as well as the connection to a specific millennia-old lineage. Knowledge is sacred and accordingly I would invite the reader to regard the teachings in this book as having their own distinct identity and heritage.

Notes

1   See Sonu Shamdasani, "Why Are Jung Biographies so Bad? Review of Frank McLynn's *Carl Gustav Jung: A Biography*," London, *The Guardian*, 12 July 2000.

2   Francis Charet, "Understanding Jung: Recent Biographies and Scholarship," in *Journal of Analytical Psychology* 45 (2000): 195–216.

THE MOON CYCLES

Life must be lived forwards
but can only be understood backwards.[1]

As we move through our lives, we come closer to knowing, creating, and living the unknowable fiction of who we truly are. This is the place where we live our Medicine, or what heals the collective and ourselves. It is the place of what Jung called the Self, the organizing core of the personality. The closer we move to the Self—particularly in the second half of life when less is more—we grow by shedding, exfoliating, sloughing off, and stripping away what is superfluous, so what is at the center can be more clearly seen. This center is the God/Goddess-image within, the dream-maker. If we are out of balance, unconscious, then the Self will nudge us in the Asleep Dream or the Awake Dream. If we have forgotten the image and language of the dream, if we do not dream our own Dream, then the Dream of the People and the Dream of the Planet dies. In English common law, ignorance of the law is no defense. So it is with Nature; sooner or later we pay for the offense of not being known to ourselves.

Balance is when inner and outer worlds are in agreement, but how can we bring these dances into harmony? Since Always, the People have turned inward to dreams but, though they are the portals to the well of life within each of us, the inner rhythm of dreams is not the subject of this book. The People have also turned to the outer rhythm of the world of things. At its most distant, this is seen in the movement of the stars and the planets in their astrological courses, as they reflect the inner planets and constellations and sketch out the broad strokes on our personal canvas. More immediate and more personal are synchronistic events, medicine signs, or what Don Juan calls "gestures of the spirit"[2] that signify, often to the ego's irritation, spirit's interest in our doings. Synchronistic events come unbeckoned and take us by surprise; their meaning is often a puzzle, like a dream, a sign that something ineffable is at work, and only in hindsight does their import become clear. Jung said, "God is the name by which I designate all things which cross my willful path, violently and recklessly, all things which upset my subjective views, plans and intentions and change the course of my life for better or worse."[3]

Midway between the immediacy of personal synchronicities and the distant movement of the stars and the planets are the yearly and monthly cycles of Grandfather Sun and Sister Moon. This book is about the cycles of the Moon and how she teaches us about the cycles of pregnancy. The Moon Cycles sing to us about our Standing Place, where we stand at a particular age in our movement around the Wheel of Life and how the energies and powers of the eight directions of the Medicine Wheel influence us as we move through this life, this Earthwalk. They sketch a map of our spiral journey inward to the center and help us understand when we are most open for change in our lives, at what ages we are most disposed to certain archetypal energies, and how we can keep our many faces turned toward the business of the Self.

Notes

1   Søren Kierkegaard, *Journals*, IV A 164.

2   Carlos Castaneda, *The Power of Silence* (New York: Simon & Schuster, 1987), p. 32.

3   *Letters* 2, p. 525, December 5, 1959.

THE MEDICINE WHEEL

The Medicine Wheel Way begins with the Touching of our Brothers and Sisters. Next it speaks to us of the Touching of the world around us, the animals, plants, trees, grasses, and other living things. Finally it Teaches us to Sing the Song of the World, and in this Way to become Whole People . . . on this Great Medicine Wheel, our Earth.[1]

The Medicine Wheel is an archetypal image of wholeness. The wisdom of the indigenous peoples of Turtle Island, accumulated over millennia, has been distilled from inner and outer experience into a vast body of knowledge, at least as deep and as broad as the knowledge in our Western culture. There are many Shields of Knowledge that cover all facets of human life, and each Shield contains many Wheels. The Medicine Wheel (see figure 1, p. 10) is the basic Pattern for understanding the influences of the Moon Cycles. Each direction on the Wheel draws on the energies of the directions on either side of it. The cardinal directions hold or stabilize the Wheel in the *tonal* (the physical world) and are compensatory to each other. The non-cardinal directions spin or move the Wheel in the *nagual* (the world of the dream) and are complementary to each other. Each cardinal direction has a non-cardinal

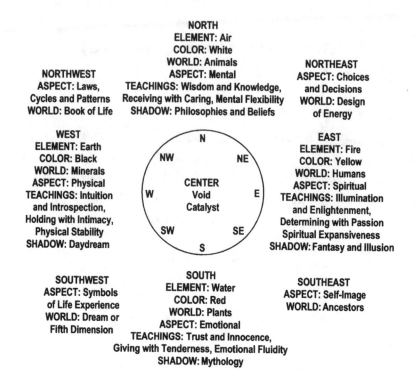

NORTH
ELEMENT: Air
COLOR: White
WORLD: Animals
ASPECT: Mental
TEACHINGS: Wisdom and Knowledge,
Receiving with Caring, Mental Flexibility
SHADOW: Philosophies and Beliefs

NORTHWEST
ASPECT: Laws,
Cycles and Patterns
WORLD: Book of Life

NORTHEAST
ASPECT: Choices
and Decisions
WORLD: Design
of Energy

WEST
ELEMENT: Earth
COLOR: Black
WORLD: Minerals
ASPECT: Physical
TEACHINGS: Intuition
and Introspection,
Holding with Intimacy,
Physical Stability
SHADOW: Daydream

EAST
ELEMENT: Fire
COLOR: Yellow
WORLD: Humans
ASPECT: Spiritual
TEACHINGS: Illumination
and Enlightenment,
Determining with Passion
Spiritual Expansiveness
SHADOW: Fantasy and Illusion

N
NW   NE
CENTER
W   Void   E
Catalyst
SW   SE
S

SOUTHWEST
ASPECT: Symbols
of Life Experience
WORLD: Dream or
Fifth Dimension

SOUTH
ELEMENT: Water
COLOR: Red
WORLD: Plants
ASPECT: Emotional
TEACHINGS: Trust and Innocence,
Giving with Tenderness, Emotional Fluidity
SHADOW: Mythology

SOUTHEAST
ASPECT: Self-Image
WORLD: Ancestors

Fig 1. The Medicine Wheel

on either side that compensates its stability, and each non-cardinal has a cardinal on either side that stabilizes its fluidity. To offer a fuller understanding of the Medicine Wheel is beyond the scope of this book, but we will amplify some of the meaning of the directions when we look at the Little Moons.

Notes —————————————————————————————————

1   Hyemeyohsts Storm, *Seven Arrows* (New York: Ballantine, 1972), p. 1.

THE MOON

The Moon is the mediator, intercessory and gateway between the realm of celestial influences and the earthly realm.[1]

The Moon governs all hidden rhythms and influences: the tides, the stages of pregnancy, the menstrual cycle, the plants, the blood. It is related to the growth of plants: the Full Moon for leaf crops, the New Moon for root crops. The Moon symbolizes the semi-darkness, the half-light of the unconscious, secrecy, hiddenness; it does not generate its own light but receives it from the sun, and then vanishes for three nights each month.

The Moon is also associated with water: sap, dew, tides, the emotions. The dew on moonlit nights is supposed to drip from the Moon. When something is too hard, the Moon brings softness, but it also brings about dissolution into madness and dismemberment when the ego is not ready for the intensity of the archetype. We can see this in the myth of Actaeon, the young hunter, who stumbles across Artemis, the Moon-goddess, bathing naked in the forest. Artemis turns him into a stag and he is torn apart by his own dogs.

The Moon, as the closest body to Earth, is the intermediary between Earth and other heavenly influences, and all descending influences that take on material form have to pass through the Moon, thus the Virgin Mary is associated with the Moon. This recognizes the psychic reality that any concrete expression of our life energies belongs to the feminine principle. In other words, the feminine incarnates and gives birth.[2] The Elders say that the First Sacred Law is: All Things Are Born of Woman.

The Moon also has a mental aspect to it. The root *me-* gave rise to such English words as moon, month, menstrual, mind, mental, measure. The Indo-European root of the word "time" is *di-*, meaning to cut up or divide, and cognate with the Latin *caedere*, to cut through or cut off, which gives the English words decide, homicide, suicide. Thus the Moon is related to the mental aspect of time; time as discriminated into observable units, subject to measurement, but still retaining some of its mystery. Time is the devourer but also the healer.

Time reflects the doings of the Creator as seen in the rhythmic changes of the seasons and the years, the planets and stars. It is often represented by several gods or goddesses, each representing a different aspect of time. In Greek mythology there is Oceanos or Cronos, the god of time as the river or ocean; Nike, the goddess of the moment of balance between victory and defeat; Kairos, the god of the opportune moment; and the Moirae, the goddesses of fate. The Maya have the year-lords and the day-gods. Buddha meditated under the banyan tree for one lunar cycle before he attained enlightenment. For indigenous cultures, time is numinous; it is a way of staying aligned with the rhythms of the Creator. Time's orderedness, observed over centuries, gives an understanding of how the movement between substance and spirit occurs. The prophecies of various cultures are the Seeing of how spirit will manifest in a particular way as matter moves through time.

In our culture, time has lost its numinosity and become a secular commodity. Time is saved or spent, wasted or bought. Those who are closer to the tempo of the Self, as expressed in the natural world or in the inner world, are more aligned with Moon Cycles, as was Jung. The archetype of time is closely related to the rhythm of the Self, so every neurotic deviation from the Self is reflected in a disturbed relationship with time.[3] Our culture has lost its connection with time as a link to what feeds the soul. So we have disorders of time, where time is lost, dismembered, or worshipped: dissociative disorder, attention deficit disorder, obsessive-compulsive disorder.

The Moon Cycles are based on a lunar measurement of time over the individual life span. The lunar cycle, the time between full moons, is 29.5 days. The length of pregnancy is about 39 weeks or 280 days from the beginning of the last menstrual period. However, ovulation, and usually conception, occurs 14 or 15 days into the menstrual cycle. Thus the time from conception to birth is about 266 days, which is also the number of days in nine lunar months (9 x 29.5 = 265.5). Part of the Mayan calendar, a highly sophisticated secular and spiritual calendar system, is the *tzolkin*, which is 260 days long. The Mayan Day-Keepers say this is based on the length of human pregnancy.

The first calendars were lunar calendars of twelve months of thirty days each, but over time the lunar calendar became out-of-step with the solar year of 365 1/4 days. The Roman, Jewish, and Mayan calendars are lunisolar calendars, and solved the problem with intercalary days or months, added or inserted, to keep the shorter moon calendar in step with the solar year. Our modern Gregorian calendar is a solar calendar.

The Moon Cycles are expressed in the months and years of our modern Gregorian calendar and are made up of three-year cycles, and each one is a Circle of Life Experience or Little Moon (see figure 2, p. 18). Each Little Moon is 1096 days long (3 x 365 1/4), which divided up into four quadrants makes a quarter round of 274 days. Similarly if we divide three years into quarters, each quarter is three-quarters of a year. The solar year is divided into quarters by the solstices and equinoxes and the length of three of these quarters (for example, from December 22 to September 22) is 274 days. So the nine months it takes to move from one cardinal direction to the next, on a Little Moon, is half-way between the length of pregnancy, as it is usually calculated (280 days), and the time from conception to birth (266 days).

Notes

1   Edward Edinger, *The Mysterium Lectures: A Journey through C. G. Jung's Mysterium Coniunctionis* (Toronto: Inner City, 1995), p. 106.

2   Edinger, *The Mysterium Lectures*, p. 109.

3   Marie-Louise von Franz, *Time: Rhythm and Repose* (London: Thames and Hudson, 1978), p. 22.

THE BIG MOONS

To every thing there is a season, and a time to every purpose under heaven.[1]

The Moon Cycles consist of five Big Moons: South, West, North, East, and Center. Each Big Moon is twenty-seven years in length, and made up of nine Little Moons of three years each. Each Little Moon embodies the influence of a particular direction of the Medicine Wheel. Every four and a half months, our perspective and the influences we stand with shift as we move through the cardinal and non-cardinal directions around each Circle of Life Experience. We enter each Little Moon through the South and exit through the East, so we do not cross the Southeast. The exception to this is during the first nine months after we are born. At all other times, as we travel from the East of one Moon to the South of the next Moon we go through a Chaotic Journey.

We are born into the Little Center Moon of the Big South Moon and at age 27 move into the Center of the Big West Moon. At age 54 we move into the Big North, at age 81 into the Big East, and at age 108 into the Big Center. Each of the Big Moons is infused with the powers and gifts of its cardinal direction and during each twenty-seven-year cycle we are most influenced by, and able to receive, the teachings and gifts of that particular direction. The name of each Moon (Child, Adolescent, Adult, and Elder) refers to the internal individuation process, which is a Moon Cycle behind the chronology of the external socially recognized stage of maturation. We are a child until age 27, an adolescent until age 54, reach adulthood in our mid-fifties, and elderhood in our eighties.

In the Big South Moon—the Child Moon from birth to 27—we learn through Trust and Innocence with the heart. Until age 27 we are still a child on the Medicine Wheel. It is the time of learning Trust in self, life, and others, through our relationships with those in our family—not only our personal family but also the other Children of Grandmother Earth: the Mineral, Plant, Animal, and Ancestor Worlds. We learn to trust, or distrust, this world of people and things. We learn this emotionally through the element of water, and the fluidity of the emotions that as children, adolescents, or young lovers, flow between ourselves and others, or later are diverted and used, dam-like, to generate power for the industrial areas of the psyche. As children we learn to swim at ease in the waters of the emotions or to mistrust this element that does not permit the breath of mind or the fire of spirit. Too much water and we drown, too little and we wither. We learn containment of it, expression of it, and how to put it to work for us. We learn of its ability to join separate bodies or islands of ideas. We learn how, in the alchemy of our own individuation, in a relationship, or in a creative work, the first step is *solutio* (Latin, meaning "dissolve"). We have to return to the unformed sea—the Dream, the unconscious—whence we came to seek guidance and give form to what is to be birthed.

During this Big Moon we also create our Mythology—the stories of who we are, or might become, the ego's view of itself, its connection to the world around it, and its history and future. The intellect views myth-making as primitive fantasy but emotionally it is the Story-that-Heals and gives life a richness, eccentricity, and depth.[2] One's personal Mythology is the tapestry of a life that collective or scientific norms can only clumsily describe and can only be expressed adequately in myth.

Throughout childhood we develop our most comfortable place on the Wheel of Life: in the North in the place of concepts and ideas; in the South in the place of emotions and relationships; in the West in the physical world and our body; or in the East, in the world of spirit and creativity. Whatever sits directly across the Wheel from our place of comfort developed in the Big South Moon, remains undeveloped and will ask for its due later in life in the Big West Moon.

The Big West Moon, the Adolescent Moon, is from age 27 to 54. Here we learn through Death and Change with the body, and learn that death is a part of life. It is the place of Introspection and Intuition, and Looks-Within. Jung said, "Who looks outside dreams; who looks inside awakes."[3] Here we learn primarily through action, the body, and the element of earth. If we are not able to look within and take responsibility for our own soul, we blame others and life for our circumstances and remain in the shadow side of the West, the Daydream. Until the age of 27 we are still considered a child. If we linger in the water consciousness of the Big South Moon past our time we have what Jung called the *puer* or *puella aeternus* (Latin for "eternal boy" or "eternal girl"). If we do not meet Life as Death and Change, then death—physical or spiritual—will meet us.

The Big North Moon, or Adult Moon, is from 54 to 81. This is the time of learning through Harmony and Balance with the mind. This Moon teaches Wisdom and Logic; not the logic of the intellect, but what Jung called the *logos spermatikos*, the fertilizing voice of the Holy Spirit, the understanding of the lawfulness of the Will of the Great Mystery. It is also the understanding of the inner laws of the Self, the Great Mystery within which allows us freedoms and imposes restrictions on us that are our own unique fate. On the shadow

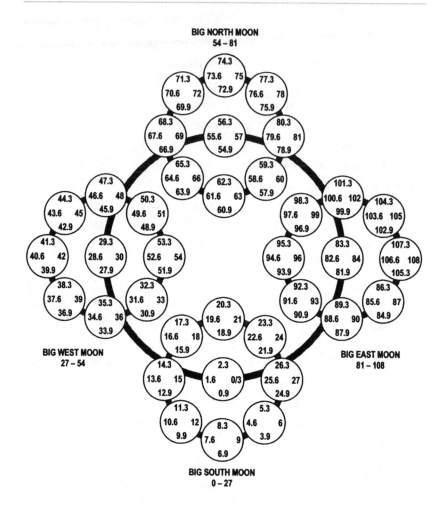

Fig 2. The Moon Cycles

side, if we remain in the earth Moon of the West too long, we become unable to receive new knowledge, unable to look at things from a different place on the Wheel, and our Philosophies and Beliefs become fanatical, rigid, and stagnant. We become the negative *senex* or *seneca* (Latin for "old man" or "old woman"). On the light side, this is the place of the sage or crone, the wise man or wise woman, who has married both thinking and feeling and birthed Wisdom.

The Big East Moon, or Elder Moon, is from 81 to 108. Here we learn through Illumination and Enlightenment with spirit as we look back on our Earthwalk, and look forward to the Dropping of the Robe, and the journey back to the Great Light. If we remain with the air of the North too long, we are unable to touch the light and warmth of the fire of spirit in the East, and we fall back into the shadow side of the South in childish nostalgia, or into the West at the prospect of the barren coldness of physical death.

Notes ───────────────────────────────────

1   Ecclesiastes 3:1.
2   *MDR*, p. 300.
3   *Letters* 1, p. 33.

THE CHAOTIC JOURNEYS

In all chaos there is a cosmos, in all disorder a secret order.[1]

P attern born amid formlessness: that is life's basic beauty and its basic mystery. Life sucks order from a sea of disorder. Order and chaos are not the best of friends, and like jealous sisters or hostile brothers, they have an uneasy peace. Set, the Egyptian god of chaos, was the enemy and brother of Osiris, the Sun god, who he dismembered. In ancient Greece, Set was known as Typhon and was associated with bad dreams, horrors, irrationality, murderous inclinations, self-sabotage, and temptation to rape.

The original chaos is the absence of order, the darkness, the unknown, the down as opposed to the up, the inward, implosive spiral to the center, contrary to the outward explosive movement to the periphery. It is the Void where space is so infinite that it has no meaning, and time, by which the formation and destruction of all things is measured, is not yet born. In chaos there are no horizons, no landmarks, no elements, no earth or sky by which to establish ourselves as having substance and existence. The Void is the mother of all things, the dark within the light. The very darkness and moistness of her womb yearns for seeding, for penetration, to see within herself her son, brother and lover and opposite. So chaos births order, but as an equal and as a lover. Order is the light within the dark, the father of all things.

So we live between order and chaos. To join with the Great Spirit in the dance of co-creation and become what we will, we must return, after times of order and structure, to the dark ground of chaos where there is no Pattern. Only there can we fully choose with the decks cleared, and all accounts settled.

Every three years, we arrive in the East of a Little Moon. Instead of journeying around the wheel through the Southeast, we travel through nine months of chaos to arrive in the South of the next Little Moon. For the first month of this Chaotic Journey we stand in the light of consciousness of the East and look back over the last three years, or in the case of the Big Moons, the last twenty-seven years. The Chaotic Journey is so called because we are between Moons and no longer subject to the archetypal patterning of those Moons.

Eighty percent of all movement of energy in the universe is patterned, and twenty percent is the Great Spirit's Free Will, or the Laws of Chance, as an expression of its Desire to birth itself anew. Because this Will is unknown and unknowable, it appears to us as chaos, both externally in that our lives may not follow their usual pattern, and also internally as the doings of the Self. The Chaotic Journey is a time of internal reflection on the Northwest-Southeast axis, or the ego-Self axis, and unexpected changes—fortunate or unfortunate— can happen to us. It is often a time of disorientation and confusion, when the veil between spirit and substance is thinnest, and when both the physical and spiritual aspects of the archetypes are most likely to be constellated. It is what Sherry Salman calls the "archetypally determined 'magical' pre-Oedipal field to which we must periodically return if any fresh development is to take place."[2]

The journey between the Big Moons is called the Big Chaotic Journey (27.0 to 27.9; 54.0 to 54.9; 81.0 to 81.9), and between the

Little Moons, the Little Chaotic Journey. When discussing ages, the numerical notation I shall use is in years and months. For example: 27.3 = twenty-seven years and three months; 33.11 = thirty-three years and eleven months.

In the accompanying graphics, you should assume that any Little or Big Moon begins in the East and ends in the East. That is, the Chaotic Journey is at the beginning of a Moon, and as such, it is the first 9 months of the 3 year cycle. However, this is only a convention with regard to the constraints of two-dimensional illustration. Because the Chaotic Journeys are outside of Pattern, and are an "in-between" time, the events that occur during a Chaotic Journey can be considered as belonging to either the Moon that comes before or the Moon that comes after, or to both. For the most part, I shall consider the Chaotic Journeys and their events as belonging to the Moon that comes after. However, at times they more clearly resonate with the previous Moon and will be considered under that Moon.

Time is not a line, it is a sphere. The ripples set off by Decisions in our lives radiate out in all eight cardinal and non-cardinal directions, "forward" into the future, and "backward" into the past. These waves in turn combine with other waves to create Patterns in the Dream. Accordingly, I invite you to play with time, and not be overly burdened by linearity and precision. Allowing a generous distance from the details enables us to see the Pattern of Jung's Dreaming.

Notes ————————————————————————

1   *CW* 9i, § 66.
2   Sherry Salman, "Dissociation and the Self in the Magical Pre-Oedipal Field," *Journal of Analytical Psychology* 44 (1999): 71.

THE LITTLE MOONS

God didn't want everything to happen all at once,
so he invented time.
(ANON.)

Each twenty-seven-year Big Moon cycle is divided into nine
Little Moons: eight around the Wheel and one in the
Center, each of three years duration. For example: at 27.9
we arrive at South of the Little Center Moon of the Big West after our
Big Chaotic Journey, then travel clockwise around this Little Center
Moon until age 30.0. We then stand for one month after our 30th
birthday at the beginning of the Little Chaotic Journey, and then
arrive in the South of the Little Southeast Moon at the age of 30.9.
This pattern is repeated nine times until we leave the Big West Moon
at age 54. At each Little Moon, we enter in the South and leave in the
East. At each Big Moon we enter in the South of the Little Center
Moon and leave from the East of the Little East Moon.

So at any one time we are subject to the alchemy of three archetypal forces: the energy of the particular direction of the Little Moon
we are in; the energy of the Little Moon itself; and the energy of the

Big Moon. So, for example, at age 32.3 we are in the North of the Little Southeast Moon of the Big West Moon. Here, we are influenced by the energies of: the place where we stand, the North, Wisdom and Knowledge; the Little Southeast Moon, Images of Self; and the Big West Moon, Death and Change. This can be expressed in several ways, for example: the Death and Change of Wisdom and Knowledge of the Images of Self, or the Self-Image of Knowledge of Death and Change, or the Wisdom and Knowledge of Self-Images of Death and Change.

Modern developmental psychology, with its largely cognitive, behavioral or biological orientation, has lots to say about child development but much less about adult development. All the action is before age 6, and by the end of adolescence everything is pretty much developed. From then on, development slows to a crawl with not much happening between the late teens and death. However, when the body and the mind have run their course, it is then that spiritual development begins to hit its stride. Jung was one of the first to consider that the second half of life has its own tasks and was not just an inevitable by-product of childhood. The Moon Cycles offer an alternative view of our development throughout the life span, and remind us that each age has its particular dignity and place in the business of soul-making.

The energy of the Little Moons determines the critical learning periods or developmental learning tasks at a particular age. For example, in childhood, in the Big South Moon, the Little Center Moon (0-3) is critical for learning about the Catalyst energy, Love; the Little Southeast Moon (3-6) for learning about Self-Image; the Little South Moon (6-9) for learning about Trust and Innocence and Giving with the emotions; the Little Southwest Moon (9-12) for learning about the Symbols of Life Experience; the Little West Moon (12-15) for learning about Death and Change and Holding with the body; the Little Northwest Moon (15-18) for learning about ceremony, Rules, Laws and Patterns; the Little North Moon (18-21) for learning Knowledge and Receiving with the mind; the Little Northeast Moon (21-24) for making Decisions about how to live one's life; and the Little East Moon (24-27) for learning about consciousness and Determining with Spirit.

LITTLE CENTER MOONS
(0–3, 27–30, 54–57, 81–84 YEARS) —
CATALYST ENERGY

The center is the place of the Catalyst energy, the Void. It produces change without itself being changed, it unites the opposites, and makes the Wheels spin without itself turning, or as Jung said, "Only absolute totality can renew itself out of itself and generate itself anew."[1] These years are the ones that catalyze or set the trajectory at the beginning of a Big Moon. Jung wrote about this Catalyst energy in his paper *The Spirit Mercurius*[2] and referred frequently in his writings to the alchemical Mercurius as the union of the opposites and a symbol of the Self. The Roman god Mercury was the god of commerce and communication and the messenger of the gods. Mercury is the swiftest planet, and the element mercury (quicksilver) is a potent accelerator of chemical reactions.

In the final analysis, the Catalyst energy in our lives is love; this is at the Center of all the Wheels. In the South is parent-child love, whether that is for our physical children, the inner child, our creative births, or the other Children of Grandmother Earth (the Stone Peoples, the Plant Nations, the Animal Brothers and Sisters). In the West is sexual, physical love. In the North is compassion or mental love. In the East is spiritual love, our love of spirit, our longing to touch the Mystery. In the Center of the Center is the Great Mystery's Love for us.[3]

LITTLE SOUTHEAST MOONS
(3–6, 30–33, 57–60, 84–87 YEARS) —
SELF-IMAGE, THE ANCESTORS, THE SEVEN ARROWS

The Southeast is the place of the Images of Self, the Seven Arrows, and the Dream of the Ancestors. It embodies the Self-Image (the ego's image of itself) and the Image of Self (the ego as the dream of the Self, and the vehicle of the Self in the world). In a dream, that richly illustrates how the ego is an Image of the Self, Jung came upon a small wayside chapel and, going inside, he found a yogi in deep meditation. Looking at him more closely Jung realized that the yogi's face was his face. He woke with the thought that the yogi was dreaming him and that when the yogi awakened, Jung would no longer exist.[4]

The Image of Self is one of the four faces of the Self that sit in the non-cardinal directions and move the Medicine Wheel. The Image of the Self sits in the Southeast, the Dream of the Self in the Southwest, the Pattern of the Self in the Northwest, and the Choices of the Self in the Northeast. The totality of the Self, the unknowable Great Mystery, sits in the Center. Shortly before his death, Jung said to the soldier and writer Sir Laurens van der Post, "I cannot define for human beings what God is, but what I can say is that my scientific work has proved the pattern of God exists in every human being. And that this pattern has at its disposal the greatest transforming energies of which life is capable."[5]

All those Ancestors, spiritual or physical, who have come before us have dreamed a Dream for the People which we are living now, just as we have a Dream that those who come seven generations after us will live out. What some anthropological literature condescendingly calls "ancestor worship" is a continuing dialogue between those who have gone before and those who are living now. The Ancestors are drawn to the living as we are repairing what has been damaged, are completing what has been left incomplete, or are damaging what has been whole. We are their dream in physical form, we dream their dream onward.

The archetypes as Ancestors are the cumulative residue of the Dreaming of the People. We are an Image in the Dream of our Ancestors. Marie-Louise von Franz said that the results of a well-lived life, a life lived consciously, which is symbolized in alchemy as the fruit of the sun and the moon tree, seem to have continuing effects in the collective unconscious and a redeeming effect on the past and on the future of humankind. She relates the story of a man who had suffered a great deal in his professional life. Shortly before his death, he had a dream in which a voice spoke to him in an oriental language, saying, "Your work and your life, which you have endured consciously, have redeemed hundreds in your generation and will have an illuminating influence upon hundreds of generations to come." Suffering that we consciously live seems to have its own rewards, its own fruit, but often only in the other world.[6]

These Southeast Moons are the years when we change our Image of Self, and are most open to the influence of the Ancestors, both in the personal unconscious (our complexes), and the collective unconscious (the archetypes). The Southeast lies between the East (spirit and fire) and the South (heart and water) and is the place of the most tension between the humanness of the heart and the inhumanness of spirit. The ego in the Southeast must mediate between the two.

The Southeast is the place of teachings of the Seven Arrows that show how our light and dark Self-Images are formed. The arrow is symbolic of the projection of a psychic content. It is in the Southeast, particularly in the first nine months of life, that the various forms of projection, introjection, and projective identification are strongly activated.

When something is unconscious, it is projected onto the outside world and distorts our view of the world around us. The unconscious, not consciousness, does the projecting, so we meet a projection in the outer world rather than making one. The effect of projection is isolation from the world as it is and our relationship with it becomes an illusory one.[7]

In Jung's view, the assimilation of a projection takes place in five stages.[8] At the first stage, on the level of archaic identity, or *participation mystique*, the person experiences the projection simply as if it were reality (South—Innocence). In the second stage, if conscious or unconscious doubts should arise from within or if the behavior of the object conflicts with the individual's ideas about it, then he begins to differentiate between the projected image and the actual object (West—Death and Change). In the third stage there is a moral judgment concerning the content of the projection (North—

Philosophies and Beliefs). In the fourth stage, the individual usually explains the projection as having been an error or an illusion (East—Fantasy and Illusion). On the fifth level (Center), however, the individual asks where the distorted image could have come from. Then it has to be recognized as the image of a psychic content, which originally belonged to the individual.

Through this process of withdrawing projections we come to change our Self-Image, our relationship with ourself. Jung said that the withdrawal of a projection was a moral accomplishment, an achievement in the area of feeling; the ego develops a different *Eros* to itself and the other.

By assimilating what we thought to be "out there" and seeing it as something of ourself of which we had been unconscious, we come to see more clearly the designs of the Pattern of the Self across the wheel in the Northwest. The ego becomes a clearer reflection of the Self. The systole and diastole that occurs between the Southeast and the Northwest is echoed in Edward Edinger's concept of the "psychic life-cycle" where there is constant dialogue between the ego and the Self.[9] The cycle of the development of consciousness follows a circular pattern, and we can begin at any point on the circle. If, on the one hand, reality is not protected against the archaic dream state, or, on the other hand, if room is not made for the dream in the world of consciousness, then an inflation will ensue where the ego appropriates energies and powers rightly belonging to the Self, and becomes puffed up with drives, unconscious pressures, and needs.[10] The balloon will eventually be pricked, a deflation ensues—the pet plan fails, you find she's going out with another guy, there's the huge speeding ticket—or more darkly, it is here Jung said that we suffer from the violence done by the Self. Then there is an alienation from the Self, a wounding, a dismemberment, which leads to a humiliation and a repentance. The ego is then reconciled with the Self and this endures until new contents emerge from the unconscious and a complacency, a passive inflation, begins to grow. Through the repetition of this cycle we discover and rediscover our own integrity, our own size, seeing ourselves as we are, not how we would like to be.

LITTLE SOUTH MOONS
(6–9, 33–36, 60–63, 87–90 YEARS)—
TRUST AND INNOCENCE

The South is the place of Trust and Innocence, the element of water, the color red, the Plants, and the number three. It is the place of the trinity, growth, and sacrifice. The number three is associated with the creative process; and dynamic, developmental and temporal processes are often configured in threes: a beginning, middle and end; past, present and future. Deities are often images of threeness, for example, the Father (Self), the Son (ego), and the Holy Ghost (ego and Self).[11] It is the place of the Triple Goddess, maiden, mother, and crone, the ones who hold the feminine cycles of life, the three times three, the nine, the pregnancy. The water in the South is symbolic of washing, purification, rejuvenation, new beginnings, amniotic fluid, emotional fluidity, and the alchemical *solutio*. In medieval alchemy, the first step of "The Work" was *solutio*, or "dissolving." The alchemists thought of this as a return to the womb for the purpose of rebirth, and that no change could come about until everything had been reduced to the *prima materia* ("the first matter"). The South is where we start to go around the Wheel, the place of the child, beginnings, futurity, and hope. So these years are the childhood years in each of the Big Moons where we are both blessed and wounded by our own innocence, and some of this innocence must be sacrificed for life to move on.

The image of the child is extravagant with opposites. It is both a link with the past (the Ancestors in the Southeast, and our complexes from the past) and the future (the Dream in the Southwest). It is both vulnerable (to abandonment, to cruelty) and invulnerable (the child-god or the child-hero). It is the divine child, like Christ, and also the earthy child, like the dummling, the slowest one, the youngest brother in fairy tales who is the one who finds the treasure. It is asexual, pre-sexual, or hermaphrodite, containing its own opposite within, but not yet penetrated, not yet born, virginal.

Virginity is sacred not because it is a condition of being physically inviolate but because it is a condition of being open to God.[12]

■ 29 ■

However, we are all virginal when we are preserved from the experience of life. James Hillman says, "For somewhere we are all virgins, sensitive, shy, psychologically naive, unexplored in our emotional life, unwilling to be called into involvements, unawakened to the terribleness of truth, resistant to major challenge, preferring where it is safe, at home, familiar and protected, with books or bits of handiwork, kindly, charitable, obedient, well meaning. Yet from all this goodness little can come unless the psyche's womb receives the fiery seed of one's own unique essence which fulfills its creative longing and from which inner fertilization issues the experience of renewal."[13]

The South, as the place of the Plants, overflows with images of abundance, profusion, growth, and greenness, a coming into the red-bloodedness of life during these years (chlorophyll and hemoglobin have similar molecular structures). So like the Plants we sit in one place, unmoving, in Trust and Innocence, innocent with all our imperfections, and are nurtured into growth toward the light. Imperfection is not the same as inferiority, which comes when we are not fulfilling our potential. Inferiority is absent when we live in accord with our true nature.

Trust is an aspect of the virgin and the anima, one who is unto herself, who is who she is. To truly know oneself engenders trust in oneself. The word trust has several roots: the Old Norse word *traust* means confidence, firmness; trust is derived from the same root as true and truth; and from the Old French *triste*, the appointed place for positioning oneself. "The development of personality ... means fidelity to the law of one's own being. For the word 'fidelity' I should prefer, in this context, the word used in the New Testament, *pistis* ... [this means] 'trust,' 'trustful loyalty.' Fidelity to the law of one's own being is a trust in this law, a loyal perseverance, and confident hope."[14]

The South is also the place of our Give-Away, our sacrifice to life, and our myth, the story we tell to ourselves and others about who we are, who we think we are, and who we think others think we are. Plants will give unceasingly and when we cut them back they regenerate in abundance; when we are who we are, there is an endless supply.

This capacity to Give-Away is linked to the notion of sacrifice. In the act of sacrifice, the ego decides against its own needs and subordinates itself to a higher authority, the Self.[15] Jung wrote about this at length in *Transformation Symbolism in the Mass*.[16] Sacrifice is payment; there is no free lunch, and the Give-Away acknowledges that as we take a life—plant or animal—to nourish our bodies, so our life will one day be taken in the cycle of creation and re-creation. We offer our Give-Away in acknowledgment of the inter-connectedness of all life. If consciousness is to flourish, we must also kill, or allow to die, plant-like inertia and animal-like impulses in ourselves, and we do this with the knowledge that they have served their purpose and their time has come to an end. The raw emotions of the Self yearn for transformation, and as the ego sacrifices its desirousness, it transforms the Self.[17]

In the stark language of the Old Testament, sacrifice is atonement for sin. If we "sin" against the Self and are not loyal to our own nature, then "punishment" will be visited on us. The restoration of the original harmony with the Self—at-one-ment—is necessary to restore balance.

Sacrifice also feeds the Creator. Our prayers are food for the Great Mystery. The ego needs to continually attend to the Self with reverie, as the mother attends to and feeds the child. Sacrifice also means being fed by the Desires of Self, as we turn our face toward it, our attention is returned in ways undreamed of by the ego.

LITTLE SOUTHWEST MOONS (9–12, 36–39, 63–66, 90–93 YEARS)— SYMBOLS OF THE DREAM, AND NEEDS, WANTS, AND DESIRES

The Southwest is the place of the Personal, Sacred, Collective and Planetary Dreams and the Symbols of Life Experience. Symbols are the best expression for something that is as yet unknown, and symbolic images or acts (ceremony) function as containers for the transformation of psychic energy. The Southwest is the place where we can develop a symbolic attitude, seeing beneath the surface of things (our Needs and Wants), what we want of life, to perceive what the Self and life wants of us (our Desires). When the shadow is made conscious it brings about a tension of opposites, which seek unity in compensation. This compensation is achieved through symbols and, *deo concedente*, the resolution appears naturally and is compellingly experienced as grace.[18]

Our Needs are those reality needs that we must have met for survival: food and water (South), shelter and clothing (West), time to Dream (North), and freedom and autonomy (East). These make up our Personal Dream, how we provide for ourselves and others in our circle, the "9-to-5," how we make a living. This work puts on psychological weight and fills out the adult emotional body. "It does not matter what job you take. The point is that for once you do something thoroughly and conscientiously, whatever it is…. the greatest help in getting over the dangers of rebirth and breaking away from the mother [is] to be in regular work…our regularly repeated efforts to throw off unconsciousness—that is, by regular work—has made our humanity. We can conquer unconsciousness with regular work but never by a grand gesture…all ceremonies may be said to be work, and our sense of work to be derivative therefrom."[19]

When the ego's shadow Needs (our idiosyncrasies, our addictions, our wounds) are not met, we find ourselves in emotional distress, for which we need the help of others to alleviate. Our Wants are those Needs where the Arrow of projection is not so firmly lodged and we are able to soothe our own distress. If we don't get our Wants satisfied, we don't lose much energy over it. But within everything is contained its opposite, and at the center of every Need is hidden a Desire, an authentic longing of the Self. As William Blake put it, "If a fool would persist in his folly, he would become wise." The longings of the Self are what we need for our Sacred Dream. They add Beauty to our Circle. Jung said that it was essential to allow our Desires absolute freedom if we are to be free from unconscious demand. In our Desires we find our self and the Self finds itself in our Desires. But the form of the desire may not be what the ego has in mind, or as George Bernard Shaw put it, "There are two tragedies in life. One is not to get your heart's desire. The other is to get it" (*Man and Superman* [1903], act 4).

Our Sacred Dream is what we have taken birth for, and the spiritual legacy we leave behind. It is the *principium individuationis*, our Give-Away to Life and the People, the permanent deposit that the individuated psyche leaves behind in the collective unconscious. The Sacred Dream is not destiny, it is not a goal, it is not a given, but is formed as we move around the Wheel of Life. We create this Dream from what life brings to us and what we bring to life.

The Collective Dream is the Dream of the People—how as a group, race, or nation we Dream our own future. Like the individual and the People, Grandmother Earth, as a living being, also has a Dream. This Planetary Dream is to take her place, as the Child planet, in the Sisterhood of the other eleven planets with Human life in this universe.

The Elders say that if all our available energy is given to our Personal Dream then we cannot feed our Sacred Dream. But as soon as twenty percent of that energy is available as *intent*—or libido at the disposal of the ego—then our Sacred Dream begins to awaken, so it is important to have time to Dream. When we feed our Personal Dream, it feeds the Sacred Dream, which feeds the Collective Dream, and this feeds the Planetary Dream. Symbolic activity converts instinctual energy into energy that is available for a new Dream. "In abstract form, symbols are religious ideas; in the form of action, they are rites or ceremonies. They are the manifestation and expression of excess libido."[20]

LITTLE WEST MOONS
(12–15, 39–42, 66–69, 93–96 YEARS) —
DEATH AND CHANGE,
INTUITION AND INTROSPECTION

The West is the place of Death and Change, the color black, the body, and the place of the woman as Life-Giver (ovulation) and Death-Bringer (menstruation). In each West Moon what already exists is destroyed in order to create new life. In adolescence, with the coming of the Sun (ejaculation) and the coming of the Moon (menstruation), the physical body changes; at mid-life the body of our lives (work, family, home, relationships) changes; in the late sixties the mental body (beliefs about life and death) changes. In these Little West Moons, we have three major life transitions: adolescence, mid-life, and retirement or the beginning of old age.

From 12 to 15 is the time of early adolescence, and on the Moon Cycles these are the years of the Little West Moon of the Big South, the Death and Change of childhood. Most notably at age 13.6, the first year as a teenager, we enter the West of the Little West Moon of the Big South, the double Death and Change of Trust and Innocence. The symbolism of the number 13 is significant here. The number 12 has been considered a perfect number, whereas 13 indicates the beginning of a new cycle and so is a symbol of death and rebirth: the thirteen at the Last Supper leading to Christ's betrayal and crucifixion; the thirteenth card of the tarot, Death; the Mayan Calendar cycle of 52 years made up of 4 x 13 year cycles; the thirteenth chapter of the Book of Revelation describes the Anti-Christ; and Odysseus, as the thirteenth member of his crew, escaped being eaten by the Cyclops.

The more known we are to ourselves, the more we can move with the deaths, changes, movements, births and rebirths that life brings us. The West is the place of Looks-Within and if we lack knowledge of death, then life imposes it. If we lack knowledge of life, then death imposes it. Jung said, "When an inner situation is not made conscious, it happens outside, as fate."[21] Spirit in the East and the body in the West, the light and the darkness, come together in this place in the longing to create new life. We bring our Sacred Dream from the Southwest into physical form in the West; through the process of bringing spirit into substance and substance into spirit, both are changed. The West is the place of Introspection and Intuition, the ability to see what is in our Earth Lodge that needs to come into the light through our own creativity. If we Look-Within to find our own answers, then we have a womb, and can conceive our creative children in the body of our lives. If we look outside for our answers, we have no womb, and we blame Life and others for our insufficiency. The result is that we fall into the shadow of the West, the Daydream, and lose the spirit out of substance. Here we become materially inflated, preoccupied with matter and the secular world. Similarly in the East when we lose the substance out of spirit we fall into the shadow of the East—Fantasy and Illusion—or spiritual inflation.

LITTLE NORTHWEST MOONS
(15–18, 42–45, 69–72, 96–99 YEARS)—
LAWS, PATTERNS, AND CYCLES

The Northwest is the place of Rules, Laws, Cycles and Patterns, and the Circle of Law. These include: the cycles and seasons of Grandmother Earth; the civil, social and religious laws of Two-leggeds; the two Sacred Laws (All Things are Born of the Feminine and Conceived by the Masculine, and Nothing Shall be Done to Harm the Children); and the Laws of the Great Spirit, how it uses its unlimited imagination to create and re-create itself. The Northwest also holds the teachings of the Patterns of movement between substance and spirit, and the Laws of transubstantiation. These Laws are not laws in the judicial or scientific sense but are descriptions of the orderliness of energy movement within and between spirit and substance over time.

In the Little Northwest Moon of the Big South, between the ages of 15 and 18, we encounter civil, social, and religious laws in the form of the rules of our family, peer group, religion, or culture. At 16, we can drive a car, and at 18, in the East of the Little Northwest Moon—the place of the Illumination and Enlightenment of Laws and Patterns—we can vote. For the adolescent, the Northwest involves modifications of the early superego structure, formed across the Wheel in the Little Southeast Moon from 3 to 6 years of age. This is accomplished through the development of an internalized value structure that reflects the amalgamation of the early superego foundations, the uniqueness of the individual personality, and the rules of the family, group, and culture. This is the time when we begin to accrue freedoms and responsibilities in society. Our early experience in the Southeast will determine whether we conform or rebel.

The Northwest is one pole of the Northwest/Southeast axis or the ego/Self axis. At ages 42 to 45 and 69 to 72, we encounter not external rules but the internal laws or "morality" of the Self. Jung said, "Just as our free will clashes with necessity in the outside world, so also it finds its limits outside the field of consciousness in the subjective inner world, where it comes into conflict with the facts of the self. And just as circumstances or outside events 'happen' to us and limit our freedom, so the self acts upon the ego like an *objective occurrence* which free will can do very little to alter."[22]

It is often a time of moral dilemma in discerning which strivings and impulses, some of which may fly in the face of convention, are ones that we should act on, sublimate, or suppress. Responsibility for this decision rests with the ego, which must decide which parts of the shadow it lives out, or with. This brings about a crucifixion: "Confrontation with the shadow produces at first a dead balance, a standstill that hampers moral decisions and makes convictions ineffective or even impossible. Everything becomes doubtful."[23]

The morality of the Self may or may not coincide with the prevailing social morality, and so places a much greater burden on us individually. We have to be honest to live outside the law. "Since real moral problems all begin where the penal code leaves off, their solution can seldom or never depend on precedents, much less on precepts and commandments. The real moral problem springs from *conflicts of duty*. Anyone who is sufficiently humble, or easy-going, can always reach a decision with the help of some outside authority. But one who trusts others as little as he trusts himself can never reach a decision at all.... In all such cases there is an unconscious authority which puts an end to doubt by creating a *fait accompli*. One can describe this authority as the 'will of God' or as an 'action of uncontrollable natural forces,' though psychologically it makes a good deal of difference how one thinks of it."[24]

Helen Luke said that, like the monastic vow of obedience, this obedience to the Self is a commitment to a total response to the voice of the Holy Spirit within and we are called, like Christ, to suffer to the death for our own truth rather than live our lives in blind conformity.[25] But this does not mean a complete rejection of collective values and norms. Jung said that the only valid reason for going outside the boundaries and conventions of one's culture or group was if, in doing so, one brought back something of greater value to the collective. "The individuated life and the collective life are two separate paths but are connected to each other by guilt. Individuation cuts one off from conformity and collective values to some extent and this is the guilt that the individual must redeem by bringing back to the collective an equivalent substitute for his or her absence in the collective sphere. Without this production of values individuation is immoral."[26]

LITTLE NORTH MOONS
(18–21, 45–48, 72–75, 99–102 YEARS)—
WISDOM, KNOWLEDGE, AND LOGIC

The North is the place of Wisdom, Knowledge, and Logic, and their shadow, Philosophies and Beliefs. The South is the place of experience whereas the North is the place of making meaning out of that experience. It is the place of the Animals, the element of air, the Gift of Mind, Earth Father, and Sweet Medicine or the Spirit of the Totem Animals. The North teaches us mental flexibility and imagination, inter-connectedness, discrimination, and receiving with consciousness from all places around the Wheel. As compensation to the South, which is all-embracing, the North is all-discriminating. James Hillman writes:

Without the father we lose also that capacity which the Church recognized as "discrimination of spirits": the ability to know a call when we hear one and to discriminate between the voices, an activity so necessary for a precise psy-

chology of the unconscious. But the spirit that has no father
has no guide for such niceties. The senex-puer division puts
an end to spiritual discrimination; instead we have promis-
cuity of spirits (astrology, yoga, spiritual philosophies, cyber-
netics, atomic physics, Jungianism, etc.—all enjoyed cur-
rently) and the indiscrimination among them of an
all-understanding mother. The mother encourages her son:
go ahead, embrace it all. For her, all equals everything. The
father's instruction, on the contrary is: all equals nothing—
unless the all be discriminated.[27]

Wisdom is associated with the archetype of the sage or the wise old
man or woman. This *sapientia dei*—the sum of the archetypal images
in the mind of God—is the matrix or the web of interconnectedness
between all things.[28] The Logic of the North is not the modern philosophical or mathematical logic, but the quality of orderedness, or
lawfulness, that arises out of this wisdom and from the understanding of the Laws and Cycles in the Northwest. This wisdom is also
symbolized in the Bible and alchemy by the feminine Sophia (philosophy is the "love of Sophia"), the Shekinah, or the *anima mundi*.
Jung, however, said that the initial encounter with the anima usually leads us to infer anything but wisdom; in fact, we experience her
as capricious, rash, and unpredictable. But when we take her seriously, we realize that behind the cruel accidents of fate lies a hidden
wisdom and the more we recognize this meaning, the more the
anima loses her unruly disposition.[29]

Knowledge that works is sacred, and it if it works it feeds the
People and brings Happiness (South), Health (West), Harmony
(North), Hope (East), and Humor (Center). Knowledge that works
can always be put on a Wheel; in other words, it always has the
four-, eight-, or twelve-fold structure of the Self. If Knowledge cannot be put on a Wheel it will not feed the People. Dead, linear
knowledge ("information") is not connected with the greater web
of Wisdom. There are two kinds of knowledge. The first works
some or most of the time but requires the constant infusion of

libido in the form of Belief (for example, most faith healing or positive thinking). This knowledge will work until the Belief that drives it runs counter to Sacred Law. The second kind, Knowledge, does not require Belief for it to work, but does require a ceremonial *temenos*, and will bring us into alignment with Sacred Law.

In the Little North Moon of the Big South, from the age of 18 to 21, is the time we look across the Wheel into our own Mythology, our story in the South, and develop our Philosophies and Beliefs about the meaning of Life, and we choose a career or profession within which to gain Knowledge. This happens again at a different level from ages 45 to 48 and again from 72 to 75. The North is the place of being able to see from multiple viewpoints, from all points around the Medicine Wheel. The shadow side of the North is closed-mindedness and mental rigidity where the world is seen in terms of unalterable, opposing dualities. If we are mentally inflexible or have sclerotic beliefs, we are unable to receive new Knowledge, unable to act without Beliefs, and become a slave to our own opinions and their attendant emotions. If the reality of the unconscious is not recognized, this leads on the one hand to fanatical ideologies or over-valued beliefs—often accompanied by ponderous pseudo-religious or patriotic affects—and on the other hand personal relationships are littered with touchiness, resentments, and irritabilities.

LITTLE NORTHEAST MOONS (21–24, 48–51, 75–78, 102–105) — CHOICES AND DECISIONS, DESIGN OF ENERGY

The Northeast is the place on the Wheel where energy moves in and out. It is the place where we use the Gift of consciousness to make Choices and Decisions about how we use our life energy (money, time, inspiration, ideas, sex, love, the car).

Through each child of Grandmother Earth—the Stone Peoples, the Plant Nations, the Four-leggeds, and the Two-leggeds—flows a life energy. The life energy of all the Children, except for Humans (the Two-leggeds), is constant; they are as they are. A rose is a rose is a rose, it knows its gift, its Give-Away, and gives this in Trust and Innocence; a rock cannot be anything more or less than a rock; the buffalo doesn't wake up in the morning and think "Today, I shall move to Florida." Jung said, "When God made animals, he equipped them with just those needs and impulses that enable them to live according to their laws."[30]

But the Gift of Humans is Free Will, and in the vast experiment of the Great Spirit to know itself more deeply, we have been gifted with the ability to choose. As Teilhard de Chardin has said, we co-create with the Creator; we are life become conscious of itself. Thus, in our choosing, our life energy can change. We can be more or less than we are. We have good days and bad days. This ability to choose, this consciousness, exacts a terrible price and is an act of primal disobedience. As punishment for stealing the fire of creation from the gods, Prometheus was chained to a rock and each day an eagle ate his liver, which grew back each night. For stealing fire we pay the price and we are stalked by spirit patiently, sweetly, cunningly, and ruthlessly.

Frances Wickes said, "The terrible gift of choice is forced upon him and must be confirmed by his own will. Often he would choose the merciful undemand of darkness.... When the ego dares not affirm the true choices of the Self, all that is spontaneous becomes suspect, tainted with undefined guilt. But the real guilt of living a lie in relation to the truth of one's own being does not become conscious. Instead, there is a vague, ghostlike, omnipresent sense of guilt that saps energy and breeds suspicion and distrust."[31]

In the Little Northeast Moon of the Big South at age 21 we get the "key to the door," in recognition of our maturity of choice, to open the doors of Life. From 48 to 51, and from 75 to 78, we look across the Wheel to Southwest to see what we have dreamed and choose whether or not to give energy to that Dream. The Southwest asks, "What do you want?" The Northeast answers, "What are you going to do?" And it is only in the Determining, the action in the

East, resulting from Choice in the Northeast, that the Dream becomes Awake in the light of consciousness.

LITTLE EAST MOONS
(24–27, 51–54, 78–81, 105–108 YEARS) —
ILLUMINATION AND ENLIGHTENMENT

The East is the place of Illumination and Enlightenment, fire and passion. Grandfather Sun, with his light and warmth and the fire that brings consciousness, sings the Song of Illumination with the other Grandfather Stars, the Song of Spiritual Memory of who we are and where we have come from. In the East is the ability to live by one's own light and vision (having seed), and the shadow side is Fantasy and Illusion (having no seed), the inability to build one's fire on the solidness of earth. The East is where we Determine with passion and spirit. It teaches us spiritual expansiveness, and is the place of the Humans. The East sits between Choices and Decisions and Design of Energy in the Northeast, and the Image of Self in the Southeast; it is the marriage of the two. It is here that we actualize the consciousness gained on our journey around the Wheel. If there has been no broadening of consciousness, or if we allow what has been gained to sink back into the unconscious, then the next Moon Cycle will present us again with what is unresolved.

The physical body is in the West, the place of Death and Change, and East and West compensate each other. Physical illness, life-threatening trauma, or spiritual practices that involve some kind of deprivation or "mortification" of the body, strongly constellate a connection with spirit in the East, and may bring some Illumination.

When we experience an Illumination we remember who we are, we regain Spiritual Memory. When the lightning bolt of Illumination jumps the gap between unconscious and conscious, there is an act of creation. What has previously been unknown and unconscious comes into the light of consciousness (the "ah-ha"). This is often accompanied by: a flow of emotion, often tears (the Inner River of Remembrance) as the previous tension between conscious and

unconscious is discharged (South); an insight, the receiving of
Knowledge (North); and a physical, autonomic reaction in the body
(West). But the Illumination birthed in the East has to walk around
the Wheel and be lived in the West. Von Franz said, "I have often
asked myself why the unconscious or nature....plays such a cruel
trick on people by first curing them and then dropping them
again.... If some people had not had a brief experience and glimpse
of how it could be when things are right, they would never hold on
through the miseries of the analytical process.... [I]t is as if it were
to say: 'That is what you will get later, but you have first to realize
this and this and this, and much more, before you can get there.'"[32]

Notes

1   CW 9i, § 221.
2   CW 14, given as two papers at Ascona in 1942.
3   Oriah Mountain Dreamer, *Confessions of a Spiritual Thrillseeker: Medicine Teachings from the Grandmothers* (Toronto: Moonfox Press, 1991), pp. 297–300.
4   MDR, p. 232.
5   Quoted in book review by Valerie Harms of Nancy Ryley, *The Forsaken Garden: Four Conversations on the Deep Meaning of Environmental Illness* (Wheaton: IL, Quest, 1998), www.cgjungpage.org/articles/harmsreview.html.
6   Marie-Louise von Franz, *On Dreams and Death: A Jungian Interpretation* (La Salle: Open Court, 1998), p. 109.
7   CW 9ii, § 17.
8   Marie-Louise von Franz, *Projection and Recollection in Jungian Psychology: Reflections of the Soul* (La Salle: Open Court, 1980), pp. 9 ff.
9   Edward Edinger, *Ego and Archetype* (Boston: Shambhala, 1972), p. 37 ff.
10   CW 9ii, § 44–47.
11   Edinger, *Ego and Archetype*, p. 179 ff.
12   Frances Wickes, *The Inner World of Choice* (Englewood Cliffs, NJ: Prentice-Hall, 1963), p. 55.
13   James Hillman, *Insearch: Psychology and Religion* (Dallas: Spring, 1967), p. 108.
14   CW 17, § 295 f.
15   Marie-Louise von Franz, *C. G. Jung: His Myth in Our Time* (London: Hodder & Stoughton, 1975), p. 229.
16   CW 11.

17 Edward Edinger, *The Bible and the Psyche: Individuation Symbolism in the Old Testament* (Toronto: Inner City, 1986), p. 60.

18 *MDR*, p. 335.

19 Carl Jung, *Dream Analysis: Notes of the Seminar in 1928-1930* (Princeton: Princeton University Press, 1984), p. 30.

20 *CW* 8, § 91.

21 *CW* 9ii, § 126.

22 *CW* 9ii, § 9.

23 *CW* 14, § 708.

24 *CW* 9ii, § 48.

25 Helen Luke, *The Voice Within: Love and Virtue in the Age of the Spirit* (New York: Crossroad, 1988), pp. 20–21.

26 *CW* 18, § 1095.

27 James Hillman, "The Great Mother, Her Son, Her Hero, and the Puer," in Patricia Berry, ed., *Fathers and Mothers* (Dallas: Spring, 1990), p. 174.

28 Edinger, *The Bible and the Psyche*, p. 132.

29 *CW* 9i, § 64.

30 *Letters* 1, p. 486.

31 Frances Wickes, *The Inner World of Choice*, pp. 275, 278.

32 Marie-Louise von Franz, *The Interpretation of Fairytales* (Boston: Shambhala, 1996), p. 79.

BIG SOUTH MOON—
TRUST AND INNOCENCE

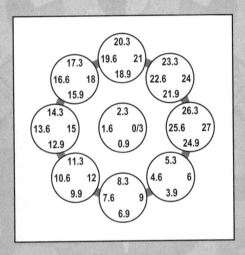

It is well for the heart to be naive and the mind not to be.

—ANATOLE FRANCE

*When innocence has been deprived of its entitlement
it becomes a diabolical spirit.*

—JAMES GROTSTEIN

LITTLE CENTER MOON
OF THE BIG SOUTH —
CATALYST OF TRUST AND
INNOCENCE

[Mythology] happens whenever people learn to recognize a meaningful texture in seemingly coincidental outward facts, joys and sorrows, human encounters, and fatefully interwoven patterns.[1]

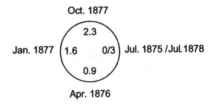

J ung was born on July 26, 1875 in Kesswil, a small village on Lake Constance, Switzerland. James Joyce called Switzerland "The National Park of the Spirit." With its high mountains and deep valleys, and as a neutral democracy often governing with the head and heart through referenda, it holds to the middle way between earth and spirit—the difficult place between the warring opposites.[2]

Jung's parents were Johann Paul Jung, a reformed evangelical minister, and Emilie Preiswerk. Emilie had given birth to a son, Paul, in 1873 but he lived just a few days and we know nothing of the effect of the elder brother's death on the family or on Jung. When Jung was six months old, his family moved to the vicarage at Laufen, near the Rhine falls. During Jung's first nine-month Chaotic Journey (July 1878 to April 1879), from the Little Center Moon to the Little

Southeast Moon, he suffered from eczema; this was related to a temporary separation of his parents, when his mother spent several months in a Basel hospital. At this time the foundations for his own Mythology of trust and mistrust were laid. He was troubled by his mother's absence and from that time felt distrustful of the word "love." For a long time he associated "mother" with unreliability and "father" with reliability but also powerlessness.[3]

THE PHALLUS DREAM

Jung said that when he was "between three and four years old" he had a striking dream, the first he could recall. In *Memories, Dreams, Reflections* he wrote that it occurred around the same time as another experience that was on a "hot summer day," thus placing the dream in the summer of 1878, at the start of his first Chaotic Journey. Jung dreamed he was in a big meadow behind the vicarage and there he discovered a hole in the ground with stone steps leading down. At the bottom was a dimly-lit room with a red carpet and a throne at the far end on which stood what at first looked like a tree trunk a dozen feet high. But it was made of flesh with a rounded head on top of which was an eye that gazed upward. Jung was paralyzed with terror and in the dream he heard his mother's voice call out above, "That is the man-eater!"[4]

This dream represented the Catalyst of Jung's own mythology of the heroic journey. It required him to descend into the chthonic depths of the earth, of which the feminine above had knowledge, and to bring light to the darkness through the resurrection of the one-eyed, creative, solar phallus (*phallos*, Greek for "shining," "bright"). In ancient Rome the phallus symbolized a man's "genius" and was the source of his physical and mental creative power, inspirations, and joy in life. Jung felt that his intellectual life began with this dream. It was an initiation into the secrets of the earth, and foreshadowed Jung's destiny: freeing the "new king," a new dominant in the collective consciousness, from the depths of the collective unconscious.[5]

Notes ————————————————————————————————

1   Gerhard Wehr, *Jung: A Biography* (Boston: Shambhala, 1987), p. 169.
2   Barbara Hannah, *Jung: His Life and Work* (New York: Putnam, 1976), p. 11.
3   *MDR*, p. 8.
4   *MDR*, pp. 11–12.
5   *MDR*, p. 15.

LITTLE SOUTHEAST MOON
OF THE BIG SOUTH —
SELF-IMAGES OF TRUST AND
INNOCENCE

*There is one ego in the conscious and another made up of unconscious
ancestral elements. . . . Perhaps certain traits belonging to the ancestors
get buried away in the mind as complexes with a life of their own
which has never been assimilated into the life of the individual,
and then, for some unknown reason, these complexes become activated.*[1]

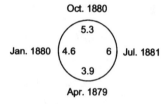

Oct. 1880

Jan. 1880

5.3

4.6

6

Jul. 1881

3.9

Apr. 1879

T he Little Southeast Moons are the place where the ego or the Image of Self is formed and re-formed. The dramas of the inner world, and the mother-child couple, predominate up to age 3, but from ages 3 to 6 the child begins to relate to the outer world. Later in life the ego's task in the Southeast is to mediate between the demands of both the inner and outer worlds, to hold the place between the warring elements of fire (East) and water (South) and, when mature, to stand for the wholeness of the personality, warts and all.

ANCESTORS

The Southeast is also the place of the Ancestors, and throughout his life, Jung was interested in his ancestors, both physical and spiritual. Lest this sound amiss to European or North American ears, we should note that Maori, the indigenous people of New Zealand or Aotearoa (The Land of the Long White Cloud), speak of their *whakapapa* or ancestral lineage when introducing themselves on the *marae* (meeting place) during the *powhiri* (welcoming) as they reconnect themselves with the *tipuna* (ancestors) and with the spirit of the land by naming their river and mountain.

The Jung family came from Mainz, and a doctor of medicine and law, called Carl Jung, was reputed to have lived in Mainz in the early 17th century (d. 1645). He was a contemporary of the alchemists Michael Maier (1568–1622) and Gerard Dorn, whose work Jung later studied. Jung's great-grandfather was the physician Franz Ignaz Jung (1759–1831), who was in charge of a military hospital during the Napoleonic Wars. He was married to Sophie Ziegler and, perhaps as a result of their unhappy marriage, there was a rumor that Sophie had an illegitimate son (Jung's grandfather) by Goethe. This paternal grandfather Carl Gustav was born in 1794 and studied medicine at Heidelberg University. He moved to Switzerland in 1820 and became Professor of Medicine at Basel University in 1822, and later, Rector. Jung's father Paul was the thirteenth child and youngest son of his father's three marriages.

As to the speculation that the elder Carl Jung was the natural son of Goethe, Jung took great interest in this rumor, although he referred to it as "annoying" and "in bad taste."[2] But Goethe's work, particularly *Faust*, was of great importance to Jung and he said of *Faust* that his "respected great-grandfather" would have approved of what he was writing because he had continued and developed his ancestor's thinking.

Jung's maternal grandfather, Samuel Preiswerk, was the Antistes, or head vicar, of Basel. He was a spiritualist and had his wife stand beside him at sermons to ward off evil spirits. A special chair was set aside in his study for his deceased first wife, and each week she came to occupy the chair and converse with her husband. He was said to have second sight and to talk with the dead. Jung's mother, Emilie, was also interested in the supernatural and left behind a diary in which she noted all the strange phenomena she experienced.[3] Like Jung's father, Emilie was also the thirteenth and youngest in her family![4]

Jung struggled intellectually with his father in his late teens, but his mother had a much greater, subterranean, effect on him. He said that she was extremely good to him and in the long run contributed more to his development than his father. Jung would say fondly that she was "also a bit of a witch" and also had a No. 1 and No. 2 personality, which helped him honor his obligation to his own No. 2 personality.[5] Jung felt her to be deeply connected to nature—despite her conventional assertions of Christian faith—and, although it never occurred to him how pagan this foundation was, it gave him security.[6]

The Earth Astrology Wheel teaches that we are each born into a different place on the Medicine Wheel depending on our date of birth.[7] The Medicine Animal of those born in the South (July 22 to August 21), as was Jung, is the sturgeon, the Keeper of the Memory of the Ancestors. Phylogenetically, the sturgeon is a very primitive fish, found very early in the fossil record, and is the longest-living freshwater fish. In England, if one is caught, it must first be presented to the monarch, and in Europe it is the source of caviar, an aristocratic food. People born in the South have a strong connection with lineage, biography, family history, previous incarnations, and their royal heritage, inner or outer. Jung felt that the unconscious was naturally aristocratic, and much of his life's work was the recollection of the phylogenetic and archetypal memory that the unconscious holds. As we shall see later the Northwest-Southeast axis was important in Jung's life. His fate (the Northwest) was to make the Ancestors—the archetypes and the collective unconscious—his "main business."

Notes

1 C. G. Jung, *Dream Analysis: Notes of the Seminar Given in 1928-1930*, William McGuire, ed. (Princeton: Princeton University Press, 1984), p. 37.

2 MDR, p. 36.

3 Aniela Jaffé, *From the Life and Work of C. G. Jung* (New York: Harper, 1971), p. 2.

4 Barbara Hannah, *Jung: His Life and Work* (New York: Putnam, 1976), p. 22. In many folk traditions there are references to the seventh son of the seventh son having "second sight" or healing powers.

5 Laurens van der Post, *Jung and the Story of Our Time* (London: Penguin, 1976), p. 77. In *Memories* Jung wrote of his No. 1 and No. 2 personalities. His No. 1 personality was caught up in concerns of the present and the everyday world, while No. 2 was deeply connected with God, history, spirit and nature.

6 MDR, pp. 19–20.

7 For a full discussion on the Earth Astrology Wheel, see Sun Bear, *The Medicine Wheel: Earth Astrology* (New York: Prentice-Hall, 1986).

LITTLE SOUTH MOON
OF THE BIG SOUTH—MYTHOLOGY
OF TRUST AND INNOCENCE

What is it at this moment and in this individual, that represents the natural urge of life? That is the question.[1]

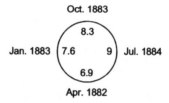

n 1879 the family moved to Klein-Huningen near Basel. At about age 7, Jung began to suffer from a pseudo-croup that was caused, as he later saw it, by a psychogenic factor: the atmosphere of the house was beginning to be unbreathable. During one of the croup attacks, he saw a glowing, blue circle about the size of a full moon, and moving inside it were golden figures he thought were angels.[2] Jung's most important works, *Aion*, *Mysterium Coniunctionis*, and *Answer to Job* all grew out of experiences while he was physically ill.

THE CHILDHOOD OF CHILDHOOD

The age of 7 is important in many indigenous cultures. In some Native traditions, when a young boy is born, a piece of the afterbirth is placed in a medicine pouch, which he wears around his neck. At the age of 7, he is taken out into the bush by the older men, the medicine pouch is buried in the ground and the young boy cuts his tie with his personal mother and reconnects with the Great Mother; the first part of his childhood dies and he is born into a greater circle. At this age, the child is in the South of the Little South Moon of the Big South (6.9 years to 7.6 years)—the childhood of childhood of childhood—and it is between 6 and 9 that we often recall the most intensely pleasurable or painful memories of childhood. Jung said that from age seven to nine he was fond of playing with fire and kept a fire burning in "caves" in his garden wall. No one but him watched over this living fire, which had an aura of sacredness.[3]

Notes

1   *CW* 7, § 487.
2   *MDR*, p. 18.
3   *MDR*, p. 20.

LITTLE SOUTHWEST MOON
OF THE BIG SOUTH—
DREAM OF TRUST AND INNOCENCE

Psychic development cannot be accomplished by intention and will alone;
it needs the attraction of symbol, whose value quantum
exceeds that of the cause.[1]

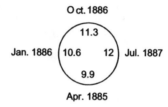

T he Southwest is the place of the Dream and Symbols of Life Experience, a time to seek a new Dream of childhood, a time for initiation, to seek symbols of Life as it might become. When he was almost 10, Jung was in the South of the Little Southwest Moon of the Big South—the double Childhood of the Sacred Dream. In *Memories, Dreams, Reflections*, after describing the fires in the garden wall, Jung wrote that he continued his "instinctive self-initiation" in his tenth year.

THE MANIKIN

Around this time, he made a manikin that was symbolic of his attempt to bridge the gap between the two worlds he found himself in. From the end of a school ruler he carved a little man, painted it, added a coat, hat, and boots, and made a bed for him in a wooden pencil case. He placed a stone with the manikin, and scrolls, or notes that he wrote, as a "library" and, like his dream of the phallus, kept it hidden, visiting it secretly in the attic. Jung said that the dream of the ithyphallic god was his first great secret; the manikin was the second and he had a vague sense of the relationship between the "soul-stone" and the stone that was he.[2] The episode with the manikin was the conclusion of his childhood and lasted about a year. Afterward, he forgot the matter until he was 35. Then, a clear memory of the manikin rose up again from childhood, together with the conviction that there are archaic components that enter the individual psyche without any direct transmission.[3]

The manikin also reminded Jung of a *Telesphoros*, one of the little cloaked gods of the ancient world that were often associated with Aesculapius, the Roman god of medicine. The dream symbol of the impersonal god/phallus in his first dream at age 3 had now become more humanized in the symbol of the manikin, which wove together his Sacred Dream (the exploration of the unconscious), his Personal Dream (being a doctor), his Ancestors (the archetypal creative phallus), and the Little People or Cabiri who appear in Goethe's *Faust*.

We see Pattern here in that Jung recalled this memory at the age of 35. He turned 35 in July, 1910 and in September, 1910 he returned prematurely from a holiday in Italy to continue his work on *Symbols of Transformation*, and it is likely that his recollection was around this time. In 1910 he was in the Little South Moon of the Big West, the place of Death and Change of Trust and Innocence. At that time he was beginning to formulate his own Dream in his writing *Symbols of Transformation*, which eventually led to his break with Freud in 1912. He was leaving behind his childhood with Freud, the father figure, and entering a stormy adolescence with him, and it was then that he recalled the manikin, a symbol of his Dream. Jung also refers to this period, the childhood of his Sacred Dream, when describing, later in *Memories*, his initial encounter with alchemy around 1928. He regarded his work on alchemy as an indication of his inner relationship to Goethe who was also captured by the same archetypal dream, and from his "eleventh year" (age 10 in the Little Southwest Moon) he had been engrossed in his "main business."[4]

Jung linked the phallus dream, the manikin, and a numinous experience he had in the cathedral square in Basel (which we shall discuss later) when he wrote in *Memories* that it would never have occurred to him to speak of these experiences and he did not say anything about the phallus dream until he was 65.[5] These experiences fed Jung's Dream throughout his whole life; it is in the Southwest that we dream the Dream that feeds us around the Wheel. Jung made the manikin when he was in the Little Southwest Moon of the Big South, and at age 65 he was in the Little Southwest Moon of the Big North. This was also when he began writing *Mysterium Coniunctionis*, perhaps the most profound expression of his creative impulse.

Notes ───────────────────────────────────

1   *CW* 8, § 47.
2   *MDR*, p. 27.
3   *MDR*, pp. 22–23.
4   *MDR*, p. 206.
5   *MDR*, pp. 41–42.

LITTLE WEST MOON
OF THE BIG SOUTH —
DEATH AND CHANGE OF TRUST
AND INNOCENCE

Modern rites of passage are unconscious ones;
they range from accidents to depression.[1]

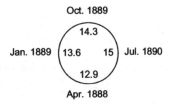

Oct. 1889

Jan. 1889   13.6   14.3   15   Jul. 1890

12.9

Apr. 1888

On his twelfth birthday, Jung stood in the East of the Little Southwest Moon of the Big South, about to begin his nine-month Chaotic Journey (July 1887 to April 1888) into the Little West Moon.[2] He said his twelfth year was a fateful one, and he devotes considerable space to the year 1887 in *Memories*.

THE DEATH OF CHILDHOOD

One day in the early summer of 1887, a month or two before he began his Chaotic Journey, he stood in the cathedral square, when suddenly, another boy gave him a shove and he struck his head against the curbstone so hard that he almost lost consciousness. At the moment he felt the blow the thought flashed through his mind: *Now you won't have to go to school any more.* From then on, he began to have fainting spells whenever he had to return to school or do homework. For more than six months he stayed away from school and he spent the time daydreaming, in the woods, by the water, or drawing.

His parents became concerned, and one day Jung eavesdropped on a conversation his father was having with a friend. He heard his father talk about how worried he was, that his son may have epilepsy or might not be able to earn his own living. Jung was stunned, and from that moment on he got back to work, crammed intensely, and gradually mastered the fainting fits. A few weeks later he returned to school and never suffered another attack. From this experience he learned that knowing one's own guilt, however painful that knowledge, is essential in being able to live freely, and it taught him what a neurosis was.[3] It also brought him diligence and conscientiousness, not for appearances but for their own sake.[4]

Around this time, Jung also began to develop an embryonic sense of his own inner authority, and also an intimation of what he later referred to as his No. 1 and No. 2 personalities. After taking a rowboat out on Lake Lucerne, he was reprimanded by a friend's father. Jung was both chastened and enraged, and to his bewilderment it occurred to him that he was two different people. One was an uncertain schoolboy, the other was an old man of high authority, who lived in the 18th century, wore buckled shoes and a wig, and went driving in a carriage.[5] As No. 1, he saw himself as somewhat disagreeable, ambitious and undisciplined, someone who fluctuated between enthusiasm and disappointment, had moderate talents, but was essentially a hermitic scholar. No. 2 was like the spirit of one who was long dead and felt himself in sympathy with the Middle Ages as embodied in *Faust*, but was unable to express himself through No. 1.[6]

Jung recognized that this split in himself, between the No. 1 and No. 2 personalities, was non-pathological and was played out in every individual.[7] This capacity is a flexibility of consciousness, or ability to Dream, that is the mark of many medicine people or intuitives, and is distinct from the defensive, or pathological, dissociation that is the product of the Self's archetypal defenses. The former is the result of conscious knowledge of and working with spirit in an individual with good ego strength, skill, and social adaptation; the latter is by definition unconscious, and the result of severe trauma in early development.

Another experience during this Little Moon marked the end of Jung's childhood when Death and Change in the West constellated an Illumination and Enlightenment in the East. Coming back from school one day he had the impression of emerging from a dense cloud where everything had happened to him, but now, as he emerged from the cloud, he happened to himself, he existed.[8]

THE SHADOW OF GOD

Finally, during this Little Moon, Jung had an encounter with the shadow side of God, again in 1887 in the cathedral square in Basel, which was significant as a prefiguration of his later work. The experience was also characteristic of the cataclysmic change that the West can bring and the unpredictability of Chaotic Journeys. Jung was standing in the cathedral square and feeling overwhelmed by the beauty of the day and how God made all this and sat above on a golden throne, far away in the blue sky. Suddenly he felt he was about to think a sinful thought that he did not want to think, and was very troubled by this for several days. He struggled with why a creator who had created such beauty and majesty would want him to think a blasphemous thought amid all that beauty. He came to the conclusion that God himself had arranged this torment for him and that he wanted to see if Jung was able to obey God's will, even if it meant going against conventional morality and his own reason. Jung gathered his courage and let the thought come. From under the throne an enormous turd fell, shattering the sparkling roof and destroying the walls of the cathedral. Jung experienced an illumination and felt an enormous relief that instead of the expected damnation, he had been graced, and wept with gratitude. He realized that God calls upon the free will of humans to fulfill his commands, even though it means disobeying sacred traditions.[9] This gave Jung his first experience of the miracle of grace, which heals all and makes all comprehensible. He realized that this was the result of his obedience to the inexorable demands of God who demands both "good" and "evil" of us, and we must obey whatever it costs us. To do evil, or good, impulsively and lightly is destructive; but to do what convention might consider as "evil" consciously and when the Self requests it of us—just as Jung thought the blasphemous thought—brings about the transformation that the Self requires, and is therefore creative.

Notes ———————————————————————————————

1 Guy Corneau, *Absent Fathers, Lost Sons: The Search for Masculine Identity* (Boston: Shambhala, 1991), p. 151.
2 Because the Chaotic Journey is an ambiguous threshold period between Moons, at times I shall consider it as part of the previous Moon, and at times as part of the next Moon. Jung's experiences on this Chaotic Journey clearly belong to the Death and Change Little West Moon.
3 Barbara Hannah, *Jung: His Life and Work* (New York: Putnam, 1976), p. 81.
4 *MDR*, pp. 31–32.
5 *MDR*, p. 34.
6 *MDR*, p. 87.
7 *MDR*, p. 42.
8 *MDR*, p. 32.
9 *MDR*, p. 40.

LITTLE NORTHWEST MOON
OF THE BIG SOUTH —
LAWS AND PATTERNS OF TRUST
AND INNOCENCE

We know there is no human foresight or wisdom that can prescribe direction to our life, except for small stretches of the way. . . . Fate confronts us like an intricate labyrinth, all too rich in possibilities, and yet of these many possibilities only one is our own right way.[1]

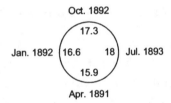

From the life-changing realizations of the West, Jung now moved into the Little Northwest Moon, the place of Law and Pattern. Often the Northwest is the place where our fate reveals itself most clearly. At about age 15 or 16, Jung's mother first introduced him to *Faust* and it came to hold great importance for him throughout his life. Fate means "that which is spoken" by the gods. It is a contradiction; some things about us are given and do not change, but fate is also something that we make up as we go along. Fate is not final, settled, or predetermined, but rather like the seed that contains the genotype of the plant, and the phenotypic expression is dependent on soil, climate, or location. The polarity in the Northwest is, on the one hand, the external civil, social, and religious laws and, on the other hand, the internal laws, the voice of the Self or *vox Dei*. Jung said, "A religious terminology comes naturally, as the only one in the circumstances, when we are faced with the tragic fate that is the unavoidable concomitant of wholeness. 'My fate' means a daemonic will to precisely that fate—a will not necessarily coincident with my own. . . . The man who submits to his fate calls it the will of God; the man who put up a hopeless and exhausting fight is more apt to see the devil in it.[2]

During these years, Jung began to experience increasing internal conflict, later to become overt with his father, between outer convention and his own inner laws. At this point, in *Memories*, Jung summarizes his experiences of adolescence and how it dawned on him that he was responsible for how his life turned out. He had a sense of being confronted with a problem he had to find the answer to and that his life ahead was predestined.[3]

THE ROOTS OF THE SUN LODGE TREE

Jung had a frequent fantasy, during the long walks home from school, of creating the world as he wished. Although Jung does not date the experience, we can assume he was in the Northwest Moon. He discusses his fantasy amid his narrative of other mid-teen events that he experienced while still at the Gymnasium in Basel, and he identifies it as occuring "a year or two" after he was 14. In the fantasy, he had a castle with a tall keep on an island connected to mainland. Inside the tower, running from top to bottom was a thick copper cable. At the top, it diverged into fine rootlets like an upside-down tree. These rootlets drew something from the air that was carried down the copper cable into a cellar below the tower, where an apparatus made gold from the strange substance that the roots had extracted. For Jung, this was an arcane and important secret of nature that had come to him by means unknown and which he had to keep hidden.[4] The fantasy, in the Little Northwest Moon, was an alchemical one concerning the transmutation of elements. Jung's last recorded dream before he died, in the Northwest of the Little Southeast Moon of the Big East, was also an alchemical one that indicated the completion of this work begun in his adolescent fantasy.

SYNCHRONICITY

The Northwest is the place of the Universal Laws, Cosmic Laws, Natural Laws and Magical Laws that govern how energy moves— inside, outside, and between—space and time. If a quantum of psychic energy is sufficient (from ceremony, or when an archetypal energy, such as death or love, is constellated) then events will occur without regard to the usual laws of causality and will operate outside and across space and time. When this "crack between the worlds" of spirit and matter opens, when the veil becomes thin, then synchronistic events occur.

In the Northwest, we stand in the place of Law and Pattern, receive Death and Change from our right, and give out Wisdom and Knowledge on our left. Or put another way: "A synchronistic event is one where an event in the physical world [West] coincides meaningfully [Pattern, Northwest] with a psychological state of mind [North]."[5] Jung's first description of a synchronistic event in *Memories* is during this Little Moon at age 15 or 16 when he paid a visit to the hermitage of Brother Klaus at Flueli.[6]

THE CHILDREN'S FIRE

One of Jung's historic contributions has been the rejoining of matter and spirit, psychology and religion. He has restored soul to a place worthy of regard, unconfined to the heights of theological inquiry, as a living presence within each person's psyche. In all of this, Jung held to the uniqueness of the individual soul, the *principium individuationis*.

In the Northwest of the Medicine Wheel sits the Children's Fire, which ceremonially symbolizes the soul of the People and of the individual. It represents the two Sacred Laws of the People: All Things are Born of the Feminine, and Nothing Shall be Done to Harm the Children. The Children's Fire is kept burning for the duration of a ceremony and must not be "crossed" or stepped over. If our inner Children's Fire is crossed, then our soul has been violated by ourselves or others. It was during this Moon that Jung wrote, and dreamed of, his own Children's Fire. In 1893, when he was 17, he wrote a poem, the last part of which reads:

> *But louder*
> *Howls the storm. It wakes the young,*
> *Urging them to live and grow.*
> *Surging, merging rise the juices,*
> *Bursting off the bud's dark shroud.*
> *Go forth to life, into the*
> *Light!*[7]

Then at age 18, on his Chaotic Journey out of the Little Northwest Moon into the Little North Moon, Jung had a dream that both frightened and encouraged him. It was about the need to keep the light of his Children's Fire kindled, leave his No. 2 personality behind, and go out into the world. In the dream he was making slow headway at night against a strong wind, and had his hands cupped around a tiny, guttering light. He looked back and saw a terrifying black figure following him. When he woke, he realized that the figure was his own shadow, cast by his light, on the swirling fog around him. He knew that the little light, though frail, was his own light of consciousness, and that was all he had. Personality No. 1 carried the light followed by No. 2 and he realized that No. 1 had to set off into the world of life and become entangled in money and matter, victories and blunders.

Notes

1   *CW* 7, § 47-48.
2   *CW* 12, § 36 fn.
3   *MDR*, pp. 47–48.
4   *MDR*, pp. 81–82.
5   Daryl Sharp, *C. G. Jung Lexicon* (Toronto: Inner City, 1991), p. 132.
6   *MDR*, pp. 79–80.
7   Aniela Jaffé, ed., *C. G. Jung: Word and Image* (Princeton: Princeton University Press, 1979), p. 18.

LITTLE NORTH MOON
OF THE BIG SOUTH — KNOWLEDGE
AND WISDOM OF TRUST
AND INNOCENCE

*Since I have not the gift of belief, I only can say
whether I know something or not.*[1]

*A belief proves to me only the phenomenon of belief,
not the content of the belief.*[2]

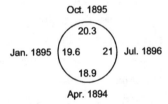

Oct. 1895

Jan. 1895   19.6   20.3   21   Jul. 1896

18.9

Apr. 1894

The North is the place of our Interconnectedness with All Things, Wisdom and Knowledge, and their shadow, Philosophies and Beliefs, the mental constructs that insulate us from our connection with All Our Relations. In *Memories*, when Jung describes his experiences in his late teens, he expresses his sense of interconnectedness with the medicine of the plants and the animals. For Jung, the countryside represented God's world, and although he admired science, he felt that it had given rise to a separation from the natural order. Humans and animals represented aspects of the Creator that had become independent, but plants directly represented the beauty and thoughts of the world of God, with no intent of their own. Woods were the place where he felt closest to the meaning of life and trees "obviously partook of the divine state of innocence."[3]

As the time for matriculation approached, Jung's No. 1 and No. 2 personalities wrestled with each other as to what career he should pursue. He wanted to study natural science but also thought about history and philosophy; then again, he was interested in archaeology, but there was no teacher for this in Basel and he had no money to study anywhere else. He then had two dreams that turned him toward science, a crucial choice for him. The first was of excavating the bones of prehistoric animals and the second was of going into a deep, dark wood, and coming to a pool. In it was a giant, shimmering radiolarian, which aroused in Jung an intense hunger for knowledge. The two dreams settled Jung on science, but he saw no future in being a "plodding" science teacher and had no money to go abroad for advanced study. Then came the inspiration to study medicine, where at least he was studying science and could do so in Basel.[4] Although Jung does not date the dreams, they probably came at the end of the school year in the early summer of 1894, when he was in the South of the Little North Moon of the Big South, the double childhood of Wisdom and Knowledge.

Later that year he was conscripted into the army for several months, as was every Swiss male over the age of 18. Then, on April 18, 1895, almost 20 years old, Jung began his studies at the University of Basel. He was in the West of the Little North Moon of the Big South, the Death and Change of the Wisdom and Knowledge of Childhood.

PHILOSOPHIES AND FATHER

The North, the place of the mind, is where we struggle to differentiate Knowledge (reality as seen through the eyes of the Great Spirit or from the point of view of the Self) from Philosophies and Beliefs (reality as seen from the point of view of the ego). Knowledge may have feeling value for us but is not weighted with emotion. Ego-driven beliefs are often rigid, and when challenged, elicit much unconscious emotion, just as undifferentiated feeling is underpinned by unconscious beliefs.

When Jung was about 17, things began to go wrong for his father and in the years until his father's death they had many vehement religious discussions. His father was a feeling type (South) and was possessed by his beliefs (North). Jung's typology, the contrary of his father's, was inferior feeling and dominant thinking, and he was always concerned with what things could mean. (Later in life, he was always astounded when feeling types were deeply moved by what he had just intended to be understood.[5]) Thinking was his father's inferior function: what things meant was always taboo, their value must never be questioned. Jung said that his father dared not think because he was consumed by doubt and was trapped by the Church and its theological thinking.[6] They had many discussions that irritated his father and saddened Jung; his father wanted belief and Jung wanted experience.[7]

Late in the summer of 1895, Jung's father fell ill with cancer. In late autumn he became bedridden and died on January 28, 1896. When his father died of cancer, his mother's No. 2 personality announced that "he died at just the right time for you." Jung said, many years later, he had no doubt that his father had died because he could not solve his religious dilemma.

When his father died, Jung was in the North of the Little North Moon of the Big South—the place of the greatest conflict between Jung's search for meaning and his father's faith—and it was a few months before Jung's Chaotic Journey out of the Little North Moon. His father (1842–1896) was 53 and about to embark on his own Big Chaotic Journey from the Big West to the Big North Moon, which he did, but in spirit. Six weeks after his death, his father reappeared to Jung in a dream in which he had made a good recovery and was coming home again. Jung had the dream again two days later. He did not dream of his father again until 1922, in the Big West Moon, when he was also in the North of the Little North Moon.

Notes

1   *Letters* 2, p. 333.
2   *MDR*, p. 319.
3   *MDR*, pp. 67–69, 83.
4   *MDR*, pp. 85–86.
5   Barbara Hannah, *Jung: His Life and Work* (New York: Putnam, 1976), p. 237.
6   *MDR*, pp. 84, 93, 73.
7   *MDR*, p. 43.

LITTLE NORTHEAST MOON OF THE BIG SOUTH— CHOICES AND DECISIONS OF TRUST AND INNOCENCE

Man was created for the sake of choice.
(HEBREW SAYING)

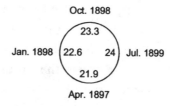

Oct. 1898

23.3

Jan. 1898 22.6   24 Jul. 1899

21.9

Apr. 1897

The Northeast is the place where we direct our use of energy around the rest of the Wheel through the decisions we make. It is the place of energy movement and how our choices, conscious or unconscious, allow energy to move. As a result of his father's death, Jung was confronted with financial choices and decisions. At age 20, he now had to support his mother and sister and pay his way through university. When they could not meet the bills for the vicarage, they moved into a house near Bottminger Mill in the suburbs of Basel. Almost in despair, Jung went to a trusted uncle and, expecting advice, told him the whole problem. However, his uncle just looked at him and said, "Well, that is how one learns to be a man, my boy." Jung was furious and stalked out of his uncle's house but stopped short before he got home and thought, "Why that's the best advice he could have given me." It was then that Jung became a man.[1]

THE KNIFE AND THE TABLE

In his second semester at university, spring of 1896, Jung came upon a small book on spiritualism in the library of a classmate's friend. This led Jung, in his early student days, to delve into occult and spiritualist literature, and he attended séances on and off for the next four years. The observations of the spiritualists were his first encounter with objective psychic phenomena and they interested him deeply, adding depth and background to his worldview.[2] In November, 1896 he delivered his first paper to the Zofingia, or student association, on "The Limits of Exact Science."

At his mother's request, in 1897, Jung visited the Rauschenbachs, old friends of the family.[3] When he entered their home, he saw a girl of about 14, in pigtails, sitting on the staircase. In his 80s, when working on his memoirs, Jung said to his secretary Aniela Jaffé, "I was deeply shaken by this, for I had really only seen her for a brief instant, but I knew immediately with absolute certainty she would be my wife."[4] Something in him had already made a decision.

One day, during the summer break of 1898, his mother was knitting in the dining room, while Jung studied in an adjoining room. A round walnut table, which had been passed down from his paternal grandmother, sat in the middle of the dining room. Suddenly, a bang came like a pistol shot from the dining room. They found that the tabletop had split all the way through the middle, not at the joints, but through solid wood. In his 80s, Jung recalled being thunderstruck at how a solid walnut table that had dried out for 70 years could split on a humid summer day.

Two weeks later, another similar incident occurred. Jung returned from university to find the women of the household in a state of agitation. Again, a noise like a shot had been heard and, in the sideboard drawer, Jung found a bread knife in four pieces.[5] Here, Jung was in the West of the Little Northeast Moon of the Big South, the place of the Death and Change of Trust and Innocence of Choices and Decisions. We shall see later that when Jung's unconscious (Trust and Innocence) was activated (Death and Change) by some not-yet-conscious decision or project, synchronicities or parapsychological phenomena tended to occur. A similar event happened in 1909 when significant decisions about Jung's relationship with Freud were still in the unconscious.

Jung suspected that the source of the disturbances at home was "Helly," or Helene Preiswerk, a maternal cousin who was fifteen years old. She spoke during séances held at a relative's house on Saturday evenings and Jung, after some initial hesitation, began to attend. He later made the séances the subject of his doctoral thesis, *On the Psychology and Pathology of So-called Occult Phenomena*, where Helly appears as "Miss S.W." In his dissertation, Jung proposed that spiritualist phenomena represented a forthcoming differentiation of personality or an attempt of the future personality to break through.[6] We shall see later that this may have been a prescient statement about his own development.

So it was here in the Northeast, the place of Design of Energy, that Jung's attention was dramatically brought to bear on phenomena that could not be explained rationally, the movement of energy between spirit and substance. "All psychological phenomena can be considered as manifestations of energy. . . . Subjectively and psychologically, this energy is conceived as *desire*. I call it *libido*, using the word in its original sense, which is by no means sexual."[7] Jung was prepared to adopt an empirical approach to non-consensual phenomena and never allowed himself the luxury of disbelief or the refuge of skepticism as easy ways out. He felt that these phenomena, such as the splitting of the table and the knife, or séances, must be investigated, even though they led into unknown and unpopular realms.[8]

PROFESSIONAL DECISIONS

In October, 1898 Jung was preparing for the state examination and was still uncertain about which medical specialty to take up. Then he happened to come across Krafft-Ebing's *Lehrbuch der Psychiatrie*, and in a flash of illumination it became clear that the only profession for him was psychiatry. At last, he had found a place where nature and spirit made contact.[9] This was the decision about his professional Dream that had been brewing. After the exams, he spent a week in Stuttgart and Munich and visited an aunt. He called this visit the final farewell to the nostalgias of his childhood.

During all these events, Jung was in the Northeast, the place where energy moves in and out of the Wheel and where we choose how we use psychological energy in our lives. When we stand in this place of choosing, we face the Southwest, the place of Needs, Wants, and Desires—our Dream—across the Wheel. The Southwest and Northeast work together. If there is no Desire, we cannot Dream; if there is no Dream we cannot Choose; if we cannot Choose, then the Dream dies.

Notes ───────────────────────────────────

1   Barbara Hannah, *Jung: His Life and Work* (New York: Putnam, 1976), p. 64.

2   *MDR*, p. 99.

3   Barbara Hannah, *Jung: His Life and Work*, p. 83. Barbara Hannah, an English woman who worked with Jung from 1929 until his death, dates this visit as "just two years" into his medical studies and "a year or so" after his father's death.

4   Gerhard Wehr, *Jung: A Biography* (Boston: Shambhala, 1987), p. 91.

5   *MDR*, p. 105.

6   *CW* 1, § 136.

7   *CW* 4, § 567.

8   Barbara Hannah, *Jung: His Life and Work*, p. 69.

9   *MDR*, p. 109.

LITTLE EAST MOON
OF THE BIG SOUTH—
ILLUMINATION OF TRUST
AND INNOCENCE

Oh! I have slipped the surly bonds of earth . . .
Put out my hand and touched the face of God.[1]

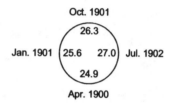

Oct. 1901

26.3

Jan. 1901   25.6   27.0   Jul. 1902

24.9

Apr. 1900

T he years from 24 to 27 are often a time of taking stock of
the end of adolescence and the early twenties. The lightning bolt of Illumination—the sudden glimpse of what has
been in darkness of the unconscious—is characteristic of the East. In
the light of the East we are more disposed to see the darkness in the
West, what has sunk into unconsciousness during the previous three
years or twenty-seven years, and also what is yet to become conscious in the next Moon. If we are able to claim for ourselves some
consciousness (Illumination and Enlightenment), we are able to
move on. If we cling to the remnants of childishness (Fantasy and
Illusion), the powers of Death and Change are increasingly constellated. Jung said, when he was almost 60, that his whole life had been
spent in eliminating his own childishness.

THE DEATH OF THE PUER

For those who are creative, who have been touched by fire, this last Moon of childhood is a crossroads between light and dark and is crucial in whether, and how, they continue their journey. The result of resisting the movement into the Big West, the next 27 years of Death and Change, is the psychology of the *puer* or *puella aeternus*. Marie-Louise von Franz said that many creative young men and women are secretly identified with another world and this closeness with the collective unconscious is both the wisdom and the folly of the young person, but if one remains in this situation "past about the twenty-fifth year" it leads to the puer aeternus neurosis, a lack of adaptation to life, often with a touch of genius, which sometimes results in early death.[2] On the light side, the puer is connected with spirit, fire, and creativity. On the shadow side, he wants to fly high and not come down to earth. The puer lives in Fantasy and Illusion and, flying too high, often dies an early, tragic death. John Keats, the poet, died at age 25 1/2, and Helly Preiswerk, the medium Jung wrote his doctoral thesis on, died at age 26. More recent examples of the puer are rock stars such as Jimi Hendrix and Jim Morrison, both dead at 27.

More commonly, as the puer grows into middle age, he dies an emotional or spiritual death, rather than a physical death. His emotional life remains at an adolescent level and he typically lives a provisional life, does not want to be committed or tied down, bucks at boundaries and limitations, and is always over- or under-reaching himself. What he has is never quite right and he is often full of big plans that are about to hatch but nothing happens. The puer is associated with the god Dionysus, the god of wine, revelry, and passion. The shadow of the puer is the *senex*, associated with the god Apollo, who is disciplined, controlled, responsible, rational, and ordered. As he moves out of late middle age (often around the mid-fifties in the transition from the Big West to the Big North Moon) he increasingly becomes his shadow—the curmudgeon, the rule-bound, grumpy old man who is impossible to please. The puer becomes what he hated a Big Moon Cycle earlier.

So Jung now entered the Little East Moon, the last Little Moon of the Big South. Here, he left behind the teachings of the first 27 years of his life and began to move into adulthood. He decided to apply for a post at the Burghölzli Psychiatric Hospital in Zurich, even though he had already been offered a prestigious post in internal medicine elsewhere, and began there on December 10, 1900. Basel had become too stuffy for him and he wanted to break the mold of being the son of the Reverend Paul Jung and the grandson of Professor Carl Gustav Jung, and a member of a definite social set. Jung did not want to be pigeon-holed.[3]

Notes

1   John Gillespie Magee, "High Flight."
2   Marie-Louise von Franz, *Puer Aeternus: A Psychological Study of the Adult Struggle with the Paradise of Childhood* (Santa Monica: Sigo, 1981).
3   *MDR*, p. 111.

BIG WEST MOON—
DEATH AND CHANGE

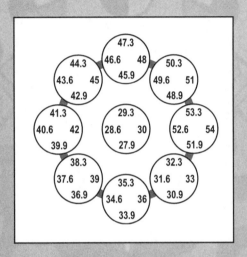

Are you willing to be sponged out, erased/cancelled/made nothing?
Dipped into oblivion?
If not, you will never really change.
—D. H. LAWRENCE, *Phoenix*

Life is trouble, only death is not. To be alive is to unhook your belt
and look for trouble.
—NIKOS KAZANTZAKIS, *Zorba the Greek*

LITTLE CENTER MOON
OF THE BIG WEST—
CATALYST OF DEATH AND CHANGE

It's good to focus your attention on one thing in life. . . .
In the process of becoming an expert you finely tune your whole being. . . .
You rid yourself of the attitudes that are not essential to your task.[1]

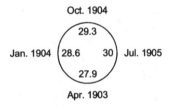

F rom birth to age 3 and from 27 to 30, we stand in the place
of the Catalyst energy, respectively in the Little Center
Moons of the Big South and the Big West. It is the Void at
the center of the Wheel, where what we do or what is done to us has
a profound impact on the course of the next twenty-seven-year cycle.
The Little Center Moon of the Big South is the story of attachment
to Life itself, the positive, nurturing aspect of the Great Mother, as
mediated through the personal mother. The Little Center Moon of
the Big West is the story of attachment to Death and Change, the
power of Life as the Death-Mother, the capacity to destroy in the service of creation, as mediated through our intimate physical relationships. In the sense that individuation is an *opus contra naturam* (a
work against nature), we begin to fashion a life out of what Life has
given us. As the years from birth to 3 are about the beginnings of the

child personality and knowing Trust and Innocence—or its violation—so the years from 27 to 30 are about fashioning the adult personality and knowing the shadow. In the Big West, now that a Big
Moon Cycle has been completed, the Little Moons begin to resonate
with similar experiences in the past, in the same moons, and opposite moons across the Wheel, of the Big South Moon.

THE FIRST BIG CHAOTIC JOURNEY

Jung's first Big Chaotic Journey was from July 1902 to April 1903,
and it was a momentous time. In July 1902, he became engaged to
Emma Rauschenbach, the young girl of 14 he had seen five years earlier on another Chaotic Journey. They were married on February 14,
1903. During the winter of 1902 to 1903, he traveled to Paris to
study with the famed Pierre Janet at Salpetrire Hospital, and returned
to Burghölzli early in 1903. In 1903, he also reread Freud's
Interpretation of Dreams, which he had first encountered in 1900, but
found it held more meaning for him this time. It eventually opened
the door to his historic and stormy relationship with Freud.

The years from 1902 to 1905 were ones in which Jung defined
himself professionally. He qualified in psychiatry under Eugen
Bleuler (1857-1939), who was Professor of Psychiatry at the
University of Zurich and Director of Burghölzli. Bleuler was a pioneer in the humane treatment of the mentally ill, and coined the
term schizophrenia. At his suggestion, Jung wrote his dissertation in
1902 on the séances of Helly Preiswerk.

Jung lived at Burghölzli and immersed himself in the treatment
of psychotic patients. In 1904 he published his *Studies in Word
Association*, an investigation into the disturbances in reaction time in
response to certain words, which led to his formulation of the complex theory. In December 1904 his first child, Agatha, was born. In
1905 he was made Senior Physician at Burghölzli, and later the same
year was appointed Lecturer (*Privatdozent*) in Psychiatry at the
University of Zurich. Jung called the time at Burghölzli under Bleuler
his "years of apprenticeship." It was here he began to explore the

symbolic content of symptoms, rather than the symptom classifications that were much in fashion at the time, and are again today. In his work with patients, Jung began to realize that psychotic delusions and hallucinations contained symbolic meaning.[2]

The Little Center Moon is a time of setting the compass and changing the trajectory of the next 27 years. During his Chaotic Journey out of this Center Moon, Jung took a step that was to change his life profoundly. In April 1906 he sent Freud his work on the word association test and in October 1906 the two men began an exchange of letters that continued at the rate of about one a week until 1913.

Notes

1   Lynn Andrews, *Crystal Woman: Sisters of the Dreamtime* (New York: Warner, 1988), p. 198.
2   *MDR*, p. 127.

LITTLE SOUTHEAST MOON
OF THE BIG WEST—
DEATH AND CHANGE OF
SELF-IMAGES

When one has not had a good father,
one must create one.[1]

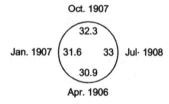

ung's first time standing on the Northwest-Southeast axis
since he was an adolescent brought him the life-changing
encounter with Freud. He was almost 32 and approaching
the Northwest of the Little Southeast Moon. This axis had immense
significance for Jung: in the Little Northwest Moon of the Big South
he was introduced to *Faust* by his mother; he had the alchemical fantasy on the way home from school, and the dream about the little
light of consciousness. In the Little Northwest Moon of the Big
North he had a near-fatal illness, and he died when he was in the
Northwest of the Little Southeast Moon of the Big East. In other
words, Jung died in the same place on the Moon Cycles as when he
first met Freud, and Freud's death also had a fateful relationship with
Jung's Moon Cycles, as we shall see later.

THE FIRST MEETING WITH FREUD

Early in 1907, Freud invited Jung to visit him in Vienna. They met at one o'clock in the afternoon of March 3, 1907 at Freud's apartment at Berggasse 19, and talked almost non-stop for thirteen hours. Jung said Freud was the first man of importance he had met and found him shrewd and intelligent but could not quite make him out. What Freud said about his sexual theory impressed him, but he also had deep reservations. Jung was too inexperienced to offer any cogent objections, however he did protest to Freud that his attitude reduced art, culture, and religion to being morbid products of repressed sexuality. Freud replied that indeed, they were, and that was a curse of fate against which protest was useless.[2] The stage was set for what was to become an intense relationship where the "puer/senex" and "gifted son/authoritarian father" dynamic was played out.

In this first meeting with Freud, Jung stood just past the West of the Little Southeast Moon of the Big West—the place of the double Death and Change of Self-Images. It was later, through Freud's insistence on the exclusively sexual and oedipal roots of neurosis, that Jung was forced to clarify his own ideas, particularly regarding the archetypes—the Ancestors—and through this, though not without struggle, he was able to develop his own view of the psyche, his own Image of Self.

During this Little Moon, the dynamics of the father-son relationship were very much alive for Jung. In 1908, he wrote *The Significance of the Father in the Destiny of the Individual* in collaboration with Otto Gross.[3] Freud had referred Gross to Jung for treatment at Burghölzli. He was just two years younger than Jung, a brilliant psychiatrist who was addicted to cocaine and opium and later became an anarchist. He had a highly antagonistic relationship with his father, a world-famous Austrian professor of criminology, who later had him committed to a mental institution in 1911 on the grounds of insanity.[4] Jung's analysis of Gross evolved into a mutual analysis, and in a letter to Freud in June 1908 he wrote, "In Gross I discovered many aspects of my own nature, so that he often seemed like my twin brother."[5] There is some evidence that he influenced Jung's theory of psychological types, as well as his views on extra-marital affairs. In January 1910 Jung wrote to Freud, "The prerequisite for a good marriage, it seems to me, is the license to be unfaithful."[6]

Notes

1   Friedrich Nietzsche, *Human, All Too Human: A Book for Free Spirits* (Cambridge: Cambridge University Press, 1996), p. 381.
2   *MDR*, pp. 149–150.
3   *CW* 4. However Jung later minimized Gross's contribution to the paper.
4   For a fuller discussion see Gottfried Heuer, "Jung's Twin Brother: Otto Gross and Carl Gustav Jung," in *Journal of Analytical Psychology*, 46 (2001): 655–688.
5   William McGuire, ed., *The Freud/Jung Letters* (Princeton: Princeton University Press, 1974), p. 156.
6   McGuire, *The Freud/Jung Letters*, p. 289.

LITTLE SOUTH MOON
OF THE BIG WEST—
DEATH AND CHANGE OF
TRUST AND INNOCENCE

Since men do live psychologically in a harem, it is useful
to get to know one's inner household.[1]

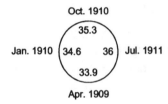

In the Big South Moon we move from mother (0-3 years, Center), to father and the family (3-6 years, Southeast), and then to the outside world and peers (6-9 years, South). The story in childhood is one of our relationship to the smaller collective, dominated by the archetype of the mother and the protective small group. In the Big West Moon the same story is repeated but within the larger circumference of the culture or society, dominated by the archetypal father.

TRIANGLES

The South is the place of the number 3. All the southern moons (Southeast, South and Southwest) in the Big West occupy the years of our 30s. It is a time of threes and triangles, a time of standing in the place of emotions, against the background of the earlier oedipal triangle writ on a larger canvas. It is the psychology of the thirty-something sitcoms.

Jung's professional and personal life during these years revolved around an oedipal triangle of issues: his relationships with his own anima, other women, and Freud. Of the anima, von Franz astutely observes, "The animus fosters loneliness in women, whereas the anima thrusts men headlong into relationships and the confusion that accompanies them."[2] The crucible of relationships and the marital triangle forces the unconscious to the fore and brings about a differentiation of Eros. When a man (let's say) is caught between his marriage to his wife and his desire for another woman, he feels, "If I don't see the other woman, I am betraying my feelings. If I leave my wife and children, I am behaving irresponsibly and chasing a passing infatuation. I can't do either and I can't keep this up." His wife's animus says, "Her or me!" And the other woman's animus says, "Make a decision!" In such a situation, he cannot make a "correct" decision.

The anima forces a man into a situation that is meant to be without a solution. Jung said that to be in such a conflict is the classical beginning of the process of individuation. The unconscious wants the hopeless conflict in order to put the ego up against the wall and temper its omnipotence. "If he is ethical enough to suffer to the core of his personality, then generally, because of the insolubility of the conscious situation, the Self manifests. In religious language you could say that the situation without issue is meant to force the man to rely on an act of God. . . . Normally, the anima does not take a man by the hand and lead him right up to Paradise; she puts him first into a hot cauldron where he is nicely roasted for a while."[3]

Much has been written about Jung's relationships with Sabina Spielrein and Toni Wolff. My intent here is not to moralize about Jung's relationships—as many others have taken upon themselves to do, with motivations we can only wonder at—but to discern the weaving with the Moon Cycles.

Significantly, he met both women when he was in the West of a Little Moon. He first met Spielrein in August 1904, when he had just turned 29, and was in the West of the Little Center Moon. He met

Toni Wolff in early 1910, when he was almost 35, in the West of the Little South Moon. The West is the place of Woman—as Life-Giver and Death-Bringer.

SABINA SPIELREIN

Sabina Spielrein was admitted, at age 18, to Burghölzli on August 17, 1904. She was brought from Rostov in Russia for treatment of severe hysterical symptoms, as a result of repeated, sexualized physical beatings by her father. Spielrein was Jewish—the significance of which we shall come to later. Prior to her admission, she had been unsuccessfully treated at a private clinic, and had already "fallen in love" with two doctors. Although Jung had little experience with such patients (and at Burghölzli they were treated, if at all, with hypnosis), he used Freud's technique of psychoanalysis for the first time, and the result was decisive. By the spring of 1905, Spielrein was free of her symptoms, she was able to begin medical studies, and was discharged on June 1, 1905.[4] Jung published a paper in 1905 on the treatment of a hysterical patient, which in all probability was Spielrein, and also presented her case to a conference in Amsterdam in 1907.[5] Spielrein saw Jung regularly for analysis, as a private outpatient, the year following her discharge, and during 1907 she was still seeing Jung intermittently for analysis.

Spielrein's diaries and her letters to both Jung and Freud were discovered in 1977, in Geneva.[6] The January 2001 issue of the *Journal of Analytical Psychology* was devoted to the English translations of the recently available Burghölzli records of Jung's treatment of Spielrein, as well as Jung's letters to her.[7] From the outset, it seems that Spielrein developed an intense erotic transference toward Jung, transferring onto him the "painful" love of her father. Jung was unable to manage this and responded in kind. He spoke of her glowingly as an intelligent and gifted person with great sensitivity and once said to her, "Minds such as yours help advance science. You must become a psychiatrist."[8] From Jung's letters to Spielrein we see that by mid-1908 he and Spielrein were arranging trysts. Jung was clearly attracted to her but seemed less fatally in love with her than she with him. During the latter period of their relationship he frequently attempted to distance himself from their tempestuous, on/off affair, only to approach again. In a letter of June 30, 1909, she wrote that she had loved him for "four, five years," and it's likely, for some period between 1906 and 1909, that she and Jung were lovers.

Spielrein was nothing if not perceptive. Toward the end of 1908, she wrote to her mother: "Just recently Junga [sic] finished his paper that created such a stir, ('The significance of the father in the destiny of the individual'), in which he shows that the choice of the future (love) object is determined in the first relations of the child with his parents. That I love him is as firmly determined as that he loves me. He is for me a father and I am a mother for him or, more precisely, the woman who has acted as the first substitute for the mother (his mother came down with hysteria when he was two years old); and he became so attached to the (substitute) woman that when she was absent he saw her in hallucinations, etc., etc. Why he fell in love with his wife I do not know... Let us say, his wife is 'not completely' satisfactory, and now he has fallen in love with me, a hysteric, and I fell in love with a psychopath, and is it necessary to explain why?"9 Later, I will explore the notion of the "second mother" in connection with Jung's book *Answer to Job*.

From his late 20s to his late 30s (1904 to 1912), in the Little Center and Little Southern Moons, Jung was vulnerable to acting out strong erotic transferences with his female patients, and to other affairs. In these relationships he would replicate the early triangle of his close relationship with the maid who looked after him (Spielrein, and later Toni Wolff), and the more estranged one with his mother (Emma), with both of these set against the contrary desires to be accepted by, and to be better than, the distant father (Freud).

Naturally, Jung's affair did not go unnoticed. In mid-January 1909 Spielrein's mother received an anonymous letter (possibly from Emma Jung) urging her to rescue her daughter and Mrs. Spielrein wrote Jung a letter to which he replied. In February 1909, responding to Freud's letter about the arrangements for the upcoming trip to Clark University, he said that he had been under enormous strain both night and day. We can assume that this was probably because of the Spielrein matter. It seems this turmoil was going on from late 1908 to the spring of 1909. In March 1909 he wrote to Freud, again likely referring to Spielrein, saying that a female patient had raised a fuss because he had declined to be the father of her child. Then, on January 10, 1910, he wrote to Freud, saying that Emma was acting jealously, but without grounds. It was in 1910 that Jung's name was also associated with several other women in Zurich. In April 1909, Jung was in the South of the Little South Moon of the Big West—the Death and Change of double Trust and Innocence, and in January 1910, he arrived in the West of the Little South Moon, the place of the double Death and Change of Trust and Innocence.

By 1911, Jung's relationship with Spielrein had cooled, and the general tone of their letters changed to discussions of clinical matters. Spielrein matriculated in psychiatry from Zurich medical school in 1911, and she then left Zurich and later joined the Vienna Psychoanalytic Association and worked with Freud, who described her work as "magnificent." In 1912 she published her best known paper, "Destruction as the Cause of Coming into Being," which can be considered a precursor to Freud's theory of the death instinct. From 1921 to 1923, she worked in Geneva where Jean Piaget, the renowned developmental psychologist, underwent analysis with her, and later she returned to her home of Rostov. When the Nazis invaded Rostov in June, 1941 they herded the Jews into a local synagogue, and shot them. Tragically, among the victims were the 55-year-old Sabina Spielrein and her two daughters.

In his penultimate letter to her on September 1, 1919 Jung wrote, "The love of S. for J. made the latter aware of something he had previously only vaguely suspected, namely of a power in the unconscious which shapes one's destiny, a power which later led him to things of the greatest importance. The relationship had to be 'sublimated,' because otherwise it would have led to delusion and madness (a concretization of the unconscious). Sometimes one must be unworthy to live at all."[10]

TONI WOLFF

Much less is known about the relationship between Jung and Toni Wolff, as after her death he burned all his correspondence with her. He referred to his wood stove at Bollingen as "his discretion."[11] Toni's mother brought her to Jung early in 1910 for treatment of depression following the death of her father in 1909. She was 22 (b. September 18, 1888) at the time, and Jung was 34. Within two years she was regarded as Jung's colleague and appeared with Jung and Emma in the photograph taken at the September 1911 Weimar Psychoanalytic Congress. Following Jung's affair with Sabina Spielrein and other putative affairs, there was increasing conflict between him and Emma. Jung agonized over his attraction to Toni because he did not want to inflict any suffering on his wife and family. But it was his family that gave Jung the motivation to seek a resolution. He was well aware of the damage that fathers can do by not living their erotic life to the fullest, and projecting that unlived life onto their daughters. He knew that if he refused the relationship with Toni Wolff, which had come to him against his conscious will, it would have repercussions in his family. It seems that around 1916, at the depths of his descent into the unconscious, Emma made accommodations for the relationship between Jung and Toni. She continued as Jung's lover and colleague for the rest of her life often joining the family for Sunday dinner and accompanying him to Bollingen.

For a long time Emma and Toni were painfully jealous of each other but Emma said years later, "You see, he never took anything from me to give to Toni, but the more he gave her, the more he seemed able to give me." Toni also realized later that Jung's unwavering devotion to his marriage gave her more than she could possibly have had without it. Jung said he could never forget what Toni did for him during his descent into the unconscious: "Such things stand forever, and I shall be grateful to her for all eternity."[12] No doubt Jung had this experience in mind when he wrote in 1958: "There are women who are not meant to bear physical children, but they are those that give rebirth to a man in a spiritual sense."[13]

TRIANGLES AND TRUST

It seems that the soul needs these erotic entanglements to experience itself emotionally. The tumultuous intensities, attractions, betrayals, crucifixions, and abandonments of triangles that occur in the thirties are archetypal necessities. "Love, in the sense of *concupiscentia*, is the dynamism that most infallibly brings the unconscious to light . . . we always find two main causes of psychic catastrophes: on the one hand a disappointment in love and on the other hand a thwarting of the striving for power."[14] Here we might also remember that Christ's ministry occupied the three years of the Southeast Moon, and he was betrayed, crucified, nailed thrice to cross, and forsaken by the father, at age 33. Our thirty-third year spans the nine months of the Illumination of Death and Change of Images of Self and the first three months of double Trust and Innocence of Death and Change.

Triangular passions and betrayals often surface in the Southern moons (Southeast, South and Southwest) of the Big West as they point to a necessary transformation of the earlier experiences of trust and its twin, betrayal. All of the emotional residues of the Southern moons in childhood from 3 to 12, and particularly all emotional residues from the South of all the Little Moons in childhood around ages 4, 7 and 10, come to the fore. The full weight of the emotion and feeling experiences in the South and the reworking of previous residues sets the stage in adulthood for the constellation of Desire in the Southwest, and realization of the shadow in the West. James Hillman says, of the erotic nature of triangles:

> For our psyche to unite legitimately with the creative and bring sanctified birth to what it carries, we evidently need to realize both our loss of primordial love through betrayal and

separation, and also our wrong relation to eros—the enthrallment, servility, pain, sadness, longing: all aspects of erotic
mania. . . . The arrow strikes us into triangles to such an
extraordinary extent that this phenomenon must be examined for its creative role in soul-making. The sudden dynamic effect on the psyche of jealousy and other triangular fears
and fantasies hints that this constellation of "impossibility"
bears as much significance as the conjunction. So necessary
is the triangular pattern that, even where two exist only for
each other, a third will be imagined. . . . Perhaps this is its
necessity: the triangles of eros educate the psyche out of its
girlish goodness, showing it the extent of its fantasies and
testing its capacities. The triangle presents eros as the transcendent function creating out of two a third, which, like all
impossible love, cannot be lived fully in actuality, so that the
third becomes imaginal reality.[15]

When we are betrayed, a wound is opened in our most vulnerable
spot—our original trust—and we can only be betrayed by those we
trust. The person who betrays is perversely being faithful to Life and
Death and Change, because the unconscious desire behind betrayal
often springs from a need to transform the relationship in some way.
Betrayal, or being betrayed, initiates us into the realization that Life
is greater than the word that has been exchanged between lover and
beloved. Our naiveté is transformed in an Illumination of the shadow of others and ourselves. As we travel around the Wheel, each
place yearns for union with its opposite. Naïve, maternal *eros* in the
South leads us to some Wisdom about the fragility of the word, the
logos of the father, in the North. Hillman elaborates on betrayal:

Could it be that the capacity to betray belongs to the state of
fatherhood? . . . The paternal image—that just, wise, merciful figure—refuses to intervene in any way to ameliorate the
suffering which he himself has brought about. He also refuses to give an account of himself. . . . The conscious use of
brutality would seem a mark common to paternal figures.

The unjust father reflects unfair life. Where he is impervious to the cry for help and the need of the other, where he can admit that his promise is fallible, he acknowledges that the power of the word can be transcended by the forces of life. . . . It means further that one has to some extent overcome that sense of uneasy guilt which holds one back from carrying out in full consciousness necessary though brutal acts. (By conscious brutality, I do not mean either deliberately perverse brutality aimed to ruin another, or sentimental brutality as found sometimes in the literature and films and the code of soldiers). . . . This hardheartedness shows an integration of brutality, thereby bringing one closer to nature—which gives no explanations of itself.[16]

Isak Dinesen said, "The cure for anything is salt water—sweat, tears, or the sea." The woundedness that we experience in triangles evokes images of salt, the salt rubbed in the wound, the bitter herbs of the Seder. Salt is the uniting symbol between the wounding and suffering from relationships in the South and the gifts of understanding to be reaped in the North. The conflict between the two constellates a third factor that unites the warring opposites.[17] In *Mysterium Coniunctionis* Jung writes of North and South:

The most outstanding properties of salt are bitterness and wisdom. . . . Tears, sorrow, and disappointment are bitter, but wisdom is the comforter in all psychic suffering. Indeed, bitterness and wisdom form a pair of alternatives: where there is bitterness wisdom is lacking, and where wisdom is there can be no bitterness. . . . Salt, as the carrier of this fateful alternative, is coordinated with the nature of woman. . . . The novilunium of woman is a source of countless disappointments for man which easily turns to bitterness, though they could equally well be a source of wisdom if they were understood.... Disappointment, always a shock [the withdrawal of projections in the South leads to Death and Change in the West] to the feelings, is not only the mother of bitterness but the strongest incentive to a differentiation of feeling. The failure of a pet plan, the disappointing behavior of someone one loves [our mythologies or projections], can supply the impulse either for a more or less brutal outburst of affect [the shadow side of the South] or for a modification and adjustment of feeling, and hence for its higher development. This culminates in wisdom if feeling is supplemented by reflection and rational insight. Wisdom is never violent: where wisdom reigns there is no conflict between thinking [North] and feeling [South].[18]

From the Relationships Wheel, a teaching about the different for of human relationship, we learn that, in the East, celibacy teaches Illumination and Enlightenment through spirit; in the West, monogamy teaches Death and Change through the body; in the South, triangular relationships teach Trust and Innocence through the heart; in the North, group relationships teach Wisdom and Knowledge through the mind; and in the Center, omnisexuality, our erotic relationship with all forms of all things, is the Catalyst that sources Life from its own presence. Although the prevailing moral code at any time may judge otherwise, there is no preferred place on the Wheel—they are all equal but differing. Enduring triangular relationships are often comprised of a Sun, a Moon, and an Earth. Emma Jung, who by her own account was an introverted sensation type, was an Earth; Toni Wolff, an intuitive hetaera (consort), was a Moon; and Jung himself was a Sun.

In reading the various biographies of Jung, particularly about his relationships with women, what is striking is the ill-temper of many of the authors.[19] They write with great attention to fact and detail, but are highly emotional in their attitude toward Jung. With the historical perspective they enjoy, and with thinly-veiled sanctimony, they stake claim to large areas of moral high ground. Much of the writing seems anima-driven, the tone is churlish, catty, defamatory, and spiteful, and their motivations are at best unclear and at worst suspect. Those who are most vocal about boundaries and probity seem unable to contain their voyeuristic need to peer into the lives of others, and tut-tut at what they see.

Although in the age of attention to dual relationships and codes of ethics (both advances in differentiation of feeling in regard to patients, and requiring fate and the unconscious to find other avenues) Jung's relationships seem highly unprofessional, we should remember that he was no exception, among the psychoanalysts of the time, to romantic entanglements. "Otto Gross' exploits were legendary, [Wilhelm] Stekel had long enjoyed a reputation as a 'seducer,' [Ernest] Jones was paying blackmail money to a patient, and even good Pastor [Oscar] Pfister was lately being entranced by one of his charges. Indeed, the most extraordinary entanglement was [Sandor] Ferenczi's, the amiable Hungarian having taken into analysis the daughter of a woman he was having an affair with and then fallen in love with the girl."[20]

However the DNA of Jung's personal life may have been inherited by later generations of Jungians. James Astor, a Jungian of the British school (which was more influenced by Freudian psychoanalysis), observes in his review of Thomas Kirsch's history of the Jungians: "Certain themes recur. One is the difficulty non transference based Jungians have had in maintaining boundaries. There is a reminder in the book of the muddle the Zurich Institute got into when it could not decide whether [James] Hillman had violated the ethical code of behaviour required of a practising analyst and was therefore liable to expulsion; this happened when the issue was already a matter of public record and subject to a court case. . . . It is not clear why Hillman's boundary infringing behaviour is included but [Nathan] Schwartz-Salant, who is often quoted on the subject of countertransference and who was disciplined for having sexual relations with patients, is not."[21]

We might remember that humanity has attempted to balance order and disorder in the sphere of human relationships for thousands of years. No culture has ever got it right, and the more sensible ones created space for both. Social norms serve the group, and desires serve the individual. Each serves as counterweight to the other, and at the balance point something happens. There is an eternal tension between socially sanctioned forms of relationship, and what people actually do, or wish to do, with each other sexually and emotionally. This might alert us to the fact that this Pattern is needed—because God learns something in the process.

Abiding by the law, the social mores, or the professional code of ethics is meet and fitting—these things provide the decent floor on which we stand. But Life is always larger than ethics. The destructive and creative waters of the unconscious always find a way around the latest ethical patch that has been applied to a leaky area. It is only in being ethical and having integrity when there are no ethical codes at hand that we make our Give-Away to Life.

STRUGGLES WITH FREUD

Between their first contact by letter in 1906 and their eventual split in 1912, the years from 1908 to 1911 were the perigee of contact between Jung and Freud. Freud stayed with Jung in Kusnacht for three days in September 1908 and Jung visited Freud for the second time, accompanied by Emma, from the 25th to the 30th of March, 1909. Although Jung was a staunch supporter of Freud, they had increasingly disagreed about the nature of the libido, the role of sexuality and incest in psychopathology, and on what Freud called Jung's "spook complex."

During their visit, Freud asked him to promise never to abandon the sexual theory of neurosis, and went on to say that they must create a dogma, an "unshakeable bulwark . . . against the black tide of mud . . . of occultism." This alarmed Jung because, like his father, Freud had asked him just to believe, to have faith. Jung felt faith and dogma that suppressed doubt had less to do with scientific inquiry than with a personal drive for power. He saw Freud's struggle as a mythological one between the light of his rational belief and the tides of darkness; as a result, he retreated to dogma as a religiose defense against an archetypal struggle.[22] "When Freud was talking of sexuality it was as though he were talking of God . . . Freud for all his repudiation of spirituality has in reality a mystical attitude to sexuality."[23]

Jung's assessment of Freud's religious transference toward sexuality illustrates how, when a conflict or imbalance comes about on the Wheel, the opposite side is the way out, either as a creative solution or a defense. Spirituality is in the East of the Wheel, the body, matter, and sexuality is in the West. Freud, trained as a neurologist, was eager to fit psychoanalysis into the Procrustean bed of rational science and precisionist technique. Sexuality, in particular, didn't fit. The rule is that what is bent out of shape reappears in unnatural form across the Wheel. Thus, we see Freud's religiose attitude to his sexual theory arising to compensate his overly scientific attitude. This seeming disavowal of spirituality has continued among psychoanalysts, a state of affairs summed up by Thomas Kirsch who, in response to a question about the emphasis on spirituality in Jung's school and its absence in Freud's, said, "How can there be said to be no spirituality in a psychoanalysis that took Freud to be God?"[24]

The same applies to the North and South. When an emotional conflict is engendered in the South it requires the discrimination of the mind in the North to navigate one's way between conflicting emotions. Likewise, when the rational problem-solving and weighing of pros and cons comes to a standoff in the North, then the ultimate arbiter is discrimination by feeling values in the South. Overdetermined emotional complexes in the South are defensively rationalized with dogma, opinion, and argument, and precious, over-valued intellectual constructs in the North are fiercely defended with great emotion—as witness, much heated scientific debate. To put it another way, from the point of view of psychological type, thinking types are touchy about their emotions, feeling types (as was Freud) are touchy about their beliefs.

It was during this visit—seemingly after Freud made the comment about the black tide of occultism—that the now-famous incident with the bookcase occurred. While Freud was speaking against parapsychology, Jung had a sensation in his diaphragm as if it was made of iron and becoming red-hot. At that moment, there was a loud report in a bookcase that stood right next to them. They both started in alarm, fearing it was going to fall over. Jung immediately pointed out that this was a parapsychological phenomenon and, to Freud's disbelief, he predicted that shortly there would be another report. No sooner had he said the words than another bang went off in the bookcase.[25]

Two similar events had previously occurred to Jung (the splitting of the wooden table and the shattering of the knife) in the summer of 1898. It seems that such events occurred when a creative decision was not yet conscious for Jung and the unconscious was preparing a change in direction. He often experienced these phenomena as a precursor to a creative effort before he realized he was going to write. They were to recur in 1916 in the middle of his confrontation with the unconscious and they also acted as the impetus to write *Septem Sermones ad Mortuos* (Seven Sermons to the Dead).[26]

The detonations in the bookcase were perhaps a prefiguration of Jung's final break with Freud. From the beginning, Jung was somewhat skeptical about Freud's attitude toward libido, but had remained publicly loyal to Freud during the early years of the psychoanalytic movement and its attendant politics, despite his increasing private ambivalence. Although the loud crack in the bookcase as a symbol of the coming intellectual split between Freud and Jung may seem too patent an interpretation, I suggest it because the phenomenon preceded their parting of ways by exactly three years. It was while finishing the final chapter of *Symbols of Transformation*, in March 1912, that Jung realized the inevitability of his break with Freud.

It is an old saw in psychotherapy that any real change, or the mourning of a significant loss, takes three years. The first year after a loss involves getting over it; in the second year you think you're over it; and in the third year, you realize you aren't and reach some closure. A completed analysis often takes three years. We can see from the bookcase incident that one of the periodic rhythms of deep change is three years. The reports in the bookcase in 1909 announced the birth of the death of the relationship between Jung and Freud in 1912.

Jung felt that from the moment of the report in the bookcase, things were never the same between them. Shortly after returning from Vienna, he wrote to Freud on April 2, 1909, that his visit had relieved him of the oppression of Freud's paternal authority, and that his psyche had celebrated this release with a dream that I will explore further on.[27] On April 16, Freud replied that on the same evening as the bookcase incident he had anointed Jung as his "successor and crown prince" but with regard to his forays into parapsychological realms, Jung must be content with not understanding rather than make such great sacrifices for the sake of knowledge.[28]

We see here the tensions of the father-son struggle that had been in the air for several years. Freud and psychoanalysis in general embodied a vigilance for pathology, Judas-like betrayal, patricidal wishes, competitiveness, and a paranoid, laager mentality that characterizes father-oriented groups. However, without this keen eye for the role of aggression and destructiveness in human relationships, and the strong loyalty to the archetypal and professional father that characterized psychoanalysis, the clarity of later (and particularly Kleinian) psychoanalytic views might have been lost.[29] One of the cornerstones of Freudian psychoanalysis was the oedipal myth in which Oedipus' tragedy is that he unwittingly kills his father and marries his mother, which is indeed what happened with Jung, but on a symbolic level. Jung later abandoned the masculine psychology of Freud and fashioned a more feminine psychology.

David Rosen says, "Freud was convinced as early as 1909 that Jung wanted to kill him. Most likely this was in part true for both men. Freud must have projected his desire to be killed onto Jung. After all, in the end, Freud had his internist kill him with two lethal injections of morphine. Symptomatic of Freud's death wish was the fact that he fainted twice in Jung's presence. . . . [In the April 1909 letter] Freud grandiosely claims to be Jung's father and a king who can anoint Jung as his successor and crown prince. It took Jung three years to convince himself that he had to let go of his No. 1 Freudian personality and kill off his false self. No wonder Freud felt Jung wanted to kill him, but actually it was to be the death of Jung the Freudian."[30]

Shortly after his visit with Freud, Jung had a dream in two parts that he refers to in the April letter to Freud. The dream confirmed for him their increasing differences. He dreamed he was in a mountainous region on the Swiss-Austrian border, in the early evening, and saw an elderly, stooped man in the uniform of an Imperial Austrian customs official. His expression was peevish and rather melancholic, and he paid no attention to Jung as he walked by. Someone informed Jung that the old man was not really there, but was the ghost of a customs official who had died years ago, and he was one of those who still couldn't die properly.[31]

This dream has been interpreted in various ways by various commentators, with varying conclusions. The inner analyst—the unconscious—seems to present dreams that can only be, or more correctly need to be, interpreted by the dreamer's conscious mind. The dream is a recursive question in a finely balanced feedback loop between the conscious and the unconscious that the alchemists called the "pelican."[32] It is a question posed to the dreamer, on the dreamer's terms, and suited to the dreamer's psychology. The dream is a diagnostic probe used by the unconscious to assess the conscious attitude, to explore life on the surface, so to speak. The answer that the dreamer gives to the dream—dismissal, attentiveness, or action—is information for the unconscious to use in subsequent dreams on the same theme. In this sense, objective interpretations by others are irrelevant; the psyche will compensate one way or another.

With this in mind, Jung's interpretation of his own dream is most relevant here; it was that the old customs official, taking a sour view of the world, was symbolic of Freud. The border was the division between him and Freud; the customs examination was analysis; and the dream as a whole was a compensation for his conscious high opinion and admiration of Freud. When he had this dream, Jung was in the South of the Little South Moon of the Big West—the double childhood of Death and Change.

The second part of this dream was set in summertime in a busy Italian city, which reminded Jung of Bergamo in northern Italy. Amid the stream of people walked a knight, like a Crusader, in full armor.

In the dream, Jung knew that the knight belonged to the 12th century. Years later, Jung said that the dream foreshadowed his later interest in alchemy. The 12th century was the time when the study of alchemy had begun. Jung's 12th year had been momentous for him; he had imagined himself belonging to the 18th century, had his erstwhile neurosis and fainting spells, and embarked upon the beginning of his "main business."

But Jung was not the only one subject to fainting spells. In December 1908, Jung and Freud had received an invitation from Stanley Hall, an American psychologist, to lecture at Clark University in Massachusetts. Jung, Freud, and Sandor Ferenczi met in Bremen prior to sailing on August 21, 1909. At lunch, on the day before their departure, Freud became irritated with Jung's conversation about the local peat-bog corpses of North Germany. "Why are you so concerned with these corpses?" he asked Jung several times, and then suddenly fainted. Afterward, he said to Jung that he was convinced that all the talk about corpses meant that Jung had death wishes toward him.

Freud would also faint again in similar circumstances. On November 24, 1912, at the Psycho-Analytical Congress in Munich, after a difficult meeting on organizational matters that Jung had called, the group gathered for lunch at the Park Hotel. During lunch, Freud challenged Jung as to why, in recent articles on psychoanalysis, he had not mentioned his name. Jung replied that because it was well known that Freud was the undisputed originator of psychoanalysis, it was superfluous to do so. There was also a heated discussion among the group and, similar to the Bremen incident, it also concerned historical matters—the relationship of Pharaoh Amenophis IV to his father, Amen-hotep, about which Jung expressed himself strongly. During this discussion, Freud suddenly slid off his chair in a faint. Jung carried him to an adjoining room and said, "As I was carrying him, he half came to, and I shall never forget the look he cast on me. In his weakness he looked at me as if I were his father."[33] Freud's first words on regaining consciousness were "How sweet it must be to die." As we shall see later, these words held fateful significance for him.

Freud later wrote that in both situations he fainted because of repressed anger toward Jung, and felt that Jung entertained death wishes toward him. Freud was prone to fainting and had previously fainted in the same hotel room in the presence of Wilhelm Fliess, who Freud felt also harbored ill-will toward him. As for Jung, he was on a Chaotic Journey when he had his fainting spells at age twelve; likewise he had just come out of a Chaotic Journey when Freud fainted in his presence for the first time in Bremen, and the Munich incident was six months after he had finished another Chaotic Journey.

During the trans-Atlantic voyage to the USA in August 1909, Jung, Freud, and Ferenczi set about interpreting each others' dreams. Jung shared one with Freud that is important not only as another illustration of the tensions between the two men, but also because it led Jung for the first time to the concept of the collective unconscious. In the dream, he was in the upper story of an unknown house where there was a salon furnished in rococo style. Descending the stairs, he reached the ground floor, which he realized must date from the 15th or 16th century. Then he discovered a stone stairway leading down into a cellar that dated from Roman times. Here he saw another stairway, and after descending it, he entered a low cave cut into the rock. The floor was covered with thick dust, and in the dust were the ancient bones and broken pottery of a primitive culture. Among these he discovered two very old human skulls. Freud was interested in the two skulls and pressed Jung for some insight into his unconscious death-wishes, wanting to know whose skulls they were, to which Jung replied, in a tricksterish way, "my wife and my sister-in-law," perhaps alluding to Freud's supposed affair with his sister-in-law, Minna Bernays.[34]

As an aside (with triangles there are always asides), John Billinsky, an American psychology professor, reported that Jung told him in 1957 that on the first visit to see Freud, Minna, who assisted Freud in his work, drew Jung aside and confided in him that she and Freud were having an affair.[35] Freud had possibly had an affair with Minna as early as 1900, but there is no evidence that Freud knew that Jung knew. There is no record of Jung mentioning it to anyone else during his lifetime, and once, when asked, he specifically declined to speak of it saying that some matters go to the grave. However, Jung did refer to Minna as Freud's "second wife" and felt she was his true wife. Jung saw Minna as being much more intellectually capable than Freud's wife, Martha. We might suppose that their secret, if it were true, was a form of psychological incest between Minna and Jung, and had oedipal overtones for Jung as Freud's professional son and heir.[36]

This is worthy of mention here for several reasons. It points to a Pattern where Jung's inferior feeling function and triangular tendencies were constellated in, or close to, the South. The Little Southeast and Little South Moons in the Big West were when he likely had several affairs. When he split from Freud in 1912 he was in the South of the Little Southwest Moon of the Big West. In 1933 when he was amid controversy about his attitude to Nazi Germany, he was in the South of the Little Southeast Moon of the Big North, and in 1957, when he made the disclosure about Minna and Freud to Billinsky, he was close to the South of the Little Center Moon of the Big East. The disclosure to Billinsky also came at a significant time when the Nazi question re-emerged from the past, as we shall see.

On their USA voyage, Jung also interpreted a dream for Freud and in doing so asked for more details of his private life. Freud's response was a look of utmost suspicion and he replied that he could not risk his authority. At that moment, in Jung's eyes, Freud lost what he wanted to preserve. He had privileged his own authority above the truth.[37]

Each place on the Moon Cycles can sing with the same place or the opposite place across the Wheel in previous Moons. We see this resonance here in that the differences with Freud, leading to the death of his relationship with Freud (his professional father), and the death of Jung the Freudian (the internalized father), began in 1909 when Jung was in the South of the Little South Moon of the Big West at age 33. His theological differences with his own father, leading up to his father's death, happened in the North of the Little North Moon of the Big South. Like Jung's father, who had unquestioning faith in religion, Freud had unquestioning faith in sexuality.

In the early months of this Little South Moon of the Big West we see the beginnings of Jung's later thinking on the collective unconscious. In April 1909, almost thirty-four, Jung went into the South of the Little South Moon—the Death and Change of double Trust and Innocence. In March 1909 he began writing to Freud about the prospective versus the reductive tendencies of the psyche, and said that if there is a psychoanalysis that proposes the present is created by the past events, then there must also be a psychosynthesis that creates future events according to the same law. It was in 1909 that he also realized that he could not treat latent psychoses if he did not understand their symbolism.[38] On returning to Kusnacht from the USA at the end of September 1909, he began reading widely on mythology and Gnosticism to understand the dream he had shared with Freud on their trip. In a letter to Freud on October 14, 1909, he wrote that archaeology and mythology fascinated him and he was finding a wealth of marvelous material.

During this eventful Little Moon, he also left Burghölzli. Although Eugen Bleuler had welcomed psychoanalysis at Burghölzli even before Jung joined its staff, and had recognized Jung's talent, he later became ambivalent about psychoanalysis and Jung himself. The tension between the two increased over the years and was somewhat similar, for Jung, to his relationships with Freud and his father. At the beginning of 1909, Jung was passed over by Bleuler for a university post in mental hygiene, and in March 1909 he left the hospital after being there for nine years. He had entered the secular monastery of Burghölzli as a young, unmarried man of 25 and left as a married man of 35 with a child and a growing reputation in psychiatry. He had spent three Little Moons there, the Little East Moon of the Big South, and the Little Center and Little Southeast Moons of the Big West, and began and ended his time at Burghölzli on a Chaotic Journey. After living in their flat at Burghölzli for many years, he and Emma built a house on a piece of land they had bought on the shores of Lake Zurich. In May 1909 they moved into 228 Seestrasse in Kusnacht, where Jung was to live the rest of his life.

Notes

1   James Hillman, *Insearch: Psychology and Religion* (Dallas: Spring, 1967), p. 101.

2   Marie-Louise von Franz, *The Interpretation of Fairytales* (Boston: Shambhala, 1996), p. 183.

3   Von Franz, *The Interpretation of Fairytales*, pp. 95–96.

4   Today we might say that this was a transference cure where the patient represses conflicts through an intensely positive but defensive identification with the therapist.

5   *CW* 1, *Cryptomnesia* and *CW* 4, *The Freudian Theory of Hysteria*, pp. 10–24.

6   See Aldo Carotenuto, *A Secret Symmetry: Sabina Spielrein between Jung and Freud* (New York: Pantheon, 1982).

7   "Burgholzli Hospital Records of Sabina Spielrein," in *Journal of Analytical Psychology* 46 (2001): 1–214.

8   Letter from Spielrein to Freud, June 13, 1909. Carotenuto, *A Secret Symmetry: Sabina Spielrein between Jung and Freud*, p. 101.

9   Quoted in Zvi Lothane, "Tender Love and Transference: Unpublished Letters of C. G. Jung and Sabina Spielrein," in *International Journal of Psychoanalysis* 80 (1999): 1196.

10 Carl Jung, "The Letters of C. G. Jung to Sabina Spielrein," in *Journal of Analytical Psychology* 46 (2001): 194.

11 Aniela Jaffé, *From the Life and Work of C. G. Jung* (New York: Harper, 1971), p. 117. Bollingen was Jung's country retreat on the shores of Lake Zurich.

12 Barbara Hannah, *Jung: His Life and Work* (New York: Putnam, 1976), pp. 119–120.

13 *Letters* 2, p. 455.

14 *CW* 14, § 99.

15 James Hillman, *The Myth of Analysis* (New York: Harper, 1978), pp. 92 *ff.*

16 James Hillman, *Loose Ends* (Dallas: Spring, 1975), pp. 75–76.

17 For a further discussion of triangles, salt, betrayal, and suffering see James Hillman, "Salt: A Chapter in Alchemical Psychology," in Joanne Stroud and Gail Thomas, eds., *Images of the Untouched: Virginity in Psyche, Myth and Community* (Dallas: Spring, 1982); Aldo Carotenuto, *Eros and Pathos: Shades of Love and Suffering* (Toronto, Inner City, 1989).

18 *CW* 14, § 330, 332, 334. Brackets mine.

19 See Paul Stern, Vincent Brome, Colin Wilson, Frank McLynn, particularly Richard Noll, and to some extent John Kerr.

20 John Kerr, *A Most Dangerous Method: The Story of Jung, Freud, & Sabina Spielrein* (London: Sinclair Stevenson, 1994), p. 379.

21 James Astor, Review of *The Jungians: A Comparative and Historical Perspective*, by Thomas B. Kirsch, in *Journal of Analytical Psychology* 46 (2001).

22 *MDR*, p. 150.

23 C. G. Jung, *Analytical Psychology: Notes of the Seminar Given in 1925*, William McGuire, ed. (Princeton: Princeton University Press, 1989), p. 21.

24 Judith Vida, "Book Review of Thomas Kirsch, *The Jungians: A Comparative and Historical Perspective*," in *Journal of Analytical Psychology* 46 (2001): 223.

25 *MDR*, p. 155.

26 See Appendix V, *MDR*, pp. 378–390.

27 *Letters* 1, p. 10.

28 *MDR*, p. 361.

29 Melanie Klein (1882–1960) was a child psychoanalyst who was very influential in the development of psychoanalysis, particularly the British school.

30 David Rosen, *The Tao of Jung: The Way of Integrity* (London: Penguin Arkana, 1997), pp. 56–58. Brackets mine.

31 *MDR*, p. 163.

32 *CW* 14, § 8.

33 *MDR*, pp. 156–157.

34 *MDR*, p. 159.

35 John Billinsky, "Jung and Freud," *Andover Newton Quarterly* 10 (1969): 39–43.

36 Kerr, *A Most Dangerous Method*, p. 136.

37 *MDR*, p. 158.

38 *MDR*, p. 131.

LITTLE SOUTHWEST MOON
OF THE BIG WEST—
DEATH AND CHANGE OF
THE SACRED DREAM

Dreams are the driving force of life. Strangely enough they are the
awakener.... The challenge is to bring the dream into reality as a gift to the
People. Every dream is either a question or an answer to
a question that is needed among the human beings.[1]

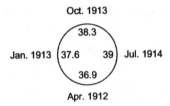

Oct. 1913

Jan. 1913   37.6   38.3   39   Jul. 1914

36.9

Apr. 1912

D uring his Chaotic Journey, Jung had scheduled a bicycle
trip for the first two weeks of October 1911. At Arona, on
the shores of Lake Maggiore, he had a dream that left him
with such strong feelings of inferiority that he cut short his trip and
hurriedly took the train back to Zurich to continue work on
Symbols of Transformation. In the dream Jung was with an "assemblage of distinguished spirits" from earlier times who were convers-
ing in Latin. A gentleman in a wig asked Jung a difficult question,
which he understood, but did not speak Latin well enough to
answer. He felt so profoundly humiliated that he woke up.[2] Jung did
not understand until years later that by working on *Symbols* he
would be answering the questions that had been asked by the
bewigged gentleman.

THE BREAK WITH FREUD

The Southwest is where we touch our own Dream and Symbols of
Life Experience. Coming from the Little South Moon and his struggles with Freud, into the Little Southwest Moon, Jung increasingly
walked his own path. It was in 1911 that Jung realized his friendship with Freud was doomed[3] and the years from 1911 to 1914 were
filled with the final break with Freud, writing *Symbols of
Transformation*, and the beginning of his confrontation with the
unconscious. Jung was beginning to live his own Dream. *Symbols of
Transformation* originally appeared in two parts published separate-
ly in the *Jahrbuch der Psychoanalyse*. The first part, published in
1911, was more or less acceptable to Freud, who had seen the first
draft in 1910, but the second part, including *On the Concept of the
Libido* and *The Origin of the Hero*, led to the final break. In his revi-
sion of *Symbols* in 1950, Jung said that he never felt happy about the
book. It was written hastily, amid the press of his medical practice,
and it came upon him like a force of nature. The urgency behind it
became clear to him later: "[I]t was an explosion of all those psychic
contents which could find no breathing space in the constricting
atmosphere of Freudian psychology."[4]

In the spring of 1911, Jung began writing the second part and in
January 1912 began work on the final chapter, "The Sacrifice."
Approaching the end of writing the chapter, he knew that its publication would cost his friendship with Freud.[5] It was finished in March
1912. The rift between him and Freud became public when, in
September 1912, Jung traveled again to the USA to lecture at Fordham
University and he began to speak openly of their theoretical differences. The correspondence with Freud became increasingly acerbic.
On December 18, 1912 he wrote an emotional letter to Freud, chiding
him to take his bit of neurosis seriously: "I would, however, like to
point out that your technique of treating your pupils like patients is a
blunder. In that way you produce slavish sons or impudent puppies....
You go around sniffing out all the symptomatic actions in your vicinity, thus reducing everyone to the level of sons and daughters who

blushingly admit the existence of their faults. Meanwhile you remain on top as the father sitting pretty. . . . You see, my dear Professor, as long as you hand out this stuff I don't give a damn for my symptomatic actions; they shrink to nothing in comparison with the formidable beam in my brother Freud's eye."[6] Freud replied, "None of us need feel ashamed of his own bit of neurosis. But one who while behaving abnormally keeps shouting that he is normal gives ground for the suspicion that he lacks insight into his illness. Accordingly, I propose that we abandon our personal relations entirely."[7]

Jung's final letter on January 6, 1913 read, "I shall submit to your wish to discontinue our personal relationship, for I never force my friendship on anyone. For the rest, you yourself know best what this moment means to you. 'The rest is silence.'"[8]

The last personal contact between Jung and Freud was at the last Congress of the International Psycho-Analytical Association on September 7, 1913. For the rest of Jung's life, and after his death, the tensions between psychoanalysis and analytical psychology lived on. Jung's was a feminine psychology and attracted women, Freud's was a masculine psychology and attracted men. In the 1950's it was bruited about in Freudian circles that on Jung's death there would be multiple suicides of his women adherents. Even such maternal a figure as Donald Winnicott, the British psychoanalyst, suggested in his review of *Memories* after Jung's death that Jung suffered from childhood schizophrenia as a result of his parent's separation.[9] Only in the past twenty years has there been a long overdue *rapprochement* between Jungian, classical Freudian, Kleinian, and other psychoanalytic schools.

THE SHIELDS

Jung was in the Little Southwest Moon from April 1912 to July 1914. After the parting of the ways with Freud, he felt disoriented, as if suspended in mid-air, and beset with a constant inner pressure. Around Christmas 1912 he had a dream where he found himself sitting, in an Italian loggia, on a gold Renaissance chair in front of an emerald stone table. A dove alighted on the table and transformed into a little girl, about 8 years old, with golden, blonde hair, who put her arms tenderly around his neck and then changed back into the dove.[10]

The Elders say that in the Luminous Cocoon, or energy field surrounding our physical body, are four Shields, or energetic fields through which we perceive reality. The Child Substance Shield (the Little Boy Shield for a man, the Little Girl Shield for a woman) is the water shield that carries all our past history and emotions, both painful and joyful. It usually sits behind us or, drawn on a Wheel, is in the South. The Adult Substance Shield (the Man Shield for a man, the Woman Shield for a woman) is our air shield that is focused on the now and the future, and is usually in front of us. The Adult Spirit Shield is the anima or animus (the Woman Shield for a man, the Man Shield for a woman), the earth shield that links us with the Dream and Symbols of Life Experience, seeks Death as an Ally, and usually sits to our left. The Child Spirit Shield (the Little Girl Shield for a man, the Little Boy Shield for a woman) is the fire shield that knows no fear, wants to know the unknown, has insatiable curiosity, and usually sits to our right. It is the contrasexual opposite to the anima or animus and adds a fourth to the trinity of the ego, shadow, and anima/animus. At the Center is the Elder Shield, or Grandmother and Grandfather Shields that dream for us and are our direct connection to the unseen. The Elders also say that the Winged-ones are the messengers of spirit, and in the Christian tradition the dove is associated with the presence of the Holy Spirit. The little girl in the dream was Jung's Child Spirit Shield, his Little Girl Shield, the harbinger of his descent into the unconscious.

In 1916 Jung began painting mandalas and the first one he painted corresponded closely to a Medicine Wheel, and another is of his Shields (see figure 3), which he later amplified.[11]

> At the four cardinal points we see human figures: at the top, an old man [the Adult Substance Shield] in an attitude of contemplation; at the bottom, Loki or Hephaestus [the Child Substance Shield] with red, flaming hair, holding in his hands a temple. To the right and left are a light [the Child

Spirit Shield] and a dark female figure [the Adult Spirit Shield]. Together they indicate four aspects of the personality, or four archetypal figures belonging, as it were, to the periphery of the self. The two female figures can be recognized without difficulty as the two aspects of the anima. The old man corresponds to the archetype of meaning, or of the spirit, and the dark chthonic figure opposite to that of the Wise Old Man, namely the magical (and sometimes destructive) Luciferian element."[12]

Fig 3. Mandala by C. G. Jung

As Jung was strongly identified with the archetype of meaning, it is not surprising that his Adult Substance Shield in the mandala should appear as a contemplative old man with a beard and, in compensation, his Child Substance Shield takes on a tricksterish quality.

As Jung moved into 1913, his feelings of disorientation and inner pressure deepened, and he was unable to make headway in understanding the dreams of the dove, the assemblage of spirits, and other subsequent dreams. So he examined his life to find out if the cause of the disturbance lay in his childhood, but this led to nothing but recognition of his own ignorance. He then decided to do whatever spontaneously occurred to him, consciously surrendering himself to the unconscious.[13] This led him to building sandcastles and "waterworks" on the shore of Lake Zurich outside his home. The first thing that surfaced was a childhood memory from his "tenth or eleventh year" of playing with building blocks, and this was accompanied by deep emotion. At this time, presumably in the late winter or spring of 1913, at age 37, Jung was in the West of the Little Southwest Moon of the Big West—the double Death and Change of his Sacred Dream. In his tenth or eleventh year he would also have been in the Little Southwest Moon. As he gathered stones from the lakeshore, he also found a red stone that reminded him of the underground phallus of his very first dream.

VISIONS OF WAR

Toward the autumn of 1913 the pressure that seemed to be inside him moved outward, and he felt it as more of a concrete outer reality. In October 1913, on entering the North of the Little Southwest Moon of the Big West (the Wisdom and Knowledge of the Dream of Death and Change), he had a vision that was repeated even more vividly two weeks later, in which he saw an enormous flood covering all the land between the North Sea and the Alps, but around Switzerland the mountains grew higher to protect the country. He saw mighty yellow waves, the flotsam of civilization, thousands of drowned bodies, and then the sea changed into blood.[14] Later in life he told the dream to Laurens van der Post. "He would suddenly see visions of a great tide of blood coming up over Europe from the north. It rose higher and higher until it lapped at the rim of the Alps like floodwaters at the top of a dam. And in this vast swollen tide of blood was a porridge of mangled corpses and torn-off limbs until he could almost cry aloud at the horror of it."[15]

On January 22, 1914 he had another dream, which he painted in 1920—a "ring of flames floating above a world of war and technology."[16] At that time the idea of war did not occur to Jung at all; it was, however, what war looked like in the Dream, from the point of view of the unconscious. The vision of the flood occurred nine months before the outbreak of WWI on August 1, 1914. War had been conceived in the Dream and Jung had seen it.

Jung's descent into the unconscious was a shamanic journey and December 1912 was the beginning of this *nekyia*.[17] Jung took the term *nekyia* (or night sea journey) from the title of the eleventh book of the Odyssey, to describe the descent into Hades and the quest for the treasure hard to obtain.[18] The term "night sea journey" was coined by the German ethnologist Leo Frobenius to describe the worldwide mythologem in which the hero is swallowed by the sea monster, travels from West to East (the night sea journey of the Sun) in its belly, and then escapes. Jung used these terms as illustrations of psychological rebirth.

In order to grasp the fantasies and emotions that were stirring, Jung knew that he must go down into them. At Advent 1913 (December 12), he was sitting in his study and he let himself "drop" and plunged downward into a dark cave. He waded through icy water to the other end of the cave where he saw a glowing red crystal. Grasping it, he discovered a hollow underneath, where there was flowing water. The corpse of a youth, with blond hair and a wound to the head, floated by, followed by a gigantic scarab beetle, and then by a red, newborn sun rising out of the depths of the water. He tried to replace the crystal but a jet of blood leapt up and continued to spurt for an unendurably long time.

It was a vision of death and rebirth. On the collective level, the corpse represented the naïve rationalism of the 20th century that had become moribund. In Egyptian mythology, the scarab beetle creates the new Sun god, the coming dominant consciousness, and pushes him up over the horizon. But these deep collective transformations are never possible without great blood sacrifice on another level, as Jung had dreamed.

The personal dimension of this vision emerged six days later when Jung had a dream in which he was with a brown-skinned man on a deserted, mountain landscape. He heard Siegfried's horn sounding over the mountains and he knew they had to kill him with their rifles. When Siegfried appeared they shot him. Jung was filled with disgust and remorse for having destroyed somebody so great and beautiful, and feared the murder might be discovered, but a downpour of rain obliterated all traces of his deed.

Jung awoke with a tremendous feeling of guilt and tried to go back to sleep, but a voice said to him that he must understand the dream immediately, and if he didn't, then he must shoot himself. In his bedside drawer lay a loaded revolver (at age 19 Jung had begun his annual army service as is usual for Swiss citizens and so owned a revolver). But Jung realized that the Siegfried problem—the heroic imposition of the will—was being played out within himself and in the world by the German nation. The dream showed him that the Siegfried attitude no longer suited him and therefore had to be killed.[19]

This is a typical mid-life dream, when all the goals of achievement have been met and the Sun hero must die to allow life to flow onward.[20] The dream cleared the path toward his Dream. Here, Jung was in the Northeast of the Little Southwest Moon of the Big West—the place of Choices and Decisions in the Death and Change of the Sacred Dream. So he began to cut away those things that kept him tied to the surface. He had already resigned from his position as editor of the *Jahrbuch* in October 1913, on April 20, 1914 he resigned as President of the International Psycho-Analytical Association, and on April 30, 1914 he gave up his post as Privatdozent at the university.

Notes

1   Hyemeyohsts Storm, *Song of Heyoehkah* (New York: Ballantine, 1981), pp. 54–55.

2   *MDR*, p. 307.

3   Barbara Hannah, *Jung: His Life and Work* (New York: Putnam, 1976), p. 103.

4   *CW* 5, p. xxiii.

5   *MDR*, p. 167.

6   William McGuire, ed., *The Freud/Jung Letters* (Princeton: Princeton University Press, 1974), pp. 534–535.

7   McGuire, *The Freud/Jung Letters*, p. 539.

8   McGuire, *The Freud/Jung Letters*, p. 540.

9   Donald Winnicott, Review of *Memories, Dreams, Reflections*, in *International Journal of Psychoanalysis* 45 (1964): 450–455.

10 *MDR*, p. 172.

11 For color illustrations of the mandalas, see Aniela Jaffé, ed., *C. G. Jung: Word and Image* (Princeton: Princeton University Press, 1979), pp. 75–76, 95.

12 *CW* 9i, § 682. Brackets mine.

13 *MDR*, p. 173.

14 *MDR*, p. 175.

15 Laurens van der Post, *Jung and the Story of Our Time* (London: Penguin, 1976), p. 155.

16 Aniela Jaffé, ed., *C. G. Jung: Word and Image*, p. 68.

17 Marie-Louise von Franz, *C. G. Jung: His Myth in Our Time* (London: Hodder & Stoughton, 1975), p. 105.

18 *CW* 15, § 214.

19 *MDR*, p. 180.

20 Von Franz, *C. G. Jung: His Myth in Our Time*, p. 109.

LITTLE WEST MOON
OF THE BIG WEST—
DEATH AND CHANGE OF
DEATH AND CHANGE

How do people change? God splits the skin with a jagged thumbnail from throat to belly and then plunges a huge filthy hand in...he pulls and pulls till all your innards are yanked out....And then he stuffs them back, dirty, tangled and torn. It's up to you to do the stitching.[1]

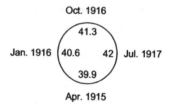

Oct. 1916

Jan. 1916   41.3

40.6   42   Jul. 1917

39.9

Apr. 1915

The Big West Moon is one of Death and Change and now Jung moved into the Little West Moon of the Big West— the Moon of double Death and Change—and began his descent into the unconscious. In the first month of a Chaotic Journey we stand in the Illumination of the East and look back on the Moon Cycles before moving ahead on our journey. Jung describes this in *Memories*, when he tells of his return, at age 39, to the slope in Klein-Huningen, and standing in front of the wall where he had made fires, suddenly he was the child of nine again. It was an unforgettable moment and "illuminated in a flash of lightning" the eternal quality of his childhood.[2]

Jung's description of this time in late 1914 and early 1915 is typical of the unpredictable energy of the Chaotic Journey, particularly into the West. He said it was a time during which a torrent of fantasies was released and he was in a continual state of tension, but he found himself calmed as he was able to transform his turbulent emotions into images which might have otherwise torn him asunder.[3]

DESCENT INTO THE UNCONSCIOUS

Jung's previous Chaotic Journey into a Little West Moon, in the Big South at age 12, had been a tumultuous one for him. Now, on this Chaotic Journey, he had more dreams of the coming catastrophe (symbolizing both WWI and Jung's inner conflict), which were repeated three times in April, May, and June 1914. In the dreams, a wave of cold descended from the Arctic in the middle of the summer and everything turned to ice. In the third dream, however, in June, there was a resolution. At the end of the dream there was a leaf-bearing tree, without fruit, but the leaves had been transformed by the cold into sweet grapes laden with healing juice. Jung plucked them and gave them to a waiting crowd.[4]

That month, on June 28, 1914, Archduke Franz Ferdinand, the successor to the Austrian throne, was murdered in Sarajevo, and on August 1, 1914, WWI began. Jung had begun his Chaotic Journey into the Moon of double Death and Change, on July 26, 1914, at age 39.

Around this time he encountered, in one of his descents into the depths, his Grandmother and Grandfather Shields: an old man with a white beard, who explained he was Elijah, and a blind, beautiful, young girl who astonished Jung by telling him that her name was Salome.[5] The figure of Elijah soon evolved into Philemon, an old man who was lame with the horns of a bull and wings the color of a kingfisher, and four keys in his right hand. While painting this image, Jung found a dead kingfisher—a rarity in that area—in his garden. The phenomenological reality of these figures brought home to Jung that there were things in the psyche that had their own life. Then he made the discovery that he could talk to the figures he encountered and find out what they wanted of him, and he made it a rule never to let a figure leave until it told him why it had appeared.[6]

He began to write his fantasies in what he called the Black Book and elaborated on them, in the form of paintings, in the Red Book.[7] In May 2000 the heirs of Jung's estate decided to permit publication of the Red Book. The announcement was made 39.0 years after Jung died in June 1961, as his death was entering the Moon of double Death and Change. Jung probably began painting in the Red Book around late 1914 and continued until the mid- to late 1920s. So three Big Moon Cycles later, at about 81 years of age, the introverted Red Book has come into elderhood and out into the world.

However, Jung was most conscious of the possibility of falling into the shadow side of the West, the Daydream, or its compensatory opposite in the East, Fantasy and Illusion. He was horrified by Nietzsche's fate[8]—uprooted from the earth and swirling in the insubstantial realms of spirit—and needed the earthy attachments of his home and family life.[9] He eventually gave up the aestheticism of the Red Book, choosing instead the rigor of understanding.

Jung pointed out that inflation is caused by the ego identifying with spirit. In the era of the New Age the danger is as Jung outlined; contact with spirit in the East leads to inflation and identification with the content of such experiences. "The conscious must keep control [of fantasy] in order to have a check on the tendency of nature to experiment. This to say, one has to keep in mind that the unconscious can produce something disastrous to us."[10] A relationship with spirit requires the willingness, and the capacity, to combine the fire of spirit with the darkness of earth in the West, to ground it in the experience of one's own shadow (the place of Looks-Within and Introspection) and the physical reality of one's body, one's Earth Lodge.

"The danger [of inflation] becomes all the greater the more our interest fastens upon external objects and the more we forget that differentiation of our relation to nature should go hand in hand with a correspondingly differentiated relation to the spirit, so as to establish the necessary balance. If the outer object is not offset by an inner, unbridled materialism results, coupled with a maniacal arrogance."[11] We could also say that if the inner object is not offset by an outer one, then unbridled holiness results, coupled with a spiritual correctness. Jung constantly warned against the danger of the illusion that one owns the spirit.

Many proponents of New Age spirituality disavow the existence of shadow, resulting in the rest of us having to carry what they disown. Too much love and light has estranged the New Age from darkness and it has become overly familiar with spirit without the proper introductions. What Jung wrote in 1945 is still true today: "One does not become enlightened by imagining figures of light, but by making the darkness conscious. The latter procedure, however, is disagreeable, and therefore not popular."[12]

SHADOW

In his descent into the unconscious, Jung experienced his own shadow and the shadow of the collective. Where there is light, there is shadow. Shadow is inevitable. If we put shadow on a Wheel, we can discern five types: two pairs of polar opposites (the personal and collective shadows, and the human and spiritual shadows) and one at the center that reflects and contains all the others (see figure 4 below). Each place on the Wheel has a positive and negative shadow, and over time, each polarity changes into and redeems, its opposite.

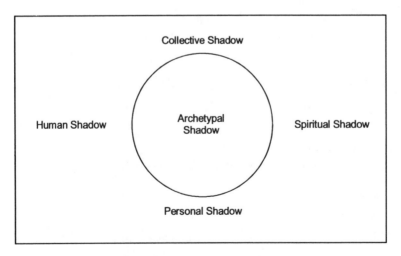

Fig 4. The Wheel of Shadows

The most accessible is the personal shadow in the South. It contains the longings, talents, needs, joys, and pains that we have had to forget in order to survive, and then we forget that we have forgotten. The personal shadow is who we hope we are not, but if we are, we hope others won't notice. On both the light and dark sides, the personal shadow holds repressed contents that have at one time been conscious, as well as contents that have yet to become conscious. On the light side, the personal shadow is the best of ourselves that we vowed never to be because the tender ego was ashamed, it is what we hoped we wouldn't have to be in order to speak with our own voice, it is our talents that we refuse to claim. It is our positive shadow. "The shadow is merely somewhat inferior, primitive, unadapted and awkward; not wholly bad. It even contains childish or primitive qualities which would in a way vitalize and embellish human existence, but—convention forbids!"[13] "It displays a number of good qualities, such as normal instincts, appropriate reactions, realistic insights, creative impulses, etc."[14]

On the dark side, it is the pain of growing up in the particular place, with the particular parents, in the particular time, and being born the particular person we are. In psychotherapy, this is where we start. W. B. Yeats wrote:

> Now that my ladder's gone,
> I must lie down where all the ladders start,
> In the foul rag-and-bone shop of the heart.[15]

These pains are exquisitely ours and rightly so; they make us unique, but they also make us common. It is an antinomy, like falling in love; it is unique but as common as potatoes. The personal shadow is personal but is also an archetype.

Carlos Castañeda's benefactor Don Juan said that:

> What distinguishes normal people is that we share a metaphorical dagger: the concerns of our self-reflection. With this dagger, we cut ourselves and bleed; and the job of our chains of self-reflection is to give us the feeling that we are

bleeding together; that we are sharing something wonderful: our humanity. But if we were to examine it, we would discover that we are bleeding alone; that we are not sharing anything; that all we are doing is toying with our manageable, unreal, man-made reflection."[16]

In the North, each culture, nation, organization, group, or family has a collective shadow, its form depending on the prevailing attitudes in collective consciousness and the history of the culture. The English gave the world sports and "fair play" as compensation for its colonial shadow. Jung told Laurens van der Post that one of the most striking qualities of the English spirit is their love of sport and genius for inventing games.[17] The Mafia and sibling hostility are the shadow of the close-knit Italian family. The idealization of the hero, the difficulty accepting limitations, and the fantasy of everlasting four percent per annum growth, are shadow to the magnificence of the individual freedoms of the Declaration of Independence.[18] Lest these characterizations seem stereotypical, we should remember that stereotypes exist only because an archetype stands behind them.

With his discoveries about the collective unconscious, Jung was always interested in the collective shadow and wrote frequently on cultural, racial, and national characteristics. But he warned that when the group submerges the individual, then the collective shadow may be mobilized and incarnated, as history has repeatedly shown us.

In the West, the human shadow only emerges after a prolonged effort at viewing oneself from the perspective of the Self—after some humble pie has been eaten, some personal shadow digested. It has nothing to do with personal history, it cannot be analyzed or psychologized away. It is the shadow of the ascensionist, growth fantasies underlying some psychotherapy today. It is the shadow of simply being human; where we cannot grow and are always stunted; the places where we feel insufficient for life and others, bitter, powerless, shameful, forsaken, alienated, and unhuman. Some Native prayers start with the words "Great Spirit, this pitiful one sends a voice..."

and in *Amazing Grace* we hear of "a wretch like me." This is not masochistic self-negation but a relativization, a humble reminder how frail our humanness is and, as the Buddha said, all life is suffering.

The light side of this human shadow is the profound magnificence of being human, being given the gift of Life, our grandeur, our exhibitionism, our extravagance, our joy of displaying our beauty and human finery. It is being true to ourselves no matter how large or small we are or feel. Robert Bly says of this humanness, "Most psychological systems don't want any expression of masculine grandeur. All talk of grandeur is inflation, and all crowns are to be left in the dust . . . human self-esteem is a delicate matter, and not to be dismissed as infantile grandiosity. Our 'mirrored greatness' as Heinz Kohut calls it, needs to be carefully honored, neither inflated nor crushed. If a man's or a woman's 'mirrored greatness' is entirely dismissed, he or she will be crippled, and a candidate for all sorts of invasions by the group mind."[19]

The opposite of the human shadow is the spiritual shadow in the East. It is the hard-on under the priest's robes. This shadow takes the moral high ground and is hard to argue with. It seduces us with the promise of deliverance and redemption from our human shadow. We can only judge its integrity by looking at how it is lived out in people's lives over a long period of time. If integrity is absent, we hear about the exploits of Rajneesh, Werner Erhard, Jim Bakker, Oral Roberts, institutional abuse within religious orders, the dark side of the guru-disciple relationship, and the abuse of spiritual power. The casualties of this shadow of spiritual correctness are just beginning to be recognized. Jung related how he once talked to a spiritual leader who impressed him with his asceticism, purity, and high-mindedness, and he left the encounter feeling quite diminished. Several days later the man's wife called wanting to talk to Jung about their marital difficulties! The light side of the spiritual shadow is what Jung called the religious impulse and the search for meaning—the yearning for spirit.

When we come to know these light and dark shadows around the Wheel, we gain substance and shape, ballast and protection. Agnes Whistling Elk (a Twisted Hair Elder) says to her apprentice:

"Because evil wants to know you. In a way, evil is trying to help you."

"How could evil help me?" I asked.

"You see, in the Dreamtime your image, your spirit, appears to be frayed. You are not clearly defined..."

"What does that mean?"

"It means that the light that you are needs a distinct darkness to define it. The darkness that provides your balance and cosmic equilibriums is now only a gray shadow. By witnessing true evil, the opposite of the goodness that you are, your spirit will become more clearly defined. On the other side, the allies of darkness will see that and know your strength and they will leave you alone."[20]

The shadow at the center of this Wheel is the dark side of the Great Mystery. This condensate of all the other shadows occasionally appears in psychotherapy, and perhaps with increasing frequency in this age. Throughout his life, from the faint beginnings at the cathedral in Basel, Jung engaged himself in resolving the problem of evil and the dark side of God, which culminated in *Answer to Job* in 1952. When this archetypal shadow, evil, or Stalking Death does emerge, we can only protect ourselves, as all shamanic traditions know how to do, and look within to see where we have denied our own darkness and so left the door ajar. Like cures like, and the best protection against evil is knowledge of one's own shadow.

ANIMA

It was during the years from 1914 to 1917 that Jung encountered the reality of the anima. As he was writing down his fantasies in the Black Book, he asked himself what he was really doing, as it certainly had nothing to do with science. A woman's voice within answered, "It is art." Jung recognized it as the voice of a patient who had had a strong transference toward him, and he was intrigued by the fact that a woman should interfere with him from within. As he wrote down his reactions, he began to distinguish between himself and the interruptions of the anima and to take a position toward them. This relativizing of the conscious will (which has been the Siegfried-like standard bearer of modern science), granting the unconscious an autonomy of its own (which, if denied, it will claim anyway) and then meeting it on its own terms, has been one of Jung's unique contributions to Western psychology. However, he cautioned that the critical factor is consciousness, which can comprehend the expressions of the unconscious and take up a position with respect to them.[21]

On the Medicine Wheel, Jung's move from passive imagination to actively relating to the inner figures was the shift from the shadow side of the West, the Daydream, to the light side of the West, a dialogue with the unconscious, or Introspection. Active imagination, as Jung came to term this dialogue, is an aspect of Dreaming and as such involves neither Fantasy nor Daydream. It requires an ethical, discriminating, human standpoint so that the ego becomes neither positively inflated in the East nor negatively inflated in the West. This is brought about by the very human faculties of thinking in the North and feeling in the South that hold the tension between spirit in the East and matter in the West.

Along with this increased awareness of unconscious contents comes the challenge of accepting the responsibilities, to oneself and others, that comes with increased consciousness. Sooner or later, we have to take responsibility for what we are not responsible for. In a letter to Victor White on April 10, 1954 Jung cautioned against wanting to know more of the unconscious than one gets through dreams and intuition. The more one knows the greater becomes the ethical burden, as the knowledge becomes one's individual obligations and responsibilities when it enters consciousness.[22]

TRIPLE DEATH AND CHANGE

The whole Little West Moon of the Big West, from 39 to 42, is three years of double Death and Change. At the age of 40.6, we pass through the West of the West of the West—the place of triple Death and Change—and it is where we choose between Life and Death. The place of triple West sings with ages 7 (6.9 – triple South), 74 (74.3 – triple North), and 108 (108.0 – triple East) as being the apogee of each of the Big Moons. It is the pivot point of adulthood as the others are of childhood and elderhood. It is the place of the mid-life crisis, the place of the greatest darkness across the Wheel from the light of the East. Jung said that in the middle of life, death is born, and after the midpoint of life, the task becomes to put down inner roots to complement the outer roots already laid down. This does not mean that we are not obligated to deal with the claims of the world when they come to us, but we no longer seek them in the same way.

The number 40 symbolizes waiting, preparation, testing, and punishment. This number frequently marks major events in the Bible. David and Solomon both reigned for forty years; the Children of Israel wandered for forty years in the wilderness before the Promised Land was reached; God's covenant with Noah after the flood lasted forty days; Moses was summoned by God at age 40, and spent forty days on Mount Sinai; Jesus was taken to the temple forty days after his birth; preached for forty months; was tempted in the desert for forty days; resurrected after forty days; and appeared to his disciples for forty days prior to his ascension. Lent lasts for forty days; forty days or years is the length of the alchemical opus, and forty days was the time required for the ancient Egyptian embalming process.[23] The practice of quarantine stems from the Italian word *quarantina*—the forty days that symbolizes a complete cycle. Both Buddha and Mohammed began their work at age 40, and in ancient Rome the honorific senex or seneca was given to men and women from the second half of the fortieth year onward.[24] Laurens van der Post, writing about the eruption of violence compensatory to the collective peaceful and cordial attitudes of the Malay people, said that an outbreak of violence was proclaimed by the cry of "Amok," and occurred when the man was usually at the age of 40.[25]

Jung was in the triple West on January 26, 1916 and by that year the gradual outlines of an inner change had begun to take shape. During the year he felt a growing urge to give Philemon a voice and during the summer of 1916 he wrote his unusual work, *Septem Sermones ad Mortuos: The seven instructions to the Dead. Written by Basilides in Alexandria, the city where the East touches the West.*[26] Several parapsychological events (which often occur when unconscious contents approach consciousness) occurred in the house—his eldest daughter saw a white figure pass through her room, doorbells rang and no-one was there, and the air was thick with spirits. As soon as Jung picked up his pen the haunting ceased and over the next three evenings he wrote *Septem Sermones.* He had it privately published but described it in *Memories* as "sin of his youth and regretted it."[27] However, both Barbara Hannah and Marie-Louise von Franz said that what Jung regretted was its publication (it had already been privately published in German in the early 1920s and in English in 1925), not its writing.[28] He reluctantly allowed its inclusion in *Memories,* and only for the sake of honesty.

Throughout the early years of his professional life, Jung's ambition was to become an academic with time for study and patients, but in his confrontation with the unconscious he realized that this was incompatible with his real task and he had to sacrifice this dream. He regretted this but said that if we attend to the desires of the Self, the wound heals.[29] Between 1913 and 1916, Jung said he found himself incapable of reading a scientific book but he did continue to see patients and in 1916 he established the Psychological Club in Zurich. During these years, he wrote very little until his descent came to an end. He then began work on *Psychological Types,* leading to its publication in 1921.

ASCENT FROM THE UNCONSCIOUS

Jung gradually began to emerge from the darkness toward the end of WWI by two means. The first was to break with the woman whose voice wanted to convince him that his painting was art; it is likely that this woman was Sabina Spielrein. By the beginning of WWI, Spielrein was married, had a daughter, and had analyzed with Freud. She and Jung corresponded intermittently over the years and, as we have seen, his letter to her on September 1, 1919 put an end to their entanglements. Jung was in the West of the Little Northwest Moon of the Big West, the double Death and Change of Laws and Patterns. We know that Jung's initial anima figure, Salome, was blind. He said this was because she did not see the meaning of things. She was the Jewish anima that could not see and, in turn, symbolized Jung's inability to see his own anima projections, including what was projected onto Spielrein, who was Jewish. We shall encounter the theme of Jung's "Jewish anima" again later on. In coming out of the darkness, Jung regained his sight and this enabled him to end the relationship with Spielrein.[30]

The second way he emerged from his encounter with the unconscious was to begin painting mandalas, which he did in 1916. Jung was often on military service during the war and wrote one of his papers, *The Transcendent Function*, while stationed on the Gotthard Pass.[31] During 1917 to 1918, he became Commandant of the camp for interred British POWs at Chateau d'Oex. While he was there, he made a practice of painting a mandala each morning. Aniela Jaffé felt that his time at Chateau d'Oex was the beginning of the end of his descent. Looking back on his descent, Jung said that the material that burst forth from the unconscious during the years from 1913 to 1917 laid the foundation for the rest of his life's work.[32]

Notes ————————————————————————————

1   Tony Kushner, in the play *Angels in America* (1994).
2   *MDR*, pp. 20–21.
3   *MDR*, pp. 176–177.
4   *MDR*, p. 176.
5   *MDR*, p. 181. The biblical story of Salome is well known. Having pleased her stepfather, Herod, with her dancing, she was granted a gift. At the instigation of her mother Herodias (because John the Baptist denounced Herodias' marriage to her first husband's half-brother) Salome asked for, and got, the head of John the Baptist. However there was another Salome in the Bible—she was the wife of Zebedee and the mother of the apostles James the Great and John the Evangelist. She was present at the crucifixion and among the women who were first to learn of the resurrection.

6   Barbara Hannah, *Jung: His Life and Work* (New York: Putnam, 1976), p. 115.
7   For further information see the International Association of Analytical Psychology website (http://www.iaap.org/redbook.html).
8   Friedrich Nietzsche (Oct 15, 1844 – Aug 25, 1900) was a German philosopher who suffered a mental breakdown in 1889, from which he never recovered.
9   *MDR*, pp. 188-189.
10 C. G. Jung, *Analytical Psychology: Notes of the Seminar Given in 1925*, p. 11.
11 *CW* 9i, § 393.
12 *CW* 13, § 335.
13 *CW* 11, § 134.
14 *CW* 9ii, § 423.
15 William Butler Yeats, *The Circus Animals' Desertion*.
16 Carlos Castaneda, *The Power of Silence* (New York: Simon & Schuster, 1987), p. 110.
17 Laurens van der Post, *Jung and the Story of Our Time*, p. 46.
18 See *CW* 10, *Civilization in Transition*.
19 Robert Bly, *Iron John: A Book about Men* (New York: Addison-Wesley, 1990), p. 223.
20 Lynn Andrews, *Crystal Woman: Sisters of the Dreamtime* (New York: Warner, 1988), p. 219.
21 *MDR*, p. 187.
22 *Letters* 2, p. 172.
23 Edward Edinger, *The Bible and the Psyche: Individuation Symbolism in the Old Testament* (Toronto: Inner City, 1986), pp. 51–52.
24 James Hillman, "On Senex Consciousness," in Patricia Berry, ed., *Fathers and Mothers* (Dallas: Spring, 1990), p. 18.
25 Van der Post, *Jung and the Story of Our Time*, pp. 27–28.
26 *MDR*, p. 190. "It was a bright summer day…" Basilides (117–161 C.E.) was a Gnostic who lived in Alexandria during the reigns of the Roman emperors Hadrian and Antoninus Pius.
27 *MDR*, p. 378.
28 Hannah, *Jung: His Life and Work*, p. 121, and Marie-Louise von Franz, *C. G. Jung: His Myth in Our Time* (London: Hodder & Stoughton, 1975), p. 121.
29 *MDR*, p. 194.
30 David Rosen, *The Tao of Jung: The Way of Integrity* (London: Penguin Arkana, 1997), p. 79.
31 Hannah, *Jung: His Life and Work*, p. 242.
32 *MDR*, p. 199.

LITTLE NORTHWEST MOON
OF THE BIG WEST—
LAWS AND PATTERNS OF
DEATH AND CHANGE

Empirically, the self appears in dreams, myths, and fairytales in the figure of the "supraordinate personality" such as a king, hero, prophet, saviour, etc., or in the form of a totality symbol, such as the circle, square, quadratura circuli, cross etc. When it represents a complexio oppositorum, a union of opposites, [it also appears in the form] of the hostile brothers, or of the hero and his adversary.[1]

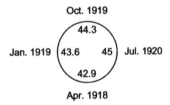

ung's Chaotic Journey into the Little Northwest Moon ended in April 1918 and WWI ended on November 11, 1918. The Elders say that the number 11 represents Spiritual Memory (Memory 10 + 1 Light) and we should note that the Remembrance Day service is held on the 11th hour of the 11th day of the 11th month. Jung's journey into the unconscious came to an end and his inner peace was restored at the same time as peace came to the fields of Europe.[2]

THE BIRTH OF THE SELF

During this Moon, Jung's work indicated his realization of form and pattern—the Northwest. Continuing his narrative in *Memories* of the post-war years, he said it was between 1918 and 1920 that he began to understand that the origin and goal of psychic development is the Self. Just at this point in *Memories,* Jung digresses to discuss his "Liverpool dream" in 1927, which he felt was crucial confirmation of his nascent ideas about the Self.[3] This archetype and image of totality, which contains all other archetypes, was the culmination of Jung's confrontation with the unconscious.[4] In 1918 he used the word "archetype" for the first time.[5] In 1921 he used the word "self" for the first time in the context of its later usage. Toward the end of the war, he had also done most of the research and writing for *Psychological Types,* in which he examines the four functions (sensing, feeling, thinking, and intuition). It illustrates how Jung's writing and conceptualizing was often in the archetypal Pattern of the Medicine Wheel. He completed the book by the spring of 1920.[6] During the summer of 1920 he decided to make an "all-out attack" on the meaning and use of the *I Ching,* the Chinese divinatory oracle which is based on patterns of changing energy polarities.

In early March 1920, at the invitation of his friend, Hermann Sigg, a Swiss businessman, Jung went to North Africa for a few weeks. The night before he left Tunisia to return to Switzerland he dreamed of being in an Arabian city with four walls and four gates. He was standing on a wooden bridge that spanned a moat surrounding the Kasbah at the center of the city. A young Arab of royal bearing came across the bridge. He and Jung wrestled until they fell into the moat, where they tried to push each other's head under water. Jung had no intention of killing the Arab, just rendering him incapable of fighting. Then the dream changed and Jung was in a large room in the center of the citadel, looking at a book on the floor, which he had written in strange calligraphy. He turned to the young prince with whom he had wrestled and said that he must read the book. The prince initially resisted but then acquiesced.

Jung's interpretation of the dream was that the royal figure coming across the bridge toward him from the Kasbah at the city's center was an emissary from the Self. Jung saw the wrestling on the bridge as akin to Jacob's struggle with the angel of the Lord. In the second part of the dream, the prince sat at his feet in order to understand his thoughts and to know man. Jung felt that in going to Africa—a psychic observation post outside his European life—he had unconsciously wanted to find that part of his personality that was unknown and invisible in Europe. Just as the Self, or the "objective psyche" as Jung later called it, is able to see a wider horizon than the ego can, so Jung in his trip to North Africa was able to see himself more objectively. This part stood in unconscious opposition to him and Jung attempted to suppress it, while it wished to keep him unconscious, thus each tried to force the other under water. The prince was a shadow figure, not associated with the persona, but a shadow of the Self.[7] The more the ego basks in its own light the darker and more threatening the Self will appear.[8]

This dream occurred when Jung was coming into the East of the Little Northwest Moon of the Big West—the Illumination and Enlightenment of the Death and Change of Laws and Pattern—and shortly before his Chaotic Journey to the North. He had already met the shadow side of the Self in the phallus dream at age 3 and the blasphemous thought at 12, both of which happened as he started a Chaotic Journey. *Answer to Job* was also written on a Chaotic Journey in the spring of 1951. Jung did not know what to make of his dream and hoped further investigation would reveal the significance of this encounter with the shadow of the Self.[9] Only when he began to study alchemy nearly 20 years later, in the early 1940s, did its full import dawn on him.

Jung's travels outside Europe, and later to central Africa and the USA, were a parallel in the outer world to his confrontation with the unconscious.[10] In his journeys, Jung's avowed purpose was to see how the white race looked from a different standpoint. He was astonished to find that his unconscious took no interest whatsoever in the journeys but it was intensely interested in what the journeys were doing to his psychology. Jung's outer travels forced him to go deeper into himself.[11]

Notes

1   *CW* 6, § 790.
2   Barbara Hannah, *Jung: His Life and Work* (New York: Putnam, 1976), p. 128.
3   *MDR*, p. 196. We shall refer to this dream as the dream of the "flowering tree."
4   For a discussion of the Self as Pattern in its triangular form see Robert Moore, "Decoding the Diamond Body," in Fredrica Halligan and John Shea, eds., *The Fires of Desire: Erotic Energies and the Spiritual Quest* (New York: Crossroad, 1992), pp. 111–125.
5   *CW* 8, *Instinct and the Unconscious*. Published 1919, presumably written in 1918.
6   Hannah, *Jung: His Life and Work*, p. 134.
7   *MDR*, p. 244.
8   *CW* 11, § 716.
9   *MDR*, p. 246.
10   Gerhard Wehr, *Jung: A Biography* (Boston: Shambhala, 1987), p. 223.
11   Hannah, *Jung: His Life and Work*, p. 179.

LITTLE NORTH MOON
OF THE BIG WEST—
WISDOM AND KNOWLEDGE OF
DEATH AND CHANGE

Turangawaewae—Maori, meaning "home ground, a place to stand,
a standing place for the feet."

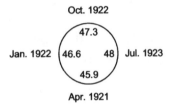

In September 1920, Jung held the first of his English seminars at Sennen Cove in Cornwall. While in England, he stayed at a country cottage in Buckinghamshire, which turned out to be haunted. Jung was in the middle of a Chaotic Journey and was beset with paranormal occurrences as he had been in 1909 with the sound in the bookcase in Freud's apartment (which also occurred when he was on a Chaotic Journey) and in 1898 with the table-splitting and the knife-shattering.

FATHER'S RETURN AND MOTHER'S DEATH

In September 1922 when he was in the North of this Little North Moon, Jung had a dream of his father. The last time he had dreamed about him was almost 27 years before, in March 1896, six weeks after his father died. In the dream, his father appeared as if he had returned from a distant journey and he said he wanted to consult Jung about marital relationships. Jung's mother Emilie was to die suddenly the following January, probably at age 74, the importance of which we shall touch on later. It was then that Jung realized that his father's return in the dream was a harbinger of his mother's death. His father was about to resume his relationship with his wife and wished for some advice![1]

These events sing with many others on the Wheel. His father died when Jung was three months past the North of the Little North Moon of the Big South. His father's return in the dream came when Jung was in the North of the Little North Moon of the Big West, a few months short of one Big Moon cycle after his father died. His mother died when she was close to the North of the Little North Moon of the Big North.[2] At her death, Jung himself was just past the North of the Little North Moon of the Big West.

Both of Jung's parents were the thirteenth and youngest in their families. Both died in the month of January. Every three years, on the anniversary of their deaths in January, Jung was at the mid-point of a Chaotic Journey. Both his parents died a few months before their own Chaotic Journeys.

Finally, Emilie died one Big Moon Cycle, 27 years to the month (January 1896-January 1923), after her husband died—perhaps just as their relationship, in spirit, was entering adulthood. From the experience-distant place of reading biography, we are not able to understand what this Pattern meant to them or to Jung, but we can clearly see the web.

THE BIRTH OF BOLLINGEN

For some time, since 1919 or 1920, Jung had been looking for land by the water on which to build a retreat. In 1922 he finally found a piece of land at Bollingen on the shores of Lake Zurich. In March 1923, two months after his mother died and approaching his Chaotic Journey in July 1923, he began building the Tower. At first, he planned a simple hut with a fire in the center and bunks around the walls, but opted for something less primitive and a two-storey tower was finished in 1923. Jung often said that Bollingen was the home of Philemon (Greek for "the loving one"), and said the Tower was a place of the Self, with a different view of things that happen in space and time.[3] At times he felt as if he were unfolded out over the land and inside the trees, waves, clouds, animals, and the rhythm of the seasons. "At Bollingen I am in the midst of my true life, I am most deeply myself."[4]

Notes

1   *MDR*, p. 315.
2   Emilie (b. 1848, d. January 1923) died sometime in her 75th year, between just before the North of the Little North Moon (74.3) and the East of the Little North Moon (75.0).
3   Barbara Hannah, *Jung: His Life and Work* (New York: Putnam, 1976), p. 266.
4   *MDR*, pp. 225–226.

LITTLE NORTHEAST MOON
OF THE BIG WEST—
CHOICES AND DECISIONS OF
DEATH AND CHANGE

It falls exclusively to the lot of human consciousness to perform the crucial action, even if consciousness fundamentally lacks the power to do so without the help of the almighty helper. This is the cosmic role that is allotted to the conscious mind in spite of its frailty.[1]

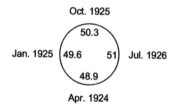

Oct. 1925

50.3

Jan. 1925 49.6 51 Jul. 1926

48.9

Apr. 1924

From a seminar that Jung gave in July 1923 in Polzeath, Cornwall we can again see how his thinking was often in the archetypal form of the Medicine Wheel. In the seminar, he spoke of how—apart from personal contents that have been repressed into the unconscious—there are several reasons why impersonal contents have been repressed. In a secular age, the influence of impersonal or spiritual ideas (which Jung later called archetypal images) wanes, because there are no adequate religious containers for such images. This archetypal energy then falls into the unconscious and returns in archaic and undesirable forms. Jung said the reasons for the repression of archetypal contents were: first, the oppression and exclusion of Nature (South); second, the exclusion of animals and the instincts (North); third, the exclusion of the body and sexuality (West)—seeing sexuality as purely reproductive and not as a way of worshipping Eros and relatedness—and the exclusion of the inferior man (the shadow) in racism; and fourth, the exclusion of creative fantasy and creative people through the routinization of work (East).[2]

The year 1923 had been an eventful year for Jung with the death of his mother and the building of Bollingen, but the following year was comparatively quiet. However it is likely that he wrote *Marriage as a Psychological Relationship* in 1924.[3] During this Little Northeast Moon he also made two major overseas journeys, to the USA and Kenya. On December 10, 1924 he left for New York, traveled by train to Chicago, and then again by train to the Grand Canyon and Taos, New Mexico, where he spent January 5-6, 1925. It was here that he met with Ochwiay Biano,[4] a spokesperson for the tribal council of the Taos Pueblo. Jung then went on to New Orleans and Washington, D.C., and arrived back in Kusnacht in mid-January, 1925.

The visit to Taos Pueblo was Jung's first contact with an indigenous culture, and it made a profound impression on him. He was in the South of the Little Northeast Moon of the Big West—the Death and Change of the Design of Energy of Mythology. Early in his confrontation with the unconscious he came to the painful realization that he could no longer live by the Christian myth. The longing to find his own myth began at that time but it had been intensified by meeting Mountain Lake who told him that his Pueblo people's reason for being was to help their father the sun cross the sky each day.[5]

AFRICA

Jung spent almost the whole of the last quarter of the Little Northeast Moon traveling in Africa from early October 1925 to April 1926; it was the longest of his overseas travels. During the late summer and autumn, Jung prepared for the long trip. Before leaving, he consulted the *I Ching* and received hexagram 53, Gradual Progress, with a nine in the third place that meant "the man goes forth and shall not return." Jung felt that this referred to himself and chose to go, even though this might mean his death. Jung survived but shortly after returning from Africa, George Beckwith, one of Jung's traveling companions, was killed in a car accident.

When he cast the *I Ching*, Jung was in the West of the Little Northeast Moon of the Big West—the double Death and Change of Choices and Decisions—and he formed a conviction at that time that one cannot live the second half of life fully unless one is willing to die. In the last decade of his life, after he had been ill, he often said that he thought his end had come and that was why he was granted a new lease on life.[6] As Jung became older, he consulted the *I Ching* less and less, feeling that "one must learn to walk in the dark, or try to discover (as when one is learning to swim) whether the water will carry one."[7]

Jung left London on October 15, journeying through the Suez Canal to Mombasa and then inland to Nairobi, where his party arrived in mid-November. From Nairobi he took a trip to the Athi Plains. Gazing out over the savannah, the cosmic meaning of consciousness became blindingly clear to him. He was envious of Mountain Lake's deep beliefs and had longed for a myth that would sustain him. Here, on the Athi Plains, he realized that Humans are the second creators who have given the world objective existence, without which life would have continued without meaning to an unknown end. It was through the creation of meaning that humankind found its place in the universe.[8] Here Jung was in the North of the Little Northeast Moon of the Big West—the Death and Change of Beliefs of the Design and Choreography of Energy—and he witnessed humankind's role in the web of creation. The idea of the created as an indispensable witness to creation was conceived in Africa and born 27 years later in *Answer to Job*, which he wrote when he was also in a Little Northeast Moon.

Although Jung was an introvert, he was able to see during these extroverted journeys that the natural world is the mirror of the inner world. While at the Mombasa railway station, he was waiting impatiently for a train to take him inland. An English gentleman, long resident in Kenya, advised him that this was "God's country," to sit down and not worry, and allow things to take their course. This advice suffered an unusual fate with Jung; he took it. So impressed was he with the advice and how helpful it was in Africa, that he passed it on to others who were fated to go through a confrontation with the unconscious. What applies in the bush also applies in the unconscious; in the bush we meet the collective unconscious outside, and in the confrontation with the unconscious we meet it inside.[9]

After three weeks on Mount Elgon, Jung's party continued north out of Kenya toward the head of the Nile. Reaching the end of the long trek, Jung's inferior sensation function was severely challenged and he said his capacity to digest new impressions was approaching its limits. It was during this lowering of the level of consciousness that he had his one and only dream of a black man on the trip. During the journey his dreams had stubbornly ignored Africa as if they considered the whole trip as symbolic. The black man he dreamed of had been his barber in Chattanooga, Tennessee on his trip to the USA in early 1925, and in the dream he was curling Jung's hair. Jung was ill with sandfly fever when he had the dream and felt it was warning him that the primitive was dangerous, so threatening in fact that the unconscious had distanced it in time, and he was in danger of "going black."[10]

One aspect of the Northeast, as the place of the Design of Energy, is how "efficiently" we use our energies. This is not in the sense of corporate efficiency but in the sense that when the universe moves and changes it does so with no wasted energy. If we move when the universe moves, if our will is aligned with the will of the Great Spirit, then we experience a flow and an effortlessness. After Jung returned from his trip in April 1926 there were tremendous demands on his time and energy from patients and pupils. He realized increasingly that it was the inner life that counted and his efficiency in outer tasks depended on how unswervingly he met the demands of the unconscious to become conscious.[11] Here, Jung was in the Northeast of the Little Northeast Moon of the Big West—the Death and Change of the double Design of Energy.

Notes

1   Alfred Ribi, *Demons of the Inner World: Understanding Our Hidden Complexes* (Boston: Shambhala, 1989), p. 23.

2   Barbara Hannah, *Jung: His Life and Work* (New York: Putnam, 1976), pp. 150–152.

3   *CW* 17.

4   Also known as Mountain Lake or Antonio Mirabal (c. 1891–1975).

5   Hannah, *Jung: His Life and Work*, p. 171.

6   Hannah, *Jung: His Life and Work*, p. 170.

7   Aniela Jaffé, ed., *C. G. Jung: Word and Image* (Princeton: Princeton University Press, 1979), p. 35.

8   *MDR*, p. 256.

9   Hannah, *Jung: His Life and Work*, p. 172.

10 *MDR*, pp. 272–273.

11 Hannah, *Jung: His Life and Work*, pp. 183–184.

LITTLE EAST MOON
OF THE BIG WEST—
ILLUMINATION OF
DEATH AND CHANGE

It is this time that is called the Time of Dreaming The World Awake!
The symbol of learning is the Maze. You wander as a guest of your world
within the wonderful Maze. It is like a great magical garden where you are
the principal person. You are protected there. You are the light
of the shadow of the flowering tree.[1]

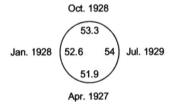

A s we have seen, the East Moon is often when previous Circles of Life Experience come into the light of consciousness for integration. They show us the way forward, or the tasks that lie before us, in the next Little or Big Moon. Every increase in consciousness in the East flows from a creative encounter with darkness in the West. During the first years in this East Moon, Jung reaped what had been sown in the West Moon during his descent. Although he led an active outer life the late 1920s, they were mainly years of inner enlightenment and were the first conscious epilogue to his earlier confrontation with the unconscious.[2] In this, the last Little Moon in the Big West, Jung had several dreams that further opened the door to his most important later contributions—alchemy and the Self.

ALCHEMY

Since 1925 Jung had had a number of dreams with a similar motif: beside his own house there stood an annex that he did not recognize, although it seemed that it must have always been there. The annex symbolized a part of his personality of which he was unconscious. Finally, he had a dream where he reached this other wing and discovered a wonderful library dating from the 16th and 17th centuries. The large books contained illustrations with curious symbols that he had never seen before and couldn't understand.[3]

After he returned from Africa, he had a dream that heralded his encounter with alchemy. We can assume Jung did not have the dream in Africa as he presumably would have mentioned it in his account of the trip. In the dream he was in northern Italy (as he had been in the dream where he met the 12th-century knight) during wartime and was being transported in a horse-drawn wagon. After driving through the countryside, with shells exploding all around, they went through a tunnel that came out in Lombardy and then they drove into the courtyard of a large manor house. As soon as they had reached the center of the courtyard, the gates suddenly shut and the peasant wagon-driver said that they were trapped in the 17th century. At first, Jung thought that he would be caught there for years, but at the end of the dream he had the final thought that years later he would get out again.

After these dreams he read widely to help him understand their meaning but it was not until much later that he realized that they referred to alchemy, which had died out in the 17th century. It was Jung's task to free it from the 17th century as something more than a historical oddity. After these first stirrings of interest, he asked a Munich bookseller to inform him whenever they found an alchemical book. Fifteen years later, Jung had assembled a library on alchemy similar to the one in the first dream.

THE FLOWERING TREE

The dream that crystallized Jung's ideas about the Self came in the first half of 1927, toward the end of his Chaotic Journey from the Little Northeast Moon to the Little East Moon. We can locate it in this period because he painted a mandala from this dream and titled it "Window on Eternity." He dedicated the mandala to Hermann Sigg, his friend who had died on January 9, 1927.[4]

Jung dreamed that he was in Liverpool, walking through dirty, sooty streets in the rain on a winter night, with about half a dozen other Swiss men. They walked up from the harbor to the top of the cliffs and there they could see that the various quarters of the city were arranged radially around a central pool. Each of the peripheral quarters was also arranged radially around its own central point, each forming a replica of the whole. In the middle of the central pool was an island and, while everything around was obscured by rain and fog, the island blazed with sunlight. On it stood a single tree, a magnolia, in a shower of reddish blossoms.[5] The tree was simultaneously in the sunlight and the source of it. His companions did not see the tree and they spoke of another Swiss who was living in Liverpool and expressed surprise that he had settled here. In the dream, Jung said to himself that he knew why.

The Elders say the human form is a configuration of energy called the Luminous Cocoon that includes the Assemblage Points, the ten Wheels or chakras, the Shields, the Dancers, and the Chiefs. It is the cast of our wholeness, the energetic form of the Self in the Dream. It is also called the Human Flowering Tree.

For Jung, this dream confirmed his first thoughts about the Self after the dream, in Tunis in 1920, of the royal figure who represented the shadow aspect of the Self. He now began to understand the Self as the principle and archetype of orientation and meaning, and therein lay its healing function. From this dream of the Self as the flowering tree Jung also began to get the first inkling of his personal myth. He described the effect of the dream, and the illumination it brought, as "an act of grace" that helped orient him after plunging into the unknown, following his break with Freud.

Jung's use of the word "grace" is significant. In *Memories* the only other time he uses the word is when he described his experience in

1887 when was 12, of his Illumination that God wanted him to sin. These Illuminations of the nature of the Self all occurred when he was in the East. At age 12, he had just left the East of the Little Southwest Moon of the Big South on his Chaotic Journey, at age 45 in Tunis he was in the East of the Little Northwest Moon of the Big West, and the dream of the flowering tree came when he had just entered the Little East Moon of the Big West. When he was 12 the Self presented itself in shadow form to his young ego. Now, at age 51, the Self presented itself in beneficent form to the mature ego. From his descent into the unconscious in the Little West Moon of the Big West, the time of choosing Life or Death, had come the flowering of the tree in the Little East Moon of the Big West. His Introspection and Intuition in the West had brought him Illumination in the East.

Other important events also happened in the East. At age 24, when he came into the Little East Moon of the Big South he decided on psychiatry as a career (his Personal Dream), in the Little East Moon of the Big West at age 51, he began to get an inkling of his own destiny (his Sacred Dream) with the dream of the flowering tree, and in the Little East Moon of the Big North, the tree would bear fruit as well as flowers. In early 1954 at age 78, one Big Moon Cycle after the dream of the flowering tree, he was to finish his major work *Mysterium Coniunctionis* (his Give-Away to the Collective Dream).

Although Jung did not mention it in *Memories*, he told Barbara Hannah that the "other Swiss" in the flowering tree dream lived in the vicinity of one of the secondary centers of the mandala-like city, and he realized that we do not live in the center but at the periphery. We are a unique replica of the Self, thus giving the Self an objective existence. Similarly, on the Wheel, we rarely experience the full power and mystery of the Self at the Center. We are more likely to experience its manifestation in the non-cardinal directions as the Symbol, Pattern, Design, or Image of the Self.

In 1927 Jung felt that Bollingen did not express everything he needed to say and that something was lacking, so he built a connecting structure to a tower-like annex. Now there was a similar second tower connected to the original central Tower. Was this the flow-ering tree dream in physical form?

In 1928, a year after the flowering tree dream, Jung painted another mandala with a golden castle at the center, which struck him as having a Chinese character. Soon afterward Richard Wilhelm, a Sinologist, sent him the manuscript of *The Secret of the Golden Flower*, a translation of a Taoist alchemical treatise. Jung was most excited to receive this as it confirmed his ideas about the mandala and the circumambulation of the center. He spent most of his free time writing the foreword to *The Secret of the Golden Flower* in late 1928 to early 1929. After 1928 he gave up painting mandalas.[6]

Notes

1   Hyemeyohsts Storm, *Song of Heyoehkah* (New York: Ballantine, 1972), p. 52.

2   Barbara Hannah, *Jung: His Life and Work* (New York: Putnam, 1976), p. 184.

3   *MDR*, p. 202.

4   Aniela Jaffé, ed., *C. G. Jung: Word and Image* (Princeton: Princeton University Press, 1979), p. 92.

5   Jung wrote extensively on the tree as a symbol. See *CW* 13, *The Philosophical Tree*.

6   *MDR*, p. 199.

BIG NORTH MOON—WISDOM AND KNOWLEDGE

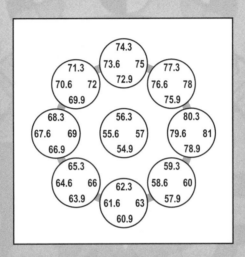

Through his historical development, the European has become so far removed from his roots that his mind was finally split into faith and knowledge, in the same way that every psychological exaggeration breaks up into its inherent opposites.

—C. G. JUNG, *Yoga and the West*, CW 11, § 868

*Where is the wisdom
We have lost in knowledge?
Where is the knowledge
We have lost in information?*

—T. S. ELIOT, "The Rock"

LITTLE CENTER MOON
OF THE BIG NORTH —
CATALYST OF WISDOM
AND KNOWLEDGE

[Y]ou never see anythng very great which is not, at the same time, horrible in some respect. The genius of Einstein leads to Hiroshima.[1]

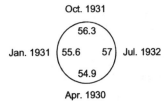

T he early 50s are the old age of youth and the youth of old age. In July 1929 Jung began his second Big Chaotic Journey at age 54.0 and entered the South of the Little Center Moon of the Big North at age 54.9. The record is curiously silent about this period from late 1929 to 1932 and as we shall see it preceded a tumultuous time for Jung in the 1930s. The various biographies on Jung seem to lose the thread of narrative between descriptions of his first encounters with alchemy in the mid- to late 1920's and his ordeals with Nazism or the beginning of the Eranos conferences, both from 1933 onward.

The events in the Center Moon we do know of are: he learned to drive in 1929, although he had long resisted buying a car; in 1930 Richard Wilhelm died; in 1931 Peter Baynes—his assistant since the early 1920s and translator of some of his works from German—got married and moved back to England; he and Toni Wolff visited Ravenna in 1932 or 1933; and in March 1933 he went on a Mediterranean cruise to Egypt, Palestine, and Rhodes, with his friend Dr. Markus Fierz. The major world event during this Little Moon was the Wall Street crash of October 1929 that triggered off the worldwide Great Depression, which did not begin to ease until 1932. From 1928 to 1930, Jung gave a series of seminars on dream analysis at the Psychological Club.[2] In the autumn of 1930 he began the Visions Seminars,[3] which were followed by the seminars on Nietzsche's *Thus Spoke Zarathustra* in March 1934, and they continued until 1939.[4]

Other events of note that occurred later but overshadowed by the more dramatic events of the 1930's were that Jung began lecturing at the Eranos conferences, on the shores of Lake Maggiore, each summer from 1934 to 1951 (with the exception of 1943-1944, on account of his serious illness). He was made Professor of Psychology at ETH and began to lecture there again for the first time since 1913 and continued almost uninterrupted until 1941.[5] In early 1934, an 18-year-old Marie-Louise von Franz (later to become one of Jung's closest colleagues) began analysis with him and, in exchange for her fee, she translated Jung's alchemical texts from Greek and Latin, thus dating his intensive study of alchemy from the spring of 1934.[6]

As he did in the Little Center and Little Southeast Moons in the Big West—first at Burghölzli and then with Freud—Jung again embarked on new endeavors. He again seemed to throw himself, or to be drawn, into the professional arena in the 1930s and much of his writing in these two Little Moons is on psychotherapy.[7]

The Little Center Moon of the Big North (from 54 to 57) sings with the Little Center Moon of the Big South (from birth to 3)—both sit in the place of the greatest tension between the opposites of matter in the West and spirit in the East. During this Little Moon in July 1931, Jung published *Basic Postulates of Analytical Psychology*, wherein he wrote, "The conflict between nature and spirit is itself a reflection of the paradox of psychic life. Whenever, with our human understanding, we want to make a statement about something . . . we must, if we are honest, be willing to contradict ourselves, we must pull this something into its antithetical parts in order to be able to deal with it at all."[8]

THE SECOND BIG CHAOTIC JOURNEY

On the Moon Cycles we travel through a Big Chaotic journey at 27, 54, and 81, all of which are major developmental turning points in our lives. Although Jung has many developmental formulations scattered throughout his works, he never wrote a great deal on developmental psychology. But during his Big Chaotic Journey at 54, he wrote one of his most significant papers on adult development. In March 1930, *The Stages of Life* was published in a Zurich newspaper. He wrote:

> Middle life begins between the thirty-fifth and fortieth year. . . . [A]n important change in the human psyche is in preparation. . . . [S]omewhere around the age of fifty, a period of intolerance and fanaticism is reached. . . . As formerly the neurotic could not escape from childhood, so now he cannot part with his youth. . . . [A]n old man who cannot bid farewell to life appears as feeble and sickly as a young man who is unable to embrace it. . . . The one hundred and eighty degrees of the arc of life are divisible into four parts. The first quarter, lying to the east, is childhood, that state in which we are a problem for others but are not yet conscious of any problems of our own. Conscious problems fill out the second and third quarters; while in the last, in extreme old age, we descend again into that condition where, regardless of our state of consciousness, we once more become something of a problem for others.[9]

In addition to the dearth of narrative in *Memories* and in his biographies, Jung's letters shed little light on this Big Chaotic Journey and Center Moon. Jung wrote his letters by hand and kept no copies, and he did not realize until later in life that others might be interested in his correspondence. There is little published correspondence before 1931, with only about sixty letters in all up to the end of 1930. During his Big Chaotic Journey there are none between early January and April 1929 and very few the rest of that year.

Other letters do exist but, understandably, the heirs to the Jung estate proscribed any publication of his letters to the family. There are also very personal letters to other recipients who felt it too soon to allow their publication in the early 1970s, just ten years after Jung's death. Jung's letters to Toni Wolff were returned to him on her death in 1953, and he later destroyed them together with her correspondence to him. Therefore, most of Jung's published letters are related to his work. He did not want his letters to Freud published until twenty years after his death, although the heirs of both families permitted publication before this hiatus, given the historical importance of the correspondence.

Of the few letters around this time, one on August 25, 1928 to Count Hermann Keyserling is particularly interesting. Keyserling, who had struck up a correspondence with Jung about spiritual matters, wrote to him and mentioned his great affection for his father and his negative attitude to his mother. He also related a recurrent dream in which his father, long dead, had not really died but lived in sad and reduced circumstances. In the dreams a meeting with his father was always frustrated by his father's hopelessness about himself and his wish to disappear.

Jung replied, commenting on Keyserling's dream, that a negative relationship with the mother was a slight against nature and led to distance from the earth and a complementary identification with the father, heaven, wind, light, spirit, and logos. He added that, although Keyserling's spiritual inclination was probably inevitable, it was too large for human proportions and was an inflation.[10]

This letter is significant for several reasons: it was written at the same time of year (late summer) that Jung's father had fallen ill with cancer, when Jung was the same age (53) at which his father had died, a few months before the anniversary of his father's death, and it is a letter about the "ill" father. Jung saw his own father's struggle as one between experience and belief, wherein belief won the day, but at the expense of his father's life. As we shall see, the 1930s were a difficult time for Jung when he attempted, with untoward consequences, to superimpose his beliefs on political events in Europe. Jung, as he did at other times, may well have intuited coming developments in his own unconscious—an inflation. Could he have projected his own complexes onto Keyserling? Did Jung fly too high in the realm of spirit and ideas leading to his deflation in the 1930s and 1940s?

The typical flow of his letters during the late 1920s and early 1930s are discussions on publications or a reply to dreams that people sent him. However, another odd letter stands out. It is dated January 8, 1932 and was sent to the editors of Jung's letters, as a fragment, without address, beginning, or end. Although Jung was not on his Chaotic Journey at this time it does give a sense of his struggles. "I have attacks of feeling horribly inferior. I have to digest a whole span of life full of mistakes and stupidity. Anyway feelings of inferiority are the counterpart of power. Wanting to be better or more intelligent that one is, is power too. It is difficult enough to be what one is and yet endure oneself and for once forgive one's own sins with Christian charity. That is damnably difficult."[11]

The only time Jung mentions this period from 1929-1932 in *Memories* is when he writes about his addition to Bollingen. In the summer of 1930 Jung was planning an addition and in 1931 he built another tower, the eight-sided retiring room. It became a place where Jung could work undisturbed, a place of spiritual concentration to which he kept the key at all times.[12]

PICASSO AND CHAOS

We have seen that, other than Jung's early childhood, there was no three-year period that was written less about than the time from 1929-1932. There seems to have been a caesura, a break in the thread of consciousness, like a break in the flow of a dream. Perhaps something sank into the unconscious? David Rosen writes of this time under the heading "The Candle Dims": "Despite the 1929 publication and promise of *The Secret of the Golden Flower*, icy and at times gale-force winds blew in from the north. The flame of the soul died down and during the 1930s it nearly went out."[13]

In early November 1932 (in the middle of his Chaotic Journey from the Little Center to the Little Southeast Moon) Jung wrote a paper on Picasso in response to a Zurich newspaper's request for his comment on a Picasso retrospective exhibition at the Zurich Kunsthaus.[14] In this paper, Jung analyzed the development of Picasso's work and, in reference to the fractured lines of his work, suggested that his painting belonged to the "schizophrenic group." He said that the healing of the schizophrenic split requires a *nekyia*, a descent into the underworld, to recover psychic wholeness, and that Picasso was in danger of succumbing to the lure of the underworld as symbolized by the ambivalent Harlequin image in his work.

Jung suggested that, although he did not wish to try his hand at prophecy (and it was for this prophesizing that he was later taken to task), there were three possibilities for the future development of Picasso's work: the inner process may continue toward its goal; it may come to standstill; or it may come to "a catastrophic bursting asunder of conjoined opposites," and Picasso must either integrate the whole of the psychic material he has expressed into a greater unity, or fragment into a psychosis.

He also drew attention to the similarity between Picasso's Harlequin images in his paintings and the buffoon in *Zarathustra* who jumps over the rope-dancer bringing about his death: "He cries out to the rope-dancer, his weaker *alter-ego*: 'To one better than yourself you bar the way!' He [the buffoon] is the greater personality who bursts the shell, and this shell is sometimes—the brain."[15]

Picasso's life mirrored Jung's in many ways. Could Jung, in his reaction to Picasso's life and work, dimly see the outline of his own future development and his later near-fatal illness? Jung's inferior function was likely his sensation function and Philemon, the figure who came to him in his descent into the unconscious, had a lame foot (although we do not know which one)[16] and Bollingen, which he called the home of Philemon, was important as Jung's contact with earthly reality. However, unlike Picasso, Jung's passage through the "doorway to God" (as he termed the inferior function) was to come through physical illness, rather than mental "bursting," and lameness was to lead him to death's door. We shall see that Picasso emerges again shortly before Jung's death.

James Wyly points out that Picasso's later work, from 1932 to the 1950s, followed the hero's journey with themes of sacrifice, descent, *coniunctio*, and then rebirth and renewal. Picasso (1881-1973) was six years younger than Jung and also went through similar upheavals but correspondingly a few years later. The 1936 Spanish Civil War was around the time of Picasso's Big Chaotic Journey. He underwent a renewal around the late 1940s and early 1950s, moving to a more objective standpoint and interest in the creative process of painting itself, and he remained fertile and creative until his death.[17]

Rosen comments that "[Jung's paper] on Picasso seems a bit odd. Jung appears to get into the persona role of psychiatrist and in an ego-dominated way makes the judgment that Picasso must be a schizophrenic. This is a strange essay, since there are certain similarities between Picasso's and Jung's troubled relationships with women (thus, mother and anima problems), but, most important, they are both profoundly creative individuals. Actually, Jung was also a very talented artist, which he denied. Therefore, could this condemnation of Picasso be a projection? This issue is raised here because at about the same time, Jung was already displaying denial—one of the two most primitive defense mechanisms, the other being projection—in his reaction to the pleas of two Jewish colleagues about the rise of Nazism."[18]

If we compare this time to the same place in the Big West Moon—going from the Little Center to the Little Southeast Moon (July 1906-April 1906)—we see that Jung had gone through tumultuous times then: he made his first contact with Freud, was in the throes of his relationship with Sabina Spielrein, and his three-year-old marriage to Emma was going through difficult times.

Notes ——

1   Pablo Picasso, in Françoise Gilot and Carlton Lake, *Life with Picasso* (New York: Anchor, 1989).

2   C. G. Jung, *Dream Analysis: Notes of the Seminar in 1928-1930* (Princeton: Princeton University Press, 1984).

3   C. G. Jung, *Visions: Notes of the Seminar Given in 1930-1934* (Princeton: Princeton University Press, 1997).

4   C. G. Jung, *Nietzsche's Zarathustra: Notes of the Seminar Given in 1934-1939* (Princeton: Princeton University Press, 1988).

5   Eidgenössische Technische Hochschule: Swiss Federal Institute of Technology, Zurich.

6   Barbara Hannah, *Jung: His Life and Work* (New York: Putnam, 1976), p. 229.

7   Including *Problems of Modern Psychotherapy* (1929), *The Stages of Life* (1930), *Some Aspects of Modern Psychotherapy* (1930), *Basic Postulates of Analytical Psychology* (1931).

8   *CW* 8, § 680.

9   *CW* 8, § 759 *ff.*

10   *Letters* 1, p. 70.

11   *Letters* 1, p. 87

12   *MDR*, p. 224.

13   David Rosen, *The Tao of Jung: The Way of Integrity* (London: Penguin Arkana, 1997), p. 101.

14   *CW* 15, *Picasso.*

15   *CW* 15, § 214.

16   *MDR*, p. 185.

17   James Wyly, "Jung and Picasso," *Quadrant* 20, no. 2 (1987): 7–21.

18   David Rosen, *The Tao of Jung: The Way of Integrity*, pp. 101–102.

LITTLE SOUTHEAST MOON
OF THE BIG NORTH—
SELF-IMAGES OF WISDOM AND
KNOWLEDGE

In the unconscious of the Protestant one finds a Jew.[1]

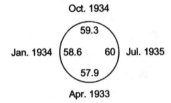

As background to the turbulent times in the 1930s, let us look at Jung's relationship with Judaism and the Jewish people. In his search for a myth of his own and a spiritual or at least religious home, Jung was on the horns of a dilemma. He was not one for the racial melting pot or adopting others' traditions. One's place of birth and the culture that one spiritually and physically grows up in leaves its mark on the soul. Jung spoke frequently of the disciplines of the East as not being psychologically or spiritually suitable for the West, as well as of the distinct differences in racial and national psychologies.

The myth and tradition that Jung longed for was not to be found in the Protestant faith, which Jung felt did not provide room for the numinous. His most important paper on religious ceremony, *Transformation Symbolism in the Mass,* was on the archetypal themes of sacrifice and rebirth in the Catholic Mass, but Jung was not Catholic, neither was he attracted to the Catholic mystical tradition. Hindu and Muslim traditions were foreign to his European sensibilities, and although he was fascinated by indigenous cultures, on his travels outside Europe he often experienced a fear of "going native."

THE JEWISH QUESTION

However Jung was well acquainted with the unbroken, four-thousand-year lineage of Judaism, in particular its mystical tradition, and had read the three-thousand-page *Kabbala Denudata* (*The Cabala Unveiled*), among other Cabalistic works. Strangely enough, Jung's father, a Protestant minister, was also an outstanding Hebraist.[2]

The Cabala embodies the Jewish mystical tradition that crystallized in the 13th century with the Zohar (The Book of Splendor) but had its roots with Rabbi Simon ben Jochai in the 2nd century C.E. According to Cabalistic writing, *En Sof* (the unknowable Godhead), emanates the ten *Sefirah* of the Tree of Life, that are the inner workings of the Godhead. The original light was poured into the ten vessels; three of these held the light and the other seven shattered into shards but with sparks of the divine light trapped within them. These shards then sank into matter and took on the quality of evil—in the Gnostic writings, they are called the Archons. The human task is, through observation of the Torah and the Commandments, a "raising of the sparks," a redemption (*tikkun*) of the world and the reunification of the Godhead.

Although the waters of Jewish mysticism, which might have slaked Jung's thirst for the *numinosum*, were not available to him, there are several significant links between Jung and Judaism. Jung's first personification of the unconscious, which came to him in his descent, was Elijah. Of all the prophets in Judaism, Elijah remains a powerful, alive personality with a paternal concern for the fate of Israel and every individual Jew.[3] It was through Jung's transformative Cabalistic visions, when he was close to death in 1944, that he was redeemed and reunited with the God-image within. His later works,

Answer to Job and *Mysterium Coniunctionis*, contain many references to Jewish mysticism.

Sabina Spielrein was Jewish, and so was the blind Salome. In *Memories*, this theme of the "Jewish anima" recurs. Jung begins a section of the chapter "Psychiatric Activities" by saying that he never tries to convert a patient to or from any religious affiliation, a Jew will remain a Jew, and the essential thing is that the patient comes to his own view. He then describes a dream in which an unknown young girl came to him as a patient, and while she was talking he thought to himself, "I don't understand her at all," but suddenly it occurred to him that she must have an unusual father complex. Jung does not date the dream, nor are there clues given by the context of the dream or its place in *Memories*.

The day after the dream, a young Jewish woman—the daughter of a wealthy banker—who was well-adapted, pretty, and highly intelligent, and "enlightened down to her bones," came to see him. She had already undergone an analysis but the doctor had referred her to Jung as he had developed a countertransference to her and begged the woman not to come any more as it would mean the end of his marriage.

At first Jung could not understand what her problem was, and then he remembered his dream. But she presented no evidence of a father complex, so he asked her about her grandfather. It transpired that he was Hassidic, in fact, a *zaddik* ("righteous one"). The center of a Hassidic group, the *zaddik* was revered as a sage, a counselor, and a mediator between the Hassidim and God. Jung then told her that because her grandfather was a *zaddik*, and her father had become an apostate to the Jewish faith and turned his back on God, she had her neurosis because the fear of God had got into her. This struck her to the core.

The following night he had another dream that this young woman was at his house. She came up to him and asked if he had an umbrella, as it was raining so hard. Jung found one and was on the point of giving it to her when he dropped to his knees and handed it to her as if she were a goddess. Frances Wickes, one of Jung's

American colleagues, gives a slightly different version of the story, adding that when the young Jewish woman came to her appointments with Jung, she in fact carried a small folded umbrella, always in its case.

In *Memories*, Jung continues the story in animated fashion, saying that the dream showed him that her superficial interests in flirtation, clothes, and sex hid her spiritual nature. His task was to awaken mythological and religious strivings in her as she was the kind of person of whom spiritual activity was demanded.[4]

When Jung saw her again he told her his dream and asked, "'What is it that you have kept folded away, something that I would go on my knees to, and would reverence as I did in the dream?' She burst into tears and told him 'I come of a line of mystics and seers. My grandfather and those before him had visions and heard words of revelation. I too hear the voice and see the vision, but when I tried to tell of them, people laughed and thought me queer. So I became ashamed and have hidden them away.'"[5]

If we look at Jung's narrative about the young Jewish woman as a dream, we might see the referring doctor as Jung's shadow who was attracted to other women, the young woman as his Jewish anima—unconscious of her own spiritual tradition and onto whom Jung projected his spiritual aspirations that Jung's ego needed to release from unconsciousness—and the grandfather as Jung's inner Jewish senex that the ego had turned its back on. The young anima is too close to the unconscious and needed protection (the umbrella) from the deluge from the unconscious. The resolution of the tension between the conscious and unconscious (the rain) resulted in Jung genuflecting and recognizing the numinous spiritual tradition that the young woman embodied. Through this tradition, which he needed to make conscious, he could relate to one of the faces of the Self—his own inner *zaddik*. Later we shall see a similar image of Jung kneeling in a dream, before Uriah, King David's general.

The theme of the "Jewish anima" is heard again in a letter of December 31, 1941, replying to Jolande Jacobi, a Jewish analytical psychologist originally from Budapest who had converted to

Catholicism, concerning the anima projections of a male patient of hers. The last sentence is his advice on how Jacobi should treat the patient, and is one of Jung's well-known maxims. He says that the Jewish anima is projected upon Jewesses not because they are Jewish but because they are "still *pagan* in their eroticism." But this eroticism "goes together with an unconsciousness which an intelligent Jewess does not have, *she upsets people by her heightened consciousness*. . . . Anyone who has unconscious assumptions must be treated like an insane person: one must let him have them until he comes into conflict with himself."[6]

We know that whatever the conscious attitude, the contrary exists in the unconscious. Was Jung consciously Swiss and Protestant, but unconsciously Jewish, and did this division in himself lead to his words and actions in the 1930s that resulted in accusations of anti-Semitism? How much was Jung conscious of the Jewish nature of his own psychology?

THE NAZIS

When the Nazis came to power in Germany in 1933, one of their first aims was to ensure that all of the country's organizations conformed to official Nazi ideology. Pressure was put on Ernst Kretschmer, President of the International General Medical Society for Psychotherapy, and editor of the *Zentralblatt* journal, to bring the society into line. As a result, Kretschmer resigned and Jung, who had been vice-president since 1930, was fervently pressed to take over the presidency and editorship to preserve the society from German domination, which he did in late 1933. In September 1933 the Germans set up a separate section of the Society, headed by Dr. Marius Göring, an aging cousin of Reichsmarshal Hermann Göring, head of the Luftwaffe. The German Society expelled some of the Jewish psychoanalysts and all the remaining Jewish analysts resigned.

Jung found himself on the horns of a dilemma and wrote at that time, "Thus a moral conflict arose for me as it would for any decent man in this situation. Should I, as a prudent neutral, withdraw into security this side of the frontier and wash my hands in innocence, or should I—as I was well aware—risk my skin and expose myself to the inevitable misunderstandings which no one escapes. . . . As conditions then were, a single stroke of the pen in high places would have sufficed to sweep all psychotherapy under the table."[7] Jung recommended that the International Society not expel the German Society in order to prevent Nazi domination of the latter and to preserve psychotherapy in Germany. He also welcomed Jewish psychoanalysts who had been expelled or had resigned from the German Society as members of the International Society.

Göring planned to bring out a supplement to the *Zentralblatt*, for circulation in Germany only, calling on all German members to conform to the tenets of Nazism. The secretary-general of the Society, and editor of the journal issue which was being published in Leipzig, was Dr. Walter Cimbal of Hamburg. Cimbal, it seems, had failed to notify Jung that this "manifesto" was to be included in the December 1933 international issue of the *Zentralblatt*. Thinking this had been done with Jung's approval, Gustav Bally, a Swiss psychiatrist, attacked Jung in the Zurich press on February 27, 1934, and this set off a wider storm of criticism directed at Jung. Unfortunately Jung never wrote an editorial denouncing the supplement's inclusion in the international journal. Then, in 1934, he wrote *The State of Psychotherapy Today*, in part about the differences between Christian and Jewish psychologies, which further inflamed matters, but after the war he said to Dr. Siegmund Hurwitz that the paper was "nonsense."

In a letter to James Kirsch (then of Berlin and later founder of the C. G. Jung Institute of Los Angeles) on May 26, 1934 Jung said that as Honorary President he could not have abandoned the Society when Kretschmer resigned, and the fact that he spoke of the differences between Jewish and Christian psychology seemed to permit anyone to call him an anti-Semite. In other letters and interviews during the years from 1933 to 1936, Jung spoke a great deal about the differences between Aryan and Jewish psychologies,[8] and the archetypal bases for these. But he had been writing about national psychologies (English, Swiss, Chinese, American, Islamic, Spanish, Slavic, Celtic, African, and Native American) since 1918. However, these public statements drew intense criticism about his dealings with National Socialism and led to a great polarization as to his views.

Those who knew Jung—Jewish and non-Jewish—thought for the most part that he made some tactless comments and his timing was off, but they also staunchly defended him. In the last ten years, an avalanche of criticism has been directed toward Jung. These more recent critics have lamely written off the support Jung's contemporaries gave him as a positive transference toward Jung.

Aniela Jaffé, herself Jewish and the editor of *Memories*, said, "Jung was neither a Nazi nor an anti-Semite," yet, "Criticism of Jung's attitude during the years 1933–1934 is justified by the facts."[9] But Marie-Louise von Franz said, in response to Jaffé's assessment, "It was not a hidden shadow element but rather the 'therapeutic' optimism of his temperament which misled Jung into his 'mistake.'"[10]

Barbara Hannah's view was that, "To anyone who, like myself, was with Jung in Berlin in July 1933, and who saw and heard him frequently during the next twenty-eight years, the libel that Jung was a Nazi is so absurd and so entirely without foundation that it goes against the grain to take it seriously enough to contradict it."[11] Thomas Kirsch, James Kirsch's son and former President of the International Association of Analytical Psychology, said, "His innocence is as hard to prove as his guilt."[12] On the other hand, Andrew Samuels says: "When Jung writes about the Jews and Jewish psychology, is there something in his whole attitude, his 'take,' to use the colloquialism, that just had to lead to antisemitism [sic]? Is there something to worry about? My brief answer, in contradistinction to that of many other leading Jungian analysts, is 'yes'…"[13]

But by the 1950s Jung was a changed man from the 1930s. James Kirsch said that "Jung was the only non-Jew I have ever known who, in my opinion, truly overcame the last trace of anti-Semitism."[14] Writing in 1991, he said of his contact with Jung over the years, "I had known Jung personally since 1928 until the time of his death. I had seen him frequently before the Second World War and many times afterward; I had talked to him quite often about the

Jewish question and never found any kind of anti-Semitism in him. . . . [In May 1933] he could not accept my utterly pessimistic view and my decision to leave Germany as soon as possible. The first time I saw Jung after the war in July of 1947, the first thing that Jung did was to remember this conversation and to apologize to me . . . I knew to what extent he had become conscious of his own Jewish psychology. . . . He [also] showed a deep understanding of the psychological causes of anti-Semitism."[15]

Jung could see the collective Dream. What happens in the third dimension has already been dreamed of in the fifth dimension. But it is the spirit of the event that is dreamed, not the form. Humans have free will and an intricate web of human choices influence the form as it comes down from the Dream, if it comes at all (and there are a million dreams that never manifest). From 1933 to 1936 Jung was in the Little Southeast Moon of the Big North (the Self-Images of Wisdom and Knowledge). He tried to communicate what he saw in the Dream, and misjudged the timing and expression of his ideas. He was standing in the place of Self-Images and the Ancestors, and he was working with Law and Pattern across the Wheel in the Northwest. Both directions were his greatest gift and his greatest weakness. Ann Belford Ulanov said that during these years, "His strengths and gifts double-crossed him, in his weaknesses, in his blind spots. . . . What he relied on betrayed him, and he betrayed what he relied on."[16] After the war, in a letter of April 20, 1946, Jung wrote, "I must say that before the Hitler era I had some illusions which have been radically destroyed. . . . I really had not thought that man could be so absolutely bad."[17]

LINGERING SHADOWS

Over the years since Jung's death, the issue of his alleged anti-Semitism has been left untouched by "first generation" Jungians. Perhaps some distance was needed. However, in August 1989, a conference on the subject was held in New York, as well as workshops at the International Association for Analytical Psychology conference in Paris. The papers were published as *Lingering Shadows: Jungians, Freudians and Anti-Semitism.*

In *Lingering Shadows,* Richard Stein discusses a dream Jung had about Hitler shortly after the Hitler-Stalin nonaggression pact in 1939. He suggests that Jung interpreted the dream archetypally (Jung said Hitler was the "devil's Christ") rather than in terms of his own psychology. The latter might have indicated an explosive inflation—the dream began with Jung in a castle made of dynamite!

Stein goes on to say that Jung's "inner development, his worldly success along with an earlier denial of leadership strivings, and his unresolved transference feelings to Freud synchronistically combined with the drama of European history to thrust him into a dangerous inflation. . . . His intuitive function took off in a dangerous direction, leaving behind his feeling function and social consciousness. . . . Jung seems identified with the *mana* personality resulting from an inflation of the very real shamanic aspect of his own psyche. . . . His wish to heal the father culture of Germany [a residue of his unresolved father transference to Freud] came together with historical events in Europe as he attempted to save and lead the science of psychotherapy in the 1930s; but his failure to save the German psyche forced him to deal with the central religious problem of his life—the light and dark sides of God."[18]

Jung took the term *mana* from the Polynesian word meaning power or authority. "The mana personality is a dominant of the collective unconscious, the well-known archetype of the mighty man in the form of the hero, chief, magician, medicine-man, saint, the ruler of men and spirits, the friend of God."[19]

Stein also raises the question of why Jung did not make a public apology, after the war, in addition to the personal apologies he offered. "Was he too ashamed to express his remorse, or did he fail to understand and feel the import of his actions? Whichever is true, I suspect that the accusation of anti-Semitism had become an ongoing narcissistic wound that made it all the more difficult to apologize publicly."[20]

Philip Zabriskie suggests that Jung's "poor extroverted feeling never grasped the terrible inappropriateness and danger of pressing such discussions [on the differences between racial psychologies] at that time and place."[21] Jung himself said after the war that his "great mistake" was in talking too much, and in a letter of January 22, 1952, wrote: "You know that one of the unfortunate qualities of introverts is they so often cannot help putting the wrong foot forward."[22]

Aryeh Maidenbaum summarizes his extensive research on the allegations of Jung's anti-Semitism and concludes that: Jung was neither a Nazi sympathizer, nor an overt anti-Semite; Jung did help many Jewish people throughout his life, including in the 1930s; Jung was taken, for a time, with the resurgence of German nationalism; and Jung wished to promote the application of analytical psychology to world events.

In Maidenbaum's research, it came to light that, in December 1944, the members of the executive committee of the Analytical Psychology Club of Zurich signed an amendment to the by-laws of the Club, which was not circulated to the general members, limiting Jewish membership to twenty-five percent. The restriction had been unofficial since the 1930s, and Jung was aware of it.[23] The quota was not eliminated until 1950.

Maidenbaum's research took several years to complete before the conference in 1989. Jung's controversial actions, beginning in 1933 to 1934, were on their second Big Chaotic Journey 54 years later, between 1987 and 1988, and in 1989 were entering the place of the Catalyst of Wisdom and Knowledge. Furthermore, Jung's death was on its first Big Chaotic Journey in 1988 and entering the Little Center Moon of the Big West—the Catalyst of Death and Change.

And my take on all this? Was Jung anti-Semitic? No. (But how would one ever decide this?) Was he inflated with his own ideas in the early 1930s? Probably. Was staying President of the International Society a wise move? The intent was good, the look was bad. Or, put another way, from an introvert's point of view he was right, from an extrovert's, he was wrong. But these opinions are just that, opinions. And without dreams, there are only opinions. We know, by the volumes that have been written, what Jung's actions meant to others, but we don't know what they meant to Jung and his soul. For whatever reasons, Jung never made any public statement denouncing the Nazis, neither did he apologize for his actions, decline the Presidency of the International Society when offered, nor resign later. These things influenced how he was seen at the time and, to a great extent, for the rest of his life.[24]

Do the Moon Cycles have an "objective" comment? We find, tragically, that Jung's actions are linked with his death. He died on June 6, 1961, one Big Moon Cycle after the events of 1934. In June 1934, he was in the Northwest of the Little Southeast Moon of the Big North, the place of the Pattern of Self-Images of Wisdom and Knowledge, a resonant point that would ripple outward, 27 years into the future. If we look at Jung's letters during the month of June 1934, we find an ill-starred "coincidence"—a letter dated June 7, 1934, one Big Moon Cycle, almost to the day, before Jung's death, to Dr. Marius Göring, the Nazi President of the German Society.[25] The brief, two paragraph letter informed Göring that if "German psychiatry" (that is, the Nazis) "annexed" psychotherapy Jung would, on principle, resign his position as President of the International Society. Jung remained President until 1939.

Notes

1   C. G. Jung, *Visions: Notes of the Seminar Given in 1930-1934*, Vol. 1, p. 11.

2   For a further discussion of Jung's relationship to the Cabala and to Judaism see Sanford Drob, "Jung and the Kabbalah," in *History of Psychology* 2 (1999): 102–118. See also http://www.newkabbalah.com/index3.html

3   After Elijah's appearance in 1914 Jung's only other mention of him (*Memories*, p. 306) is to say that after a while he and Salome receded back into the unconscious but about two years later they reappeared, unchanged. Jung also says that the Elijah figure evolved into Philemon, a pagan with a Greek and Egyptian atmosphere about him. Philemon was to remain important to Jung for the rest of his life.

4   *MDR*, pp. 139–140.

5   Frances Wickes, *The Inner World of Choice* (Englewood Cliffs, NJ: Prentice-Hall, 1963), p. 176.

6   *Letters* 2, p. 308.

7   *CW* 10, § 1016.

8   *CW* 10, *Wotan*.

9   Aniela Jaffé, *From the Life and Work of C. G. Jung* (London: Hodder & Stoughton, 1975), p. 64.

10   Marie-Louise von Franz, *C. G. Jung: His Myth in Our Time* (London: Hodder & Stoughton, 1975), p. 64.

11   Barbara Hannah, *Jung: His Life and Work* (New York: Putnam, 1976), p. 213.

12   Kirsch, *The Jungians: A Comparative and Historical Perspective* (London: Routledge, 2000), p. 146.

13   Andrew Samuels, *Jung and Antisemitism*, [sic]
     http://www.history.ac.uk/ihr/esh/jung.html

14   James Kirsch, "Jung's Transference on Freud: The Jewish Element," in *American Imago* 41 (1984): 77.

15   James Kirsch, "Carl Gustav Jung and the Jews: The Real Story," in Aryeh Maidenbaum and Stephen Martin, eds., *Lingering Shadows: Jungians, Freudians, and Anti-Semitism* (Boston: Shambhala, 1991), pp. 60, 64, 79–80.

16   Ann Belford Ulanov, "Scapegoating: The Double Cross," in Maidenbaum and Martin, *Lingering Shadows*, pp. 231, 234.

17   *Letters* 1, p. 425.

18   Richard Stein, "Jung's 'Mana Personality' and the Nazi Era," in Maidenbaum and Martin, *Lingering Shadows*, pp. 103, 105, 107, 113.

19   *CW* 7, § 377.

20   Richard Stein, "Jung's 'Mana Personality' and the Nazi Era," in Maidenbaum and Martin, *Lingering Shadows*, p. 112.

21   Philip T. Zabriskie, "Shadows and Light: Closing Reflections on Jung and Jungian Psychology," in Maidenbaum and Martin, *Lingering Shadows*, p. 308. Brackets mine.

22   *Letters* 2, p. 35.

23   Aryeh Maidenbaum, "Lingering Shadows: A Personal Perspective," in Maidenbaum and Martin, *Lingering Shadows*, p. 298.

24   Thomas Kirsch, *The Jungians: A Comparative and Historical Perspective*, pp. 133, 146.

25   The only other published letter that Jung wrote to Göring was a short note in November 1937, dissociating himself from a book review of Göring's.

LITTLE SOUTH MOON
OF THE BIG NORTH —
TRUST AND INNOCENCE OF
WISDOM AND KNOWLEDGE

Our esteem for facts has not neutralized in us all religiousness. It is itself almost religious. Our scientific temper is devout.[1]

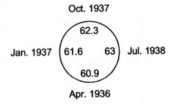

T his Little South Moon is the time of the childhood of Wisdom and Knowledge and for Jung, it was the beginning of his greatest contribution—the study of alchemy. During the summer of 1936, he found a dead snake with a fish in its mouth and was so struck by this synchronistic event that he carved it on the wall of the courtyard at Bollingen. This image, the pagan spirit eating up the Christian spirit, and the reconciling symbol that would be born from these two opposites, was the major theme of *Aion*.[2]

Continuing his Pattern of extroverted traveling in the Little Southeast and Little South Moons, Jung went abroad frequently, although travel—the long trips at least—seemed to take him away from himself. In the autumn of 1935 he traveled to England and lectured at the Tavistock Clinic, and in August 1936, he went to the USA to lecture at Harvard. In 1936 he lectured on children's dreams at ETH, and presented alchemy publicly for the first time at Eranos.[3] However, during the winter of 1936 to 1937 he cut down on his analytical hours, lectures, and seminars, and went deeper into the study of alchemy. He compared this period of intensive study to his confrontation with the unconscious.[4] Here Jung was coming out of the South of the Little South Moon of the Big North—the double childhood of Wisdom and Knowledge. This time sings with the same place in Little South Moon of the Big West when he began his study of mythology in 1909.

THE MYTHOLOGY OF SCIENCE

In October 1937 Jung again traveled to the USA to deliver the Terry Lectures on Psychology and Religion at Yale University. At the beginning of this lecture he stated that he was an empiricist and adhered to the phenomenological point of view.[5] Empiricism was the philosophical view of the 18th-century English philosophers Locke, Hume, and Berkeley that all knowledge was based on sensory experience. (However, in the last 50 years the term has become narrowly identified with the scientific method of testing hypotheses by replicable experiments.) Phenomenology was the view—held by the German and French philosophers Husserl, Heidegger, and Sartre—that consciousness exists without reference to external experiential data and can perceive the essence of things-in-themselves. Knowingly or not, Jung put his ambivalent attitude toward science in a nutshell.

Jung was always concerned with making his investigations stand up to sensation-orientated scientific inquiry—that is, if you can't count it, it doesn't exist. Although Jung took pains to present his work to the professional community as rigorously scientific, he was a pragmatist and unambiguous about the nature of reality when he said that "Reality is simply what works in a human soul."[6]

Jung's empirical method was the accumulation of evidence across times and cultures in order to amplify a symbol or theme. He said it was important for "a disciplined imagination to build up images of intangibles [East, intuition] by logical principles [North, thinking] and on the basis of empirical data [West, sensation]" from the evidence of dreams.[7] This book is an example; the Moon Cycles are a Pattern in the Dream, one of the ways the Great Mystery births itself into All Forms of All Things. Intuition is the function by which we perceive this unseen, nonphysical pattern, and it is only by amplifying it with the events of Jung's life, like morning dew on a spiderweb, that the Pattern then becomes visible to the other functions of feeling, sensing, and thinking. Once it can be apprehended by all the functions, the Pattern then becomes more available to consciousness.

While Jung's method was empirical, it was not that of modern scientific empiricism which, through the experimental method, wishes to eliminate the messy, feminine element of chance, and elevate itself as the gold standard of truth. Science is a magnificent democracy of ideas that arose in response to medieval superstition and religious dogma. Although it has brought us much benefit, modern science is inflated in its self-assessment and is unconscious of its own biases. The scientific net tends to catch the fish but not the water.

One of the collective anodynes in Western culture is that something "has been scientifically proven," and great importance is laid on research and evidence. This often leads to the confused cry from scientists that, for example, the notion of archetypes is not empirically testable. Neither are death, marriage, or taxes. We do not carry out randomized, double-blind, controlled trials to decide who we marry and all important human decisions (love, marriage, or childbearing, for example) are made on the basis of a different evidence and a different rationality than science can entertain.

Science is in the grip of an archetypal enthrallment with matter that has led to a false split between the physical world and the spiritual world. Jung pointed out that the rational strictures of modern science have compelled us to rediscover what has been known to indigenous peoples for millennia. Modern science, over the last 300 years, has taken the spirit out of matter through the privileging of trained objectivity over trained subjectivity (and science may be quite perplexed that the latter exists at all). With this withdrawal of projections from matter and the natural world, humankind's spiritual identity with the physical world has been attenuated as never before. As a result of this retraction into the psyche of psychic energy that formerly had been invested in nature, modern humanity has been forced to rediscover the existence of the unconscious.[8]

INDIA

Not long before his next Chaotic Journey into the Little Southwest Moon beginning in July 1938, Jung left on another major overseas journey, as he had done before, on his Chaotic Journeys in 1920 to Tunis, and in 1925 to New Mexico. Almost immediately after his return from the USA in 1937, he left for India at the invitation of the British government to attend the 25th anniversary celebrations of the University of Calcutta. He landed in Bombay in December 1937 and returned to Kusnacht in February 1938.

While in Calcutta, Jung became ill with dysentery. As with his trip to Africa he said that he found the busy schedule in India, and the impression of India itself, indigestible and that is why he had to get sick. Shortly after his recovery, he dreamed that he was on an unknown island off the coast of southern England. On this island was the castle of the Grail and that evening there would a celebration of the Grail. However, the Grail was not yet at the castle, and the preparations had already started. It was the task of Jung's party of six (recall that there had been half a dozen men in his 1927 flowering tree dream) to bring the Grail to the castle from the north end of the island. As the party traveled north they found that, at its narrowest part, the island was divided in two. One by one, his companions fell asleep[9] (similarly, his companions in the 1927 dream had not been able to see the flowering tree), and Jung had to swim across the channel and fetch the Grail. He took off his clothes and was ready to swim, but then woke up.

Jung said the dream wiped away all the impressions of India and reminded him that India was not his task. It was as though the dream was suggesting that he seek for himself and others the urgently needed healing vessel.[10] Although he returned via Ceylon (Sri Lanka), the journey, internally, was over for him. However, one other event in India is of note. He visited the 13th-century Temple of the Sun at Konarak with its stone carvings from the Kama-Sutra and said he was once again reminded of the numinous aspect of sexuality. In Jung's first encounters with Freud, when he and Freud had differed over this very matter, he was in the Little South Moon of the Big West. He visited Konarak in the Little South Moon of the Big North.

Notes

1   William James, in *Pragmatism: A New Name for Some Old Ways of Thinking*. Lectures delivered at Columbia University, 1907.

2   *CW* 9ii.

3   These papers became Part III of *Psychology and Alchemy*, *CW* 12.

4   Barbara Hannah, *Jung: His Life and Work* (New York: Putnam, 1976), p. 238.

5   *CW* 11.

6   *CW* 6, § 60.

7   *MDR*, p. 310. Brackets mine.

8   *CW* 11, § 375.

9   Laurens van der Post, *Jung and the Story of Our Time* (London: Penguin, 1976), p. 261.

10 *MDR*, p. 282.

LITTLE SOUTHWEST MOON
OF THE BIG NORTH –
WISDOM AND KNOWLEDGE
OF THE SACRED DREAM

How sweet it must be to die.[1]

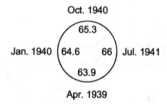

When Jung returned from India in February 1938, he was ordered to convalesce for several weeks. However, it seems he never quite recovered his health, although he resumed a full practice, his lecturing at ETH, and his seminars on *Zarathustra* at the Psychological Club.[2]

On March 12, 1938 the Nazis annexed Austria. Jung and his old colleague Franz Riklin collected together a large sum of money, and dispatched Franz Riklin Jr. to Vienna to speak directly with Freud and persuade him to come to safety via Switzerland. When Riklin knocked at the door of Berggasse 19, Anna, Freud's youngest daughter, answered the door and her father, coming to see what the visitor wanted, frankly refused Riklin's offer of help. On June 6, 1938, Freud arrived safely in London, and ironically, it was a Jungian, Dr. E. A. Bennet, who had organized Freud's safe passage out of Austria.

FREUD'S DEATH AND WORLD WAR II

Since 1923, Freud had suffered from cancer of the jaw. He had undergone an endless series of operations, and was fitted with a prosthetic jaw and palate. A year after his flight from Austria, as he lay dying and in great pain, he said to his doctor, "You remember our 'contract' not to leave me in the lurch when the time had come. Now it is nothing but torture and makes no sense."[3] Over the next day, his doctor administered two doses of morphine. Freud slipped into a coma and died on September 23, 1939, at age 83.[4]

The Pattern we see in their relationship is that Jung, at the time of the death of his relationship with Freud in late 1912, was in the Little Southwest Moon of the Big West, and when Freud died in 1939 Jung was in the Little Southwest Moon of the Big North. Most surprising, however, is that Freud's death was one Big Moon Cycle almost to the month (November 24, 1912 to September 23, 1939) since he fainted in Jung's presence in the Munich hotel room. At that time, Freud's first words on regaining consciousness were "How sweet it must be to die." It seems as if Freud's "death wish," born at that time, had reached adulthood, 27 years later.

In September 1938, Germany annexed the Sudetenland in Czechoslovakia and Neville Chamberlain signed the Munich Pact. Although war was not declared until September 1, 1939, when German troops marched into Poland, WWII had already begun for Germany. And like WWI, it had begun when Jung was on a Chaotic Journey. In March 1939 Hitler annexed the remainder of Czechoslovakia, and on August 23, 1939, the Nazi-Soviet pact was signed. Immediately after receiving the news, Jung dreamed that Hitler was the "devil's Christ."[5]

In his work, Jung was increasingly concerned with alchemy. During 1939 he gave a series of four seminars on the *Exercitia Spiritualia* of St. Ignatius of Loyola (1491–1556, founder of the Order of Jesuits). One of the meditations in the exercises is the "Anima Christi," which Jung spent some time reflecting on. One night during the period of the seminars, he awoke to see the distinct figure of Christ on the cross at the foot of his bed, and that Christ's body was greenish-gold. The image was marvelously beautiful and he was profoundly shaken by the vision. The green gold or *viriditas* of the alchemists was the symbol for the living quality of matter. In his vision Jung had seen the alchemical image of the union of spirit and matter and said, "This spirit has poured himself out into everything, even into organic matter; he is present in metal and stone."[6]

By the late summer of 1940, the threat of the German invasion of Switzerland had passed and Jung settled back into a routine of analysis, lectures, and writing. He had been studying alchemy for ten years now and it was beginning to bear fruit. In August 1940 at Eranos he gave an extemporaneous lecture, *A Psychological Approach to the Dogma of the Trinity*, and in 1941 he wrote *Paracelsus as a Spiritual Phenomenon, Transformation Symbolism in the Mass*, and *The Spirit Mercurius*.

Notes

1   Sigmund Freud, after fainting in Munich, 1912. Quoted in Ernest Jones, *The Life and Work of Sigmund Freud*, vol. 1 (New York: Basic Books, 1953), p. 317.

2   Barbara Hannah, *Jung: His Life and Work* (New York: Putnam, 1976), p. 256.

3   Peter Gay, *Freud: A Life for Our Time* (New York: W. W. Norton, 1988), p. 651.

4   Sigmund Freud was born on May 6, 1856.

5   Hannah, *Jung: His Life and Work*, p. 265.

6   *MDR*, p. 210.

LITTLE WEST MOON
OF THE BIG NORTH —
DEATH AND CHANGE OF
WISDOM AND KNOWLEDGE

*The feeling for the infinite, however, can be attained
only if we are bounded to the utmost.*[1]

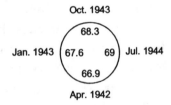

Oct. 1943

Jan. 1943   67.6   68.3   69   Jul. 1944

66.9

Apr. 1942

The major event during this Moon was Jung's near-fatal heart attack in 1944 that was to change him profoundly. It sings with his descent into the unconscious 27 years earlier in the Little West Moon of the Big West. As he did then, prior to his descent, he gave up his outer commitments. In August 1942, he gave up lecturing at ETH after seven years because of his intermittent heart problems. Then, in October 1943, the University of Basel appointed him full Professor of Psychology, but because of his later illness, he never took up the position. This gave Jung the opportunity to delve even deeper into alchemy much in the same way he had descended into himself during the Big West. *Psychology and Alchemy*, which was an expanded version of his lectures at Eranos during 1935 to 1936, with an entirely new introduction, was completed by January 1943. Soon afterward, he started on *Mysterium Coniunctionis*, the first chapters of which were completed before his illness in February 1944, but the entire work was not finished until 1954.

LAMENESS, BLINDNESS, AND THE FIBULA

The figures Jung had encountered in his descent into the unconscious were the lame Philemon and the blind Salome. Blindness—the need for, and resistance to, consciousness—is central to the Oedipus myth, and the relationship between Freud and Jung had been shot through with the oedipal struggle between the father and son.

Jung's fate was to struggle with the tension between his acute consciousness of spirit and its opposite, earth consciousness. We might think of consciousness of spirit as having to do with the polarities of vision and blindness, and earth consciousness as having to do with the polarities of mobility and lameness. Jung's struggle may have been with lameness and blindness of a certain kind. In January 1928 Jung was in the West of the Little East Moon of the Big West, one of the places where there is the most tension between spirit and matter, and on January 2, 1928 he wrote to Count Keyserling, "By temperament I despise the 'personal,' any kind of 'togetherness,' but it is so strong a force, this whole crushing unspiritual weight of the earth, that I fear it. It can rouse my body to revolt against spirit, so that before reaching my zenith I fall lamed to earth."[2]

Jung never wrote about what happened to the blind Salome figure, and we can assume that in his descent into the unconscious during WWI, he claimed the inner spiritual vision that she personified for him. But the lame Philemon continued as a figure in Jung's life in the Red and Black Books and in his carving in later life. Jung struggled with this outer connection to the earth, his earth vision, and when he attempted to apply his introverted, archetypal vision to external events, as he did in the 1930s, he fell lame.

In the Oedipus myth, the oracle at Delphi tells Oedipus' father, King Laius, that he will be murdered by his son who will marry his mother. When Oedipus is born, his father, following the practice of infanticide at the time, drills holes through Oedipus' ankles, binds his feet together, and abandons him on a hillside. There he is found by a shepherd and taken to King Polybus who raises him and he is known as Oedipus (Greek for "swollen foot"). When Oedipus is grown he meets King Laius on the narrow road to Thebes, an argument ensues, and he kills Laius.[3] Unknown to Oedipus the first part of the prophecy has come true.

Oedipus then goes on to solve the riddle of the Sphinx that has terrorized the citizens of Thebes. The riddle is about contact with the earth: "What has four legs in the morning, two at noon, and three in the evening?" Oedipus rightly answers "Man, because he walks on all fours when he is a baby, walks on two when he is an adult, and walks with a stick when he is an old man." As a result the Sphinx throws herself off a cliff and Thebes is free from the monster's tyranny. In gratitude, the Thebans welcome Oedipus and allow him to marry Laius' widow, Jocasta—his mother.

Subsequently, a plague sweeps through Thebes, and Tiresias, the blind seer, is consulted as to the reason for the plague but dares not tell the truth that Oedipus has married his mother and the murder of Laius has not been avenged. Eventually the truth comes out and, in horror, Jocasta kills herself. Oedipus blinds himself with Jocasta's pin (a piece of jewelry like a large safety pin that was used to hold robes). Oedipus wanders in exile, accompanied by his daughter Antigone, until he dies at Colonus.

Hephaestus, the Greek god of fire and metalwork, was lame and worked with matter, fashioning armor, weapons and jewelry. A common piece of jewelry found across ancient Europe as early as 800 B.C.E., was a large brooch, like Jocasta's pin, known by the Romans as a "fibula." The lower leg contains two long bones: the larger tibia or shin bone, and alongside it the thinner fibula, so-called by the Romans because, attached to the tibia, it resembles the pin or clasp of a brooch.

On February 11, 1944, while Jung was out on his daily walk, he slipped in the snow and broke his fibula (as to right or left we do not know) and was hospitalized. Ten days later, he had a near-fatal heart attack that was followed by transformative visions. He was in the

Little West Moon of the Big North (Death and Change of Wisdom and Knowledge) and from these near-death experiences his earth vision was restored and he was led back to his own path.

The Elders say that in our Luminous Cocoon there are ten eyes: our two physical eyes; the Ancestor eye, or third eye between the eyebrows, that sees the spirit world; the fourth eye, or Animal eye, in the middle of the chest sees the truth of what happens; the fifth eye, at the top of the head, sees in the fifth dimension or the Dream; the sixth eye, in the palm of the left hand, sees the spirit of what it touches; the seventh eye, in the palm of the right hand, sees the Sacred Dream of what it touches (this is what happens when people shake hands); the eighth eye, in the sole of the left foot, sees the Laws, Cycles, and Patterns of one's path; the ninth eye, in the sole of the right foot, sees the Design of Energy of one's path; and the tenth eye, at the umbilicus, sees through the eyes of the Great Spirit and sees our interconnectedness with all things.

We might conjecture that from 1929 until 1944 Jung lost his earth vision—his contact with the Design and Pattern of his own path—in the sense that he refused his own fate, the understanding of the Self and the integration of opposites. This fate had left its tracks throughout the 1920s in the Tunis dream, the dreams about being stuck in the 17th century, and the flowering tree dream. Perhaps he was also waylaid by world events that threw him off his stride until, as with Freud in the Little Center, Southeast, and South Moons in the Big South, he could find his own ground.

Although robust and active throughout his life Jung had several bouts with illness. Before we look at his almost fatal illness we should note that of the eight illnesses that he mentions in his writings, three occurred while he was on a Chaotic Journey, and the other five occurred within six months of a Chaotic Journey. It seems that on Chaotic Journeys we are most affected in the area of our inferior function. For Jung, as an intuitive thinking type with inferior sensation or feeling, this was his relational judgment or his physical health.

THE CREATIVE ILLNESS

Ten days after his hospital admission, Jung developed a thrombosis in his heart and lungs and was critically ill for three weeks. During these weeks he had a vision or a dream of being high up in space, looking at part of the earth bathed in a glorious, blue light. Several years after the dream he wrote to Dr. Markus Fierz, inquiring how high he would have to be to see what he saw—the whole of India and Ceylon.[4] The answer he received was one thousand miles high.

This initial scene of India and Ceylon reminds us that two Little Moon Cycles before Jung had visited those two countries, and shortly before leaving India in February 1938, he had a dream of searching for the Grail, the healing vessel that was needed. In his vision high above the earth, Jung turned toward the south and saw a huge block of dark stone about the size of a house. An entrance led into an antechamber where a Hindu man sat. As Jung approached the chamber, he experienced everything he was being painfully stripped away, leaving a feeling of both great poverty and great richness. He existed in objective form; there were no wants or desires, he simply was what he was. He also had a conviction that he was about to enter an illuminated room where he would meet all those people he knew in life and would understand what historical context he fitted into. At that moment an image of his physician, Dr. H., floated up from the earth and Jung knew that the doctor was going to tell him that he must return to earth. Then the vision ceased.[5]

It was three weeks before Jung could make up his mind to live again because life and the whole world struck him as a prison and he had been so glad to be rid of it. During the period he was ill, he was in the Northeast of the Little West Moon of the Big North—Wisdom and Knowledge of Choices and Decisions of Death and Change. On some level Jung made a decision to return to life, and he did bring great Wisdom.

Almost every night for these three weeks, as he floated between life and death, he experienced many visions. During the night his nurse brought him food, and he saw her as an old Jewish woman ritually preparing kosher dishes for him. After falling asleep for an hour, he would wake and the visions would last for about an hour before he fell asleep again. Jung found himself in the *Pardes Rimmonim*, the garden of pomegranates, where the Sacred Marriage of Tifereth and Malchuth was taking place, or he was the Rabbi Simon ben Jochai, whose wedding in the afterlife was being celebrated.[6] Night after night, Jung experienced states of utter bliss and joy, and by morning the visions would fade and he would again face the drab world.[7]

As he drew closer to life, the visions grew fainter and after three weeks they ceased altogether, but afterward he never entirely freed himself of the impression that life is only one aspect of existence contained in a three-dimensional universe specially created for it.[8] During the first month he suffered from deep depression because he felt he was on the road to recovery. Paradoxically, he felt he was dying and did not want to return to the disconnected, narrow world of matter subject to the laws of gravity and time.[9]

Although he did not write of it in *Memories* he told Barbara Hannah and Emma Jung that as he was recovering from his illness, he felt that his body had been dismembered and cut up into small pieces, and then, over a long period, he collected it together with the greatest care.[10] This is a widely documented shamanic ceremony in indigenous cultures.[11]

The Elders say that the phenomenal, physical world makes up the first three of the seven dimensions of the Great Spirit. The fourth dimension is time and the fifth dimension is the Dream. When the Assemblage Point[12] on the Luminous Cocoon is located at the usual position, we maintain a temporally and physically consistent view of the three-dimensional world, and are "within" time. When we dream at night our Assemblage Point moves and we assemble another reality but we do not usually retain our waking consciousness. Then we are in the fifth dimension or the Dream. We are "outside" time and everything happens in the Now, where subjectivity and objectivity are woven together.[13] However under certain conditions, like a life-or-death situation, we move back and forth between the third and the fifth dimensions and may carry some degree of waking consciousness with us (as did Jung when he was ill). Here we are in the fourth dimension, the place of the "crack between the worlds" (equivalent to the bardos of the Tibetan Buddhist tradition), where time is greatly expanded or contracted, and we are "across" time.

Jung was concerned that his doctor's (Dr. H.) life was in danger, for the doctor had called him back to earth. If the law against resurrecting the dead was broken, then the doctor must pay for it with his own life, just as Zeus had killed Aesculapius with a thunderbolt because he had brought back patients from the dead. On April 4, 1944 Jung had sufficiently recovered to sit up in bed, and on that same day Dr. H. became ill, and within a short time died from septicemia. Jung was concerned that the death of his physician may have been connected with his miraculous recovery. However, he was somewhat consoled when he heard that another Zurich specialist had been concerned about Dr. H.'s health for some months before Jung's illness.[14]

The illness wrought deep changes in Jung. On February 1, 1945 Jung wrote to Kristine Mann, a terminally ill American colleague, "When you can give up the crazy will to live and when you seemingly fall into a bottomless mist, then the truly *real* life begins with everything which you were meant to be and never reached. . . . Death is the hardest thing from the outside and as long as we are outside of it. But once inside you taste of such completeness and peace and fulfillment that you don't want to return."[15]

He found in himself a "strange cessation of human warmth" after the illness, and that the visions and the objectivity he had experienced had led to a detachment from emotional ties. Jung said that though these ties were part of the fabric of human relationship, they still contained projections and emotional coercion. Something was expected of the other person, and it was essential to withdraw these projections in order to arrive at oneself. Without this objectivity, the subjectivity of the greater *coniunctio* is not possible.[16]

In *Memories*, Jung writes that he felt there was something wrong with his attitude before his illness, and as a result he was in some way responsible for breaking his fibula. He then goes on to say that an authentic life, one's own life, would be incomplete without mistakes and it was only after the illness that he appreciated the importance of living one's own destiny. In living our own lives, for ourselves and not for others, we learn to carry our own errors and triumphs as well as the full weight of the doings and desires of the Self. "In this way we forge an ego that does not break down when incomprehensible things happen; an ego that endures, that endures the truth, and that is capable of coping with the world and fate."[17] This is the Northwest-Southeast axis. The Image of Self in the Southeast (the ego) allows the Pattern of the Self in the Northwest to manifest in the world and in life.

After his illness, Jung said that all the early chapters he had written on *Mysterium Coniunctionis* were correct, and he did not need to change a word but only now did he realize its full reality. It was after the illness that most of his principal works were written and his visions gave him the courage to follow new paths. So Jung had been restored to his rightful course. He no longer attempted to put across his opinion, as might have been the case in the 1930s, but surrendered himself to himself.

REDEMPTION

We have seen that there were strong links between Jung and Judaism, and David Rosen connects Jung's illness with losing himself in, as he terms it, the "Jewish question" during the 1930s. "My conjecture is that Jung's 'heart attack' in 1944, which occurred after a fall, was also a 'soul/spirit attack' based on the realization that he'd been wrong about the German psyche (and his own)."[18] Richard Stein also comments that "Perhaps his illness and depression in the 1940's were an inevitable part of the ensuing deflation."[19] Jung's possible guilt was two-edged: toward his misreading of outer events in the 1930s and, perhaps more importantly, toward his betrayal of his own Dream and his own fate during his Big Chaotic Journey and Center Moon from 1929 to 1932. It took a severe illness to bring him back on course.

Jung's heart attack in 1944, and a later one in 1946, happened around significant dates in the history of the Holocaust. His heart attack was in late February 1944 and Jung was poised between life and death during the month of March. Since 1942 Jews from all over Europe had been deported to the concentration camps of Eastern Europe, and following the German occupation of Hungary on March 19, 1944 the Nazi's "final solution" approached its climax. During the summer of 1944, the concentration camps of Auschwitz-Birkenau reached their highest-ever total of persons gassed per day (9,000). The first Nuremburg trial, where the full horrors of Nazi atrocities became public, began in November 1945. Those who were sentenced to death were executed on October 16, 1946. Hermann Göring committed suicide in his cell a few hours before he was to be executed. On November 4, 1946 Jung had a second heart attack. In the collective unconscious time obeys different rules, and as the heart of the world suffered, so did Jung's.

One final observation of Pattern around these issues is that the years from 1905 to 1911, in the Little Southeast and Little South Moons of the Big West, were the years of Jung's collaboration and then increasing disagreement with Freud, who was Jewish. This was followed by Jung's descent into the unconscious in the Little West Moon of the Big West. A similar sequence occurred in the Big North. The Little Southeast and Little South Moons, from 1932 to 1938, were times of controversy when he was seen by some as being sympathetic to Nazi Germany, and it was followed by his near-death experience in 1944 when he was in the Little West Moon of the Big North. Each sequence was the mirror of the other: in the Big West, the struggle with Freud was fought on an outer battlefield, and the resolution came internally through his descent into the unconscious. In the Big North, the struggle was partially an inner one, much deeper and perhaps partly unconscious, and the resolution came externally through public criticism and illness. Given his relationship with Freud, and the Nazi controversy, there was an ironic *lysis* to his psychological death during WWI, and his brush with physical death in WWII. His redemption and creative rebirth, on both occasions, came through Judaic images—first Elijah and later through the Cabalistic marriage of the Sephiroth Tifereth and Malchuth.[20]

Notes

1 *MDR*, p. 325.

2 *Letters* 1, p. 49.

3 My thanks to Dr. Dale Dodd for humorously pointing out that this was the first known incident of "road rage." Dale Dodd, "Reflections on the Analytic Mirror." *Forum: Journal of New Zealand Association of Psychotherapists* 6 (2000): 78–91.

4 *Letters* 1, p. 518.

5 *MDR*, pp. 290–292.

6 The *Zohar* speaks of the Wedding Song of Solomon as celebrating the death of the legendary Rabbi Simon ben Jochai in the form of his marriage to the other world.

7 *MDR*, pp. 294–295.

8 *MDR*, p. 295.

9 *Letters* 1, p. 358.

10 Barbara Hannah, *Jung: His Life and Work* (New York: Putnam, 1976), p. 283.

11 Mircea Eliade, *Shamanism: Archaic Techniques of Ecstasy* (Princeton: Princeton University Press, 1972).

12 A point on the Luminous Cocoon, on the upper right chest area, that assembles our perception of reality. When the Assemblage Point moves, the reality that we assemble changes.

13 *MDR*, p. 296.

14 Hannah, *Jung: His Life and Work*, p. 279.

15 *Letters* 1, p. 358.

16 *MDR*, pp. 296–297.

17 *MDR*, p. 297. The *coniunctio* was a term used in alchemy to refer to the union, marriage, or conjunction of dissimilar substances, or opposites.

18 David Rosen, *The Tao of Jung: The Way of Integrity* (London: Penguin Arkana, 1997), p. 118.

19 Richard Stein, "Jung's 'Mana Personality' and the Nazi Era," in Aryeh Maidenbaum and Stephen Martin, eds., *Lingering Shadows: Jungians, Freudians, and Anti-Semitism* (Boston: Shambhala, 1997), p. 107.

20 In the Cabala (the ten-branched image of the Tree of Life that is a pictorial representation of Creation), the masculine and feminine are represented by the Sefira Tifereth (Beauty) and Malchuth (Kingdom).

LITTLE NORTHWEST MOON
OF THE BIG NORTH —
LAWS AND PATTERNS OF
WISDOM AND KNOWLEDGE

There are two kinds of people in the end: those who say to God,
"Thy will be done," and those to whom God says,
in the end, "Thy will be done."[1]

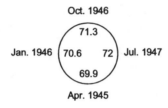

A lthough Jung described himself as an introvert, in the unconscious he was extrovertedly connected to the Patterns of his time and able to see the collective Dreaming of the People. He was an intuitive, sensitive to what was "in the air" in the collective unconscious.

DRESDEN DREAMING

In 1913, Jung had dreamed of WWI. Soon after WWI ended in 1918 he had a "visionary dream" of the coming of WWII. In a letter to Peter Baynes in August 1940, he said that in the dream he was returning from a trip to Germany and his clothes and skin were burnt. He had seen "fire falling like rain from heaven and consuming the cities of Germany. I had an intimation that the crucial year would be 1940." Jung went on to add something important about where the fire would come from. "Since 1918 I knew that a terrible fire would spread over Europe beginning in the North East."[2]

Indeed, 1940 was the crucial year of WWII. By the summer of 1940, Hitler dominated Europe from Norway to the Pyrenees, and the Nazi tide was turned back only by the Battle of Britain in September 1940. The decision that led to the consumption of Germany by fire was made in January 1943, when Jung was in the West of the Little West Moon of the Big North—the double Death and Change of Wisdom and Knowledge. In that month, at the Casablanca Conference, Churchill and Roosevelt decided to launch an around-the-clock strategic bombing offensive against Germany that resulted in the firebombing of Hamburg in July 1943 and July 1944, and more controversially, Dresden in February 1945. Both cities were destroyed by firestorms. In Dresden, 135,000 people were killed—compare that to the 50,000 British civilians killed by the Luftwaffe during WWII, and the 70,000 killed by the atomic bomb dropped on Hiroshima. Jung dreamed that the fire would come from the Northeast— Hamburg is in the north of Germany and Dresden is in the east. The Dresden bombing occurred 27 years after Jung's dream.

The Pattern of Jung's Moon Cycles sings with the great events of modern times. His first Big Chaotic Journey (1902) was at the beginning of the last century of the millennium; his second Big Chaotic Journey was at the time of the Great Depression in 1929; and his third was in 1956 at the height of the Cold War.

Both of Jung's Death and Change Little West Moons occurred at the mid-point of two World Wars. During WWI, Jung stood in the place of triple Death and Change (the West of Little West Moon of the Big West), at the age of 40.6 in January 1916. The major battles of WWI were fought that year, with the Battle of Verdun beginning in February 1916. The Battle of the Somme on July 1, 1916 had the highest ever one-day casualty rate in military history. During WWII, we have seen that the decision to firebomb Dresden was taken in January 1943 when Jung was in the West of the Little West Moon of the Big North.

Jung had encounters with death in both wars—psychological death in WWI and physical death in WWII. His emergence from both of those ordeals occurred in the same place, the South of the Little Northwest Moons—the Trust and Innocence of Laws and Patterns— and both of these redemptions coincided with the end of both wars.

RECOVERY

The world's recovery from the near-fatal illness that was WWII began on June 6, 1944, when the Allies landed on the beaches of Normandy. At the same time, Jung was beginning his own recovery in hospital, and his convalescence took a year afterward ending almost at the same time as the war.[3] Jung convalesced in Kusnacht from July 1944 until the spring of 1945. In April 1945 his doctor allowed him to return to Bollingen, and from that time on, for the first time in his life, he gave his writing precedence over his other work. His orientation to therapy had also changed. "The main interest of my work is not concerned with the treatment of neuroses but rather with the approach to the numinous. But the fact is that the approach to the numinous is the real therapy inasmuch as you attain to the numinous experiences you are released from the curse of pathology."[4]

Over the years, Jung had been pressed to say something about the transference, so in 1945 he took a part of the *Mysterium Coniunctionis* that he had written before his illness and submitted it for publication as *The Psychology of the Transference*, which was published in 1946. These two works, together with *Aion* and *Answer to Job,* form a coherent quaternary of work that came out of his illness.

In *Memories*, after the chapter on his illness, a long chapter titled "On Life after Death" relates a number of Jung's precognitive dreams and synchronistic experiences. Included in this chapter is the dream of the "assemblage of distinguished spirits" he had in 1911. He writes that it was not until many years later that he understood that by working on *Symbols of Transformation*, he would be answering the question that the spirits had asked in the dream—an answer that they had not been able to learn while alive. It was Jung's question to answer: if the solution had been eternally present, it could have been discovered by anyone else at any other time in history.[5]

In the language of dreams, when events and images occur together in the dream, it often indicates a relationship between them. In the sequence of the dream that is *Memories,* the 1911 dream is mentioned shortly after his illness, so we might assume that his life's work, beginning with his first book *Symbols of Transformation,* was the question and the larger task that he lost sight of in the 1930s, which the illness had now set him to answering.

As if Jung had not had enough reminders of his task, he got another one from his body. On November 4, 1946 he had another heart attack, and remained ill for about three months but recovered by early summer 1947. He was doubtful if he had really had a heart attack and thought that the tachycardia he had experienced was due to his being faced with the mysterious problem of the *hieros gamos.*[6] In the beginning of November, Jung had just entered the North of the Little Northwest Moon of the Big North (double Wisdom and Knowledge of Laws and Pattern).

A month later, on December 18, 1946, he wrote to Father Victor White, describing a poetic dream image of the Northwest-Southeast axis, the Self and the Image of Self. "Yesterday I had a marvelous dream: One bluish diamond like a star high in heaven, reflected in a round quiet pool—heaven above heaven below. The *imago Dei* in the darkness of the earth, this is myself. The dream meant a great consolation. I am no more a black and endless sea of misery and suffering but a certain amount thereof contained in a divine vessel."[7]

Notes

1   C. S. Lewis, *The Great Divorce* (New York: Simon and Schuster, 1996), p. 72.

2   *Letters* 1, p. 285

3   Hannah, *Jung: His Life and Work* (New York: Putnam, 1976), p. 288.

4   Aniela Jaffé, ed., *C. G. Jung: Word and Image* (Princeton: Princeton University Press, 1979), p. 123.

5   *MDR,* p. 307.

6   Hannah, *Jung: His Life and Work,* p. 294. The term *hieros gamos* (Greek, meaning "sacred wedding") refers to the union between two divinities, or between a human being and a god or goddess.

7   *Letters* 1, p. 450.

LITTLE NORTH MOON
OF THE BIG NORTH —
WISDOM AND KNOWLEDGE OF
WISDOM AND KNOWLEDGE

Individuation does not shut one out from the world,
but gathers the world to oneself.[1]

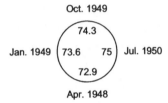

W ith more English and Americans coming to Zurich to study, the Psychological Club felt that it was necessary to offer them something more than had been available. For several years, there had been discussion about establishing an institute but Jung, with his antipathy toward groups, had resisted it. Unexpectedly, in the summer of 1947, he proposed the foundation of an Institute even though two years before he had been adamantly opposed to the idea. He said it was impossible to prevent it from happening, so he may as well have some say in it, and that, "They would start one between my death and my funeral in any case."[2] As an introvert, he preferred to leave the process of individuation to those whose fate obliged them to seek it, but he also recognized the validity of the extroverted viewpoint that wishes to make the process available to the collective. In 1948, the C. G. Jung Institute was established with the inaugural meeting on April 24, 1948—the day before Jung entered the South of the Little North Moon of the Big North, the childhood of double Wisdom and Knowledge.

During 1947 and 1948, Jung revised many of his previous works, and continued to retire into himself. On January 2, 1949 in the West of the Little North Moon of the Big North—the double Wisdom and Knowledge of Introspection—he wrote in a letter, "I too am in a retrospective phase and am occupying myself, for the first time in 25 years, thoroughly with myself, collecting my old dreams and putting them together."[3]

AION

Jung probably began writing *Aion* in late 1947 and this continued into 1950.[4] It is subtitled *Researches into the Phenomenology of the Self* and was the eventual outcome of the Pattern that began with the dream encounter with the Self, 27 years before, in Tunis. Jung had used the term Self in varying ways and contexts, and it changed over the years in his writing, but he first used the term in its later meaning in 1921.[5] His Tunis dream was in March 1920, just as he was ending a Chaotic Journey into the Little North Moon of the Big West. *Aion*, the child of that dream, was born one Big Moon Cycle later, on Jung's 's Chaotic Journey into, and during, the Little North Moon of the Big North.

We see a similar gestation of 27 years in his earlier work, *Psychology and Alchemy*. Parts I and II are extensive revisions of Eranos papers from 1935 and 1936, and he began the book in 1941 after he gave up his lecturing at ETH.[6] Jung always wrote the foreword to a book after he had completed his writing and from this we know that *Psychology and Alchemy* was completed in January 1943. We see Pattern in that when he completed the book in January 1943, Jung was in the West of the Little West Moon of the Big North. In January 1916, at the nadir of his descent into the unconscious when he laid the foundations for his life's work, he was in the West of the Little West Moon of the Big West. In writing *Psychology*

Fig 5. Aion. Roman, 2nd – 3rd century C.E., Vatican Museum.

and Alchemy he at last reached the floor that lay beneath his experiences from 1913 to 1917.[7]

Jung wrote *Aion* during this Little North Moon; it is very much a book about the North, written in the style of the North. He elaborates at some length on the symbolism of the North, and said that his model of the Self in *Aion* was based on the biblical prophet Ezekiel's vision, blown on the North wind, of the Wheels of God.[8] Jung's themes are the idea of the Aeon (Greek: *Aion*) and the changes in psyche over the Christian aeon. His vast sweep, from all points around the Wheel, of the two-thousand-year period of the Piscean age ranges from succinct summaries of ego, shadow, anima and animus, through Christ as a symbol of the Self, the symbol of the fish, Gnosticism and alchemy, to a model of the structure and dynamics of the Self.

Aion is about the archetypal significance of the Age of Pisces and coming of the Age of Aquarius, and how the workings of archetypal processes during the Christian era resulted in the Christ image becoming one-sidedly spiritual and lacking in substance and instinct. The transition from one astrological Age to another comes about as the spring equinox moves, or precesses, out of the constellation of Pisces and enters Aquarius.[9] The lion-headed Aion was a Mithraic god and Jung was intensely involved in the study of Mithraism. Since Jung's death, it has come to light that the mystery of the precession of the equinoxes was at the center of Mithraic initiatory ceremonies.[10]

ALL OUR RELATIONS

The North is the place on the Medicine Wheel of the numbers 4 and 14. The number 4 represents the Animals, those who live closest to Grandmother Earth in Harmony and Balance; they are our instincts, our animal nature. Jung wrote just prior to this Moon, "The only true servants of God are the animals."[11]

The number 14 (All Measures of Intellect, 10 + 4, Harmony and Balance) represents Sweet Medicine, Earth Father, or the Spirit of the

Animals. In the Celtic tradition he is Cernunnos, the Horned God and Lord of the Animals. It is cognate with the early Christian *logos spermatikos*, the creative word that is brought by the whirlwind, or the dove, as symbols of the Holy Ghost. The 19th century Pawnee Chief Letakots-Lesa taught that in the beginning of all things, the animals held all the wisdom and knowledge; for Tirawa—the One Above—did not speak directly to people. He sent certain animals to tell the people that he showed himself through the animals. In the Western tarot, the fourteenth card is Temperance, and depicts a divine figure who pours water from a higher container to a lower container, and in the Mayan tarot, it is a Twisted Hair, with a rainbow at his back, who pours water on the ground.[12] In the Catholic Church, the Pope fulfills the role of the *pontifex* or bridge-builder between God and the Church. All these symbolize the differentiated feeling connection between earth and spirit. In other words, 14 is spiritualized instinct, or instinctualized spirit.

The North is also the place where we see things with the mind from all places around the Wheel, and our Inter-relatedness with All Things. In *Aion* Jung discusses at great length the myths and images of Adam or the Anthropos. In many creation myths there emerges the figure of a cosmic man (the Anthropos, Adam, or original man) who represents the *prima materia* of the world and the basic substance of all later human generations, and symbolizes all human souls in a transpersonal unity. In Jewish legend, God created Adam from red, black, white, and yellow dust that he gathered from all corners of the world—Adam is the Rainbow Human. The Anthropos is another aspect of the 14 and symbolizes the resolution of conflict (4 – Walking in Harmony and Balance) from a widening of consciousness (10 – All Measures of Intellect) around the Wheel, because the paradoxes of the Self at the center have been made conscious.

Thus 14 is also the archetypal source of the feeling of being connected with all humankind, compassion, and the social aspect of the Self. The human psyche is naturally dissociative and tends to split up into different archetypal contents and personal complexes. However, this is countered in the collective unconscious by an opposite tendency that is revealed by the image of the Anthropos. The Anthropos is humankind's "group-soul," the basis of all compassion and community, as well as being the psychic counterweight to the one-sided drive to live out a single instinct.[13]

Aion is about the split that developed in the Christian era between instinct and spirit and the loss of feeling relationship between the two. The Animals and Earth Father, the 4 and the 14, instinct and spirit, balance each other in the North. "Too much of the animal distorts the civilized man, too much civilization makes sick animals."[14] This *coniunctio* in the North between these opposites can manifest in positive or negative form. Their light *coniunctio* births Wisdom and Knowledge, the word as *logos*, and the mental aspect of love, which is compassion. Their shadow *coniunctio* births Philosophies and Beliefs as prejudice and intolerance and "-isms," the word as dogma, and group possession that results in unadapted, animal-like, instinctual behavior.

As we shall see, this polarity of earth and spirit was reflected in an image of a wolverine and Bollingen in one of Jung's last dreams before he died. Jung used a picture of Aion, the highest Mithraic god, the god of "Infinite Time," as the frontispiece to *Aion* (see figure 5, p. 193). With a lion's head, large wings, and a human body encoiled by a serpent, it is a fitting image of the marriage of the spirit and instinct.

FAUST AND ALL OUR RELATIONS

We shall digress here to consider Goethe's *Faust* as symbolic of Jung's life and work and its connection with All Our Relations. Jung was deeply moved by *Faust*, and he said it was his "heritage." At Bollingen he carved the Latin words "Philemon Sacrum, Fausti Poenitentia" (Shrine of Philemon, Repentance of Faust) over the entrance to the original Tower. This was covered over when the annex was built in 1927, but Jung carved it again in 1934, above the inner door to the retiring room.

The central themes of *Faust* are searching, longing, desire, power, and love. The story opens with God and Mephistopheles bargaining for the soul of Faust, an academic who has long searched for enlightenment through scholarly knowledge.[15] Mephistopheles tricks Faust into leaving his academic pursuits. He plunges into life, and in his adventures he encounters Gretchen, the young virgin, and goes on to magically conjure up Helen of Troy. Eventually, Faust is granted rights to the coastline of the Emperor's domain and his great plan is to extend the land by draining the marshes and pushing back the sea. There he plans to establish a paradise on earth, won from the ocean bed, where he believes humankind, winning the struggle over the forces of nature, will become free.

However, Faust's plans are frustrated because an old couple, Philemon and Baucis, live on the land. Goethe took these figures from the Greek myth in which Zeus and Hermes, in human form, wandered through Phrygia seeking food and lodging. All except Philemon and Baucis, an aged couple renowned for their mutual love, turned them away. So Zeus sent a flood to destroy the people of Phrygia and made Philemon and Baucis' cottage into a temple. On their death, he changed them into an oak and a linden tree that grew from the same root.

In Celtic mythology the oak tree is connected with strength, courage, and the underworld. The linden (basswood or lime tree) and the oak are two of the few trees that form perfect circles, or rings of trees, in mature forests by putting up new shoots from suckers. Thus Philemon and Baucis represent the greater *coniunctio*—the circles of the masculine and feminine in good relation—that honors the gods. Faust, in his desire to develop the land, had Philemon and Baucis murdered.

In the last act of *Faust*, four "gray women"—Lack, Guilt, Need, and Care—knock at Faust's door. Only Care is able to get in through the keyhole, but Faust refuses to acknowledge her and, cursing him, she breathes on him, making him blind. At the end of the play, the blind Faust hears digging and thinks that his life's work of overcoming nature is being completed but in fact the workmen are digging his grave. Faust dies believing his plans are nearing fruition. It's easy to see the story as an allegory of Western culture.

The story was unsatisfactory to Jung in many ways. He thought Faust one-sided and he could not forgive Goethe for having dismissed Mephistopheles by trickery and portraying evil as innocuous.[16] Perhaps Jung saw himself as someone who could carry on from where Goethe had lost his nerve. Life had set Jung a question, or he himself was a question posed to life. He felt he must give his own answer or else be reliant on the collective answer.[17]

Jung saw individuation as an *opus contra naturam* as symbolized in the Bible by the expulsion from the Garden of Eden. Individuation is always accompanied by guilt, or original sin. "Life itself is guilt,"[18] he said, and, "We know of course that without sin there is no repentance and without repentance no redeeming grace, also that without original sin the redemption of the world could never have come about."[19]

The process of individuation demands choice, which is a theft, an act of disobedience in stealing some of God's omnipotence. Prometheus stole the divine fire, the creative flame, from the Gods and was chained to a rock as punishment. Eve ate of the Tree of Knowledge and was expelled from the Garden of Eden. This theft brings on it the burden of consciousness—responsibility, awareness, and judgment—all qualities of the North.[20]

This individualistic guilt we can take to be true in Western culture but not necessarily in indigenous cultures. The introverted, personal guilt that Jung refers to results from escaping the gravitational pull of the unconscious. It is the compensatory opposite of the extroverted social guilt, in indigenous cultures, which results from disloyalty to the group. In Maoridom in Aotearoa/New Zealand, the responsibility of the individual is towards his or her *whanau* (extended family), *hapu* (the group of extended families, or sub-tribe), and *iwi* (the tribe). It would be no exaggeration to say that, in Maori culture, there is no such thing as an individual.

Western culture has despiritualized matter and as a result has been forced to discover the obvious—that the unseen (the unconscious) exists. Because the unseen is denied and is farther from consciousness, it exerts a greater psychic influence in the process of individuation. Indigenous cultures live closer to the unconscious through a world of matter in which spirit is alive, and so Western, introverted guilt does not loom as large in the indigenous psyche.

Most importantly, indigenous cultures have not murdered Philemon and Baucis, those who offered a home to the gods. So the expulsion from the Garden of Eden is a quite literal story of the severance of Western culture from the land that supports it. That Western culture has taken this story either as theological dogma or as psychological symbolism is an indication of a blind spot, an area of unconsciousness.

In his carving "Repentance of Faust" Jung acknowledged the question that he was an answer to. This had to do with the rewriting and reparation, so to speak, of the cheap ending of *Faust*. He did this in *Answer to Job*, seeing the creator in its wholeness, both light and dark. In a letter of January 5, 1942, when he was leaving the East of the Little Southwest Moon of the Big North, the Illumination of Wisdom and Knowledge of the Sacred Dream, he wrote, "All of a sudden and with terror it became clear to me that I have taken over *Faust* as my heritage, and moreover as the advocate and avenger of Philemon and Baucis."[21]

In *Mysterium Coniunctionis* and at the end of *Answer to Job* Jung deals with the Assumption of the Virgin Mary. On November 1, 1950, Pius XII, in his papal bull *Assumptio Mariae*, proclaimed the dogma of the bodily assumption of the Virgin Mary into heaven. In *Mysterium Coniunctionis* Jung refers to an alchemical drawing (see figure 6, p. 200) in which—below the upper spiritual quaternary of Mary, God, Christ, and the Holy Ghost—a haloed man with wings, the body of a fish, and snakes for arms is being pulled out of a lump of matter.[22] "This is without doubt the *anima mundi* who has been freed from the shackles of matter, the *filius macrocosmi* of Mercurius-Anthropos, who, because of his double nature, is not only spiritual and physical but unites in himself the morally highest and lowest."[23]

This is the alchemical image of Earth Father, the Feathered Winged Serpent, the marriage of spirit and instinct. Jung assumes that the form is monstrous, and to the alchemists it likely was.

Fig 6. Speculum Trinitatis. One of a series of 18 woodcuts in the alchemical text by Hieronymus Reusner, Pandora, Basel, 1582.

However, it represents the inner 14, the internal relationship to Sweet Medicine, the Spirit of the Animals—in popular descriptions these are the "totem animals." So it is the Swimmers, the Crawlers, the Four-Leggeds, and the Winged Ones—all who live close to the body of Grandmother Earth—who are the teachers of the consciousness (10) of how to walk in Harmony and Balance (4).

Jung goes on to say "The dogmatisation of the *Assumptio Mariae* points to the *hieros gamos* in the pleroma, and this in turn implies . . . the future birth of the divine child, who, in accordance with the divine trend towards incarnation, will choose as his birthplace the empirical man. This metaphysical process is known to the psychology of the unconscious as the individuation process."[24]

Here Jung perhaps has only half the story. He was heir to the Faustian legacy both as a man of his historical time, and as an introvert who was more identified with the spiritual end of the instinct/spirit polarity. In the figure of the extracted spirit, Jung sees only the introverted aspect of the coming archetypal changes (or how the Dream of the People will come Awake in the third dimension); that is, how the God-image will incarnate, not through a collective savior, but within each individual.

Fig 7. The Rebis

However, Jung leaves out the extroverted aspect. A similar but more differentiated—and significantly twin-headed—image is seen in other alchemical pictures. For example, "The Rebis" (figure 7, p. 201) appears as the tenth picture in the *Rosarium Philosophorum* on which Jung based *The Psychology of the Transference*.[25] As the feminine is restored to its rightful place, it will conceive a divine birth in matter, but this birth will be of twins, as in the twin-headed Rebis. One twin will be the inner relationship to spirit, the other twin will be the outer relationship to matter, the renewed and reclaimed relationship with the outer ecology—the honoring of All Our Relations.

PARTICIPATION MYSTIQUE

Jung's experience of indigenous cultures was sparse, with personal contact limited to a few days in New Mexico and three weeks at Mount Elgon in Kenya. The rest of his information was derived from European anthropological texts. Some of his writings on indigenous peoples do show a "primitive" view of the "primitive mentality." From an ethnocentric viewpoint he suggests that "primitive" cultures were less differentiated, less conscious, and more subject to a participation mystique with the surrounding world, than "civilized" cultures.[26] However in reading Jung's writings on indigenous consciousness we should keep in mind that what he wrote is not necessarily what he thought, and indeed others have often described him as a "pagan."[27] Perhaps Jung did not want to commit himself publicly to a view that would have been at odds with the prevailing colonial and Eurocentric sentiment with regard to "primitive" peoples.

"Participation mystique" is a phrase that was coined by the anthropologist Lévy-Bruhl in his book *How Natives Think*, to denote a particular kind of psychological connection with objects, where the subject cannot clearly distinguish him- or herself from the object. Jung said, "It is a phenomenon that is best observed in primitives.... Among civilized peoples it usually occurs between persons, seldom between a person and a thing."[28] "The primitive cannot assert that he thinks; it is rather 'something that thinks in him'. . . . His consciousness is menaced by an almighty unconscious: hence his fear of magical influences which may cross his path at any moment. . . . Owing to the chronic twilight state of his consciousness, it is often impossible to find out whether he merely dreamed something or whether he really experienced it."[29] "I use the term identity to denote a psychological conformity. It is always an unconscious phenomenon. . . . It is a characteristic of the primitive mentality and the real foundation of *participation mystique*, which is nothing but a relic of the original non-differentiation of subject and object, and hence of the primordial unconscious state. It is also a characteristic of the mental state of early infancy, and, finally of the unconscious of the civilized adult."[30] We might liken these generalizations, based on brief contacts with a few indigenous people, to Ochwiay Biano (the Taos Pueblo Jung met in 1925) thinking that all Europeans were like Jung.

Jung posits a hierarchy: discrimination between subject and object is more "civilized," and identity between subject and object is less "civilized." Differentiation is the more conscious, and identity the less conscious, mode of being. Many individuals in indigenous cultures are differentiated and conscious, but in ways contrary to how differentiation is understood—psychologically, anyway—in Western culture. A state of identity is not always unconscious, and we need look no further than Jung to find examples. It was he who said that the meeting of two personalities is like a chemical reaction; if anything happens, both are changed. Conscious identity allows psychotherapy to take place, and it is the consciousness with which this meeting happens that differentiates therapy from most other human encounters. It is conscious identity, a conscious participation mystique, that is the basis for the Eros that the People have for the land.

However, in other writings Jung clearly understands the indigenous consciousness. In *The Spirit Mercurius*, written in 1942, he relates a story of a soldier in Nigeria who, when he heard his tree spirit calling him, desperately tried to break out of his barracks and go to the tree. When the soldier was questioned about it, he said that all those who bore the name of the tree would occasionally hear its voice and be obliged to respond. Jung elaborates:

> These psychic phenomena suggest that originally the tree and the daemon were one and the same, and that their separation is a secondary phenomenon corresponding to a higher level of culture and consciousness. . . . Since at the present level of consciousness we cannot suppose that tree daemons exist, we are forced to assert that the primitive suffers from hallucinations, that he hears his own unconscious which he had projected into the tree. If this theory is correct—and I do not know how we could formulate it otherwise today—then the second level of consciousness has effected a differentiation between the object "tree" and the unconscious content projected into it, thereby achieving an act of enlightenment. The third level rises higher still and attributes "evil" to the psychic content which has been separated from the object. Finally a fourth level, the level reached by our consciousness today, carries the enlightenment a stage further by denying the objective existence of the "spirit" and declaring that the primitive has heard nothing at all, but merely had an auditory hallucination. Consequently the whole phenomenon vanishes into thin air—with the great advantage that the evil spirit becomes obviously non-existent and sinks into ridiculous significance. The fifth level is of the opinion that something did happen after all . . . [it] assumes that the unconscious exists and has a reality just like any other existent. However odious it may be, this means that the "spirit" is also a reality . . .[31]

Shortly before he died, he said,

> As scientific understanding has grown, so our world has become dehumanized. Man feels himself isolated in the cosmos, because he is no longer involved in nature and has lost his emotional "unconscious identity" with natural

phenomena. These have slowly lost their symbolic implications. Thunder is no longer the voice of an angry god, nor is lightning his avenging missile. No river contains a spirit, no tree is the life principle of man, no snake is the embodiment of wisdom, no mountain cave the home of a great demon. No voices speak to man from stones, plants and animals, nor does he speak to them believing they can hear. His contact with nature has gone, and with it has gone the profound emotional energy that this symbolic connection supplied. This enormous loss is compensated for by the symbols of dreams.[32]

"DISSOCIATION MYSTIQUE"

Western culture has had two thousand years to negotiate the process, which Jung outlines in *Aion*, of being severed from the land, whereas indigenous cultures that have been dispossessed withstand it over the course of a few centuries. Similar to their vulnerability to alien physical diseases—like smallpox during the colonization in the Americas—indigenous cultures have little immunity against the psychic infections of Western culture, the worst of which (alcoholism, suicide) become amplified.

When there is no connection to the unconscious, then psyche goes wrong, and if there is no conscious connection with the land, then matter goes wrong. The manic, grandiose illusion that is the global economy omnipotently assumes that we have broken free of our relationship with, and are self-sufficient from, the land that feeds us. We are separate from the elements of air, earth, fire, and water that support us, and the Minerals, Plants, Animals, and Ancestors that are our Relations, and we have assumed dominion over all. As a result we are under the spell of a perverse and contrary participation mystique—a "dissociation mystique," so to speak. Like Faust, we do not acknowledge Care and are unable to tend that which gives us life. The ecology is dismembered, nature is carved at her joints, and we have lost our spiritual relationship with the world of matter.

Like Faust, in his lust for land and his turning away of the gray women, the Western psyche has ignored its obligations to the natural world, and as a result is heir to an archetypal guilt arising from the betrayal of what gives us life.[33] Indigenous cultures have not severed their relationship with the sacredness of the natural world; like Philemon and Baucis they have given shelter to the gods. Therefore, guilt in indigenous cultures is less archetypal; it is a human, everyday ledger of obligations toward, and transgressions against, one's family and community.

Western culture defends against this archetypal guilt with a catastrophic dissociation and psychotic denial of the reality that the planet we live on is alive and has consciousness.[34] The heroic world economy is unsustainable, in spite of the defensive and euphemistic rationalization of "sustainable development." Were it not for the severe breakdown in reality testing, even a single statistic would be enough to confront us with our destructiveness.[35]

These dynamics are identical with the Kleinian notion of manic defenses against the depressive position, or in Jungian terms, the denial of the shadow. Manic activity or mentation, defends the person against the depression inherent in realizing his or her own destructiveness. When the person begins to integrate his or her aggression as opposed to projecting it into others, a healthy depression ensues, leading to tolerance of goodness and badness within the same object, internal or external.

Here we might listen, with a different ear, to the apocalyptic warnings that abound at the end of the millennium. When this inflation, the mark of our Western and now global culture, undergoes an *enantiodromia*[36] and the awareness of the previously inflated state and its destructiveness, together with the accompanying guilt, reaches consciousness, then the collective ego will be overwhelmed. The collective unconscious symbolizes this in apocalyptic imagery such as Zeus's flooding the land as punishment for the deaths of Philemon and Baucis.

When the *enantiodromia* comes about it will not be a pretty picture. The global heroic ego, for all its priapic, hyper-masculine competitiveness, has fragile self-esteem and is narcissistically vulnerable. Commercial self-esteem and "business confidence" is a surprisingly delicate thing, swinging between blustering, aggressive competition, on the one hand, and tantrums and tears on the other when its omnipotence is frustrated. This omnipotent ego is in thrall to its histrionic anima—the stock market. In the psychological under-world of the global economy the libido-laden words of interest, cred-it, account, inflation, depression, and exchange, carry great weight. Like Faust's being blinded (a loss of consciousness) by Care, the unacknowledged feminine may take revenge by insinuating the fem-inine elements of chance and chaos (the commingling of order and chance accounts for the archetypal fascination with gambling and sports). The stock market, as the moody, unpredictable, irrational anima, may compensate in some way.

Some time after I wrote these words, the terrible events of September 11, 2001 took place. Given the inflation of Western cul-ture, a compensatory deflation was inevitable. I thought it would have been the stock market or the economy. No one could have imagined it would happen in such a tragic and graphic way. The ter-rorists got the penis (the World Trade Center) and the testicles (the Pentagon), but fortunately not the head or the heart (the White House or Capitol Hill, we may never know). Deeper and broader learnings seem unlikely to flow from this event, as it is viewed sim-plistically as a battle between good and evil. It has also gone unno-ticed that a similar structural collapse followed hard on the heels of 9/11. In what is the biggest bankruptcy in U.S. history, the energy corporation Enron collapsed barely two months after the terrorist attacks. Enron may be the second in a line of dominos.

Notes

1   *CW* 8, § 433.

2   Barbara Hannah, *Jung: His Life and Work* (New York: Putnam, 1976), p. 296.

3   *Letters* 1, p. 516.

4   Edward Edinger, *The Aion Lectures* (Toronto: Inner City, 1996), p. 13. The fore-word to *Aion* is dated May 1950; however, some parts were presented at Eranos in 1948.

5   Gary Hartman, *History and Development of Jung's Psychology: The Early Years, 1900 to 1935* (Analytical Psychology and Culture, http://www.cgjung.com/articles/hdself3.html, 1995).

6   Hannah, *Jung: His Life and Work*, p. 275.

7   *MDR*, p. 209.

8   *Letters* 2, p. 118.

9   The earth wobbles as it rotates and the earth's axis inscribes a cone out into space, like a spinning top that is not upright. This movement, or precession, of the earth's axis through the heavens takes 25,800 years for a complete revolution. This is called a Platonic, or Great, Year. An astrological Age is one month of this Great Year. This movement is also called the precession of the equinoxes because the position of the spring equinox gradually moves in relation to the stars.

10 David Ulansey, *The Origins of the Mithraic Mysteries* (New York: Oxford, 1989).

11 *Letters* 2, p. xxxix. June 27, 1947.

12 Peter Balin, *The Flight of Feathered Serpent* (Wilmot, WI: Arcana, 1978).

13 Marie-Louise von Franz, *C. G. Jung: His Myth in Our Time* (London: Hodder & Stoughton, 1975), pp. 122, 136, 138.

14 *CW* 7, § 32.

15 Edward Edinger, *Goethe's Faust: Notes for a Jungian Commentary* (Toronto: Inner City, 1990), p. 25.

16 *MDR*, pp. 60–61.

17 *MDR*, p. 318.

18 *CW* 14, § 206.

19 *CW* 12, § 36.

20 Frances Wickes, *The Inner World of Choice* (Englewood Cliffs, NJ: Prentice-Hall, 1963), p. 8.

21 *Letters* 1, p. 308.

22 *CW* 12, fig. 232.

23 *CW* 14, § 238.

24 *CW* 11, § 755.

25 *CW* 16, Fig. 10. "The Rosary of the Philosophers" is a series of 20 woodcuts from the alchemical text *De Alchimia opuscula complura veterum philosophorum*, Frankfurt, 1550.

26 *CW* 10, *Archaic Man*.

27 Including Richard Noll, *The Jung Cult: Origins of a Charismatic Movement* (Princeton: Princeton University Press, 1994).

28 *CW* 6, § 781.

29 *CW* 9i, § 260.

30 *CW* 6, § 741.

31 *CW* 13, § 247–248.

32 C. G. Jung, *Man and His Symbols* (London: Aldus, 1964), p. 85.

33 For a further discussion see Luigi Zoja, *Growth and Guilt: Psychology and the Limits of Development* (London: Routledge, 1995).

34 I use the terms "dissociation" and "psychotic" here in their clinical sense. Dissociation meaning a pathological alteration of consciousness as a defense against the awareness of trauma. Psychotic meaning a severe distortion in reality testing.

35 Some examples are: since 1970 nearly 80 percent of the world's indigenous forests have been destroyed; in 1992 the Grand Banks fishery off Newfoundland, the richest fishing ground in the world, was closed and ten years later cod stocks continue to decline; since 1950 more resources have been consumed by humankind than in the whole history of the human race.

36 *Enantiodromia* (Greek, meaning "running counter to"): The emergence of the unconscious opposite in the course of time. *CW* 6, § 709.

LITTLE NORTHEAST MOON OF THE BIG NORTH — DESIGN OF ENERGY OF WISDOM AND KNOWLEDGE

The things that my soul refused to touch are as my sorrowful meat.[1]

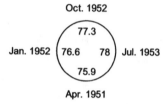

In the spring of 1951 Jung was repeatedly bedridden with a fever and liver trouble (hepatitis). During this bout of ill-health he wrote *Answer to Job*, a few months after the pronouncement of the *Assumptio Mariae* in November 1950. He said that *Aion* had been written in "polite language" but was insufficient and so he had become ill and was forced to write.[2]

We have seen that *Aion* was concerned with the Self, that his flowering tree dream of the Self was set in Liverpool, and now *Answer to Job* was written when he had "liver trouble." We might also remember Prometheus's own "liver trouble" which he suffered as punishment for stealing fire from the gods—as Jung did in confronting the dark side of God in *Answer to Job*.

JOB'S MOTHER

Answer to Job was written in a style different from *Aion*, not as a careful exegesis of symbolic material but, typical of the Northeast, as a more personal, emotional experience that flowed from him effortlessly.[3] He told Esther Harding[4] that the book was dictated to him by a figure who sat on his bedpost during his illness, and as soon as it was completed his illness was over.

In *Memories* Jung said that *Answer to Job* had been "foreshadowed in a dream." To understand the conception and birth of this major work we need to go back 3 years to January 1948 when he had the dream, which was in two parts. In the first part, he was paying a visit to his father who was living in the country in an 18th-century style house, which used to be an inn or spa. It seemed that a great many famous personages had stopped at the house; several had died and their sarcophagi were kept in a crypt below the house, and his father was their guardian. In the dream, Jung's father was also a distinguished scholar and in his study with Jung were Dr. Y., a psychiatrist about Jung's age, and his son. Whether it was in response to a question that Jung had asked, or his father wanting to explain something, he was not sure, but his father went to the bookshelf and took down a large Bible covered in fish skin. He opened it at the Old Testament (Jung guessed it was the Pentateuch)[5] and began interpreting a passage so learnedly and swiftly that Jung and the others could not follow him. Jung saw that Dr. Y. did not understand, and his son began to laugh, thinking it was senile prattle. To Jung it was obvious that his father was flooded with profound ideas, but he and the others were so stupid that they could not understand him.

From a letter of Jung's on January 30, 1948 in which he mentions the dream, we can date it as occurring in early January 1948. In the letter, however, he adds something that was not in *Memories*. In the last part of the dream he was in his father's house on the ground floor, thinking about a question that had been raised at the beginning of the dream: "How is it possible that my mother celebrates her 70th birthday in this year 1948 while I am reaching my 74th year?"[6] His father is going to answer the question but then takes him up to the first floor.

In the letter he adds a postscript, "My mother = anima is younger than myself. When I was 3 years old I had my first anima-experience, the woman at that time was *not* my mother. It [the dream] means a lot that escapes me for the time being." Here Jung refers to the time when he was ill with eczema and his mother was away in hospital—likely as a result of the difficulties in his parents' marriage—and a maid was taking care of him. We know that Jung's relationship with the maid was highly significant for him. Sabina Spielrein said that Jung was very attached to the maid, and in a letter to Spielrein in December 1908 Jung wrote, "Recently *earlier and earlier childhood memories have been surfacing*, from a time (3–4th *year*) when I often hurt myself badly, and when, for example, I was once only just rescued from certain death by a maid."[7] In *Memories* he also refers to this incident, when he almost fell off a bridge, and describes his early recollections of the maid in sensuous terms.[8]

Jung was 72.6 at the time of the dream, that is, in his seventy-third year, and reaching his seventy-fourth year. But why this convoluted reference to his age? Remember that in January 1923, twenty-five years earlier, his mother had died in her seventy-fourth year. If his mother in the dream was 70 years old in 1948, then she would have been born in 1878 when Jung was 3, and he makes a connection to that age in the postscript to the letter. It is this mother/maid, these first and second mothers, that can give birth to something in him. Recall also that in 1878, he had the dream of going down into a cellar in the earth and coming upon the phallus on a throne, which his mother, above ground, told him was the "man-eater."

At the time of the letter of January 30, 1948, Jung was in the middle of a Chaotic Journey into the Little North Moon of the Big North. He wrote it two days after the anniversary of his father's death (which occurred when Jung was in the North of the Little North Moon of the Big South, and shortly before his own Big Chaotic Journey into the Big North). In 1922, when Jung was in the North of the Little North Moon of the Big West, he had had a dream of his father asking for marital advice, and a few months later his mother died when she was in the North of the Little North Moon of the Big North.

Now, in January 1948, Jung is approaching the Little North Moon of the Big North, where his mother had died on her Moon Cycles, writing a letter two days after the anniversary of his father's death, in the same month as his mother's death, about a dream about his father that refers to a question about his mother![9]

In the dream, the potential to give birth (his mother) is not yet 70 years old and Jung is 72.6.[10] The medieval alchemists said, "The mother bore me and is herself begotten of me."[11] So we could consider the mother image as saying something like: "I am your mother. I gave birth to you and you have given birth to me. I was born when you were three years old when you had the dream about the phallus. I am not as old as you yet, but when I am, I shall give birth to something."

If we look at what happened when the "mother" in him reaches 72.6, one Little Moon Cycle later, we see that Jung was on a Chaotic Journey into the Little Northeast Moon and at the end of it he began writing *Answer to Job* in the spring of 1951. Was this the birth? We see a similar theme, of scholarly discourse, in the dream Jung had in October 1911, where he was being questioned by the "assemblage of distinguished spirits" and felt humiliated by not knowing the answer. But now Jung knows more and he is not identified with the psychiatrist persona that does not understand or thinks the old man is prattling. In the spring of 1951, the dream of the distinguished spirits would have been about 39.6 years old, and on its Chaotic Journey into the Little West Moon of the Big West, the place of double Death and Change. Was *Answer to Job* Jung's answer to the questions posed to him in the dream?

Before we go further, let us look at the second part of the dream. His father led Jung from the ground floor, up a winding staircase to a mandala-shaped, council hall that was a replica of Sultan Akbar's.[12] There was a gallery around the room with four bridges that led to the center platform where the Sultan would sit. From the center platform, a steep flight of stairs, almost a ladder, led up to a small door high up in the wall. As soon as Jung stepped onto the bridge, he fell on his knees, overcome by the realization that his father was going to lead him up to the "supreme presence," and touched his head almost to the floor.[13]

The presence in the upper room was Uriah, King David's general, who David arranged to be killed in battle so he could have Uriah's wife, Bathsheba. Some years later, Jung understood what this dream meant to him. At the center is the seat of Akbar, the "lord of the world," like David. But higher than he is Uriah, the guiltless victim, like Job and Christ, who has been abandoned by God. Similar to Uriah, Jung was vilified and severely criticized on the publication of *Answer to Job*, and later, like Uriah, his wife would be taken from him by death. In the dream Jung could not bring himself to touch his forehead to the ground; something held him back from complete submission. He said that without this free will, the story of Job would never have been written and this freedom would have been created for naught if it could not affect God in some way. The dream revealed the notion that the created went beyond the creator in the development of the fragile gift of human consciousness and free will.[14]

But there is something else that is curious about the dream. The figure of Uriah suggests an oedipal triangle, but in reverse. We have seen that Jung was caught in an oedipal triangle with Freud and Sabina Spielrein, and possibly with Minna Bernays, and the story of Oedipus and Jocasta's pin had associations with Jung's near-fatal illness. After its publication, a frequent criticism of *Answer to Job* was that Jung's sullying of the image of God was evidence of his unresolved father/Freud/anti-Semitic complex. However in Jung's dream, instead of the prototypical story of the son killing the father to gain the mother, Uriah's story is the mirror image, where the father (David) kills the son (Uriah) to gain the daughter (Bathsheba). The fruit of the union of David and Bathsheba was great wisdom—their son, Solomon, became the wisest of kings. Moreover, the story of Job is about the death of the victim complex. Job no longer fights, nor fears, the authoritarian father, but takes a third position which leads to something higher than both—human integrity. This is represented in the dream by the elevation of Uriah, the victim by whose death wisdom is born.

So let us summarize the web that this dream weaves: the first part of the dream is about Jung's personal father and the second part about the supreme father. Jung associates to a childhood dream of going down to the lowest presence, known to his mother. In the 1948 dream, he goes up to the highest presence, known to his father. Three years after the dream Jung writes a book about bringing the "man-eater"—the dark side of God—into the light of consciousness.

JOB'S FATHER

The theme of *Answer to Job* was the divine drama of the development of the God-image in the Western psyche, and how it was transformed by human consciousness. After the polytheistic pantheon of the Greek gods and goddesses (at least there *were* goddesses), when humans were forced to endure the perpetual and almost human interference by the deities in human affairs, the God-image underwent a radical transformation with the appearance in the Old Testament of Yahweh who, while more removed, would take an erratic interest in human affairs and play favorites. Like Zeus, he was a sky-god, but insisted on being the only god—displaying, perhaps, signs of dangerous inflation and fatal narcissism.

Yahweh was a mixture of unpredictable, sharply contrasting opposites: wrathful and loving; creative and destructive; generous and narcissistic; cruel and merciful; jealous and loyal. Jung hoped "to give expression to the shattering emotion which the unvarnished spectacle of divine savagery and ruthlessness [of God] produces in us."[15] Yahweh demanded praise and glory from his people and that he alone be worshipped. In the absence of this mirroring, his wrath would descend and his actions reveal a being that can only exist in relationship to an object. His existence was real only when noticed and acclaimed. "One can imagine what would happen if this assembly suddenly decided to stop the applause: there would be a state of high excitation, with outbursts of blind destructive rage, then a withdrawal into hellish loneliness and the torture of non-existence, followed by a gradual reawakening of an unutterable longing for something which would make him conscious of himself."[16]

In our age, Yahweh's behavior would attract a diagnosis of borderline personality disorder. He was the trickster, dissociated, the right hand not knowing what the left is doing, and amoral like life itself.[17] However there was no contradiction within Yahweh because no objective consciousness, within or without, had ever interceded to question the contradiction.

The next major transformation in the God-image was Job's encounter with Yahweh. By holding to his integrity and his human consciousness, Job was granted a glimpse of the shadow side of God, of which God himself was unconscious. Briefly, the biblical story of Job runs as follows: Yahweh boasts about Job's goodness to Satan, and Satan says that the only reason Job is good is because God has treated him so well. Satan wagers Yahweh that Job would curse Yahweh if things went badly for him. So Yahweh gives him leave to plague Job but spare his life. Yahweh, quite without reason and too obviously, lets himself be influenced by his eldest son. As a result, multiple calamities and catastrophes are visited on Job. He is robbed of his herds, his servants are slaughtered, his sons and daughters are killed, he is abandoned by his friends and wife, denied a fair hearing in court, and brought to the brink of death. In his dealings with Job, Yahweh displays no conscience, scruples, or consideration—only callousness and brutality—and he violates several of the commandments he himself gave to Moses on Mount Sinai.

From a human standpoint, Yahweh's behavior is so repellent that it raises the question of an underlying motive. Was Yahweh jealous of human consciousness? "Is it worth the lion's while to terrify the mouse? . . . Altogether, he pays so little attention to Job's real situation that one suspects him of having an ulterior motive which is more important to him: Job is no more than the outward occasion for an inward process of dialectic in God."[18]

Edward Edinger puts this in psychological terms: the ego is the outward occasion for a dialectical process within the Self, and indeed suggests that our affects are manifestations of Yahweh. Yahweh is the unconscious and, like God, our affects happen to us—they come from the Self and can have destructive consequences unless they are contained and transformed by the human ego.[19]

The Elders say the same thing in a different way. Humans are the Determiners and they have been given the gift of Free Will—the integrity of Job—in the Creator's desire to exercise its Free Will and birth itself into All Forms of All Things. They also say that the Creator has four Shields (as we do, being created in Its image), and each Shield is a universe. The South universe is the Child Substance Shield, the North universe is the Adult Substance Shield, the West universe is the Adult Spirit Shield and the East universe is the Child Spirit Shield. Within the South universe are twelve planets that carry human life, and Grandmother Earth is the South planet.

The South universe is the Child universe and, as the South planet in the South universe, Grandmother Earth carries the emotions of the child aspect of the Great Spirit. And, as the East child of Grandmother Earth, the Gift of Humans to the Creator is consciousness of the emotions of its Child Substance Shield.

Enduring all his trials, Job asks God to justify why this is happening to him, as his life and conduct do not warrant this kind of treatment. In other words, he asks for help with God from God. Counselors advise Job to stop his questioning and submit to his fate and accept, though he may not understand it, that God is just. But Job persists and, as he puts it, maintains his integrity: "Till I die I will not remove mine integrity from me."[20] Finally Yahweh manifests as a whirlwind and speaks at length of his might and power. Job is silenced and accepts the situation: "I will lay mine hand upon my mouth."[21] But his numinous vision earns him the right to question Yahweh as to his motivations: "I will demand of thee and deliver thou unto me."[22] As a result Yahweh restores all Job's property twofold.

At this point, the consciousness of the created (humankind in the figure of Job) surpassed the consciousness of the Creator. The result is cataclysmic. As an act of redemption and an enlargement of consciousness Yahweh was obliged to incarnate himself in the form of Christ, the good son—a form of self-punishment for his trans-gressions. Jung goes on to say, "What kind of father is it who would rather his son were slaughtered than forgive his ill-advised creatures who have been corrupted by his precious Satan?.... So it comes a nasty shock when this supremely good God only allows the purchase of such an act of grace through a human sacrifice, and, what is worse, through the killing of his own son.... One should keep before one's eyes the strange fact that the God of goodness is so unforgiving that he can only be appeased by human sacrifice."[23]

Christ died on the cross at age 33. On our 33rd birthday, we sit in the East of the Little Southeast Moon of the Big West, the Illumination and Enlightenment of the Death and Change of Self-Images. We then go on a Chaotic Journey and the last three months of this year is in the place of double Trust and Innocence of Death and Change.

Christ did indeed go to his death in Trust and Innocence, and the Self-Image that died was that of the Old Testament God. The crucifixion was the Illumination of the transformative change in God's view of himself through the incarnation and sacrifice of his only son. God's self-sacrifice is the self-destruction of the amoral God who demands human sacrifices. Yahweh was so destructive that it took the sacrifice of his son, in masochistic reparation of his guilt, to reconcile him with humanity and to broaden his own con-sciousness. In so doing, Yahweh's image was transformed from the wrathful God to that of the loving father in whom there is no dark-ness. In this process, Yahweh became man, and the collective unconscious became human. This is the Gift of the Humans as Determiners because, "If God has become man, then reality itself has become humanized. It means that reality itself has taken on a human face."[24]

So Job had integrity—he would not sell out no matter how much he was bullied from the outside or the inside. In his book, *Integrity in Depth*, John Beebe writes about how integrity is a dialectic between thinking and feeling: "The implication is that the real plea-sure in exercising integrity in dealings with others is the discovery of integrity itself.... This shared field of integrity is the ground of any depth psychotherapy, and it is impossible to understand the burgeoning of psychotherapy in our century if one does not recognize the profound pleasure that the discovery of integrity brings."[25]

But the other end of this polarity is the experience of violation. Like Job, we have all been unjustly treated, and like Faust we have all sold out, or been sold out, in childhood or as adults. Often we are unaware of the Self until the Self has been violated, until the Children's Fire has been crossed. Archetypes do not have human integrity and need to be taught good manners and human courtesy so they can come and live among us. This is the marriage of the South and the North, the judging functions of feeling (Trust and Innocence, virginity, Eros) and thinking (Harmony and Balance, structure, order, discriminating receptiveness, justice, Logos). In psychotherapy this is the maintenance of the secure frame, the transitional space that is chaste but free, where libido is contained but free to flow. This marriage constellates the Catalyst energy and contains the hostile opposites at the Center. Job is a model for the sufferings of the modern ego, where both the ego and the Self are transformed in the conscious encounter between the two and by the ego's effort to find meaning in seemingly meaningless experience.[26]

Edinger distinguishes four features of the Job archetype, which allows us to put it on the Wheel. First, there is an encounter between the ego and a greater power (South). Second, the ego is wounded as a result of this encounter (West). Third, the ego assumes the experience is meaningful and persists in searching for the meaning of the wound (North). Fourth, as a result of its persistence, a divine revelation takes place where the ego is rewarded with insight, an Illumination, into the nature of the divine—the transpersonal psyche—and this insight brings acceptance to the ego and healing of the suffering (East). In finding meaning in his painful experience, Job contributes to the transformation of the God-image through his attitude. He is concerned about the state of his very human soul, no matter how powerful, ruthless, right, and correct the forces that afflict him might be. In his many trials and hardships Job asks, "Why me?" and "Why did God allow this to happen?" Edinger goes on to suggest that there are five possible answers:

> One of them is "God has punished me for my sins." [South: Mythology]. . . . that's the Jeremiah reaction. . . . Another possible reaction is that "I'm a victim of Satan, the Evil one, who is responsible." [West: Daydream] That's the dualistic or Manichean reaction, it sees the world as engaged in a conflict between two different deities; the Good and the Evil. The third possibility is that "This catastrophe is actually good for me in a way I can't understand." [North: Belief] I call that the Apostle Paul reaction. He said "All things work together for the good to them that love God"—if you can see far enough. It usually takes some faith to assume that one. The fourth possibility is that the suffering is caused by chance, because there is no transpersonal agency in human affairs. "God doesn't exist, or if he does exist he doesn't concern himself with man." [East: Illusion] That's the secular reaction. It doesn't offer much comfort but if you believe it you can harden yourself and adopt a stoic attitude. The fifth possibility is the one that Jung has discovered, namely, "God is an antinomy who isn't quite conscious of what he is doing." [Center: Catalyst] . . . Job also realizes that by having awareness about God he is contributing to God's transformation. That's the Job reaction and it's one that never existed before in human thought until Jung interpreted it that way.[27]

In *Answer to Job,* Jung also deals with the Book of Revelation as the Western psyche's archetype of the apocalypse or last judgment. The coming of a new order from the collective unconscious emerges in the catastrophic predictions typical of apocalyptic, *fin-de-siècle* movements. Likewise, in the personal unconscious, the emergence of the Self is often experienced as a death, frequently accompanied by end-of-the-world dream imagery such as nuclear explosions. These dreams are often positive but terrifying.

Now, at the end of the Christian era, the God-image has undergone a further transformation reflected in the dogma of *Assumptio Mariae*—the elevation of Mary alongside the Father, Son, and the Holy Ghost. Jung considered this to be the most important religious event since the Reformation, as it carried tremendous archetypal significance, in that the elevation of Mary balanced the one-sided masculine trinity.

Von Franz said that, "The senex, the old man, is characterized as a worn-out image of God and world order and the puer . . . is a new God image.... If the new God image cannot be born in the soul of man, it remains an archetypal unconscious figure, which has dissolving and destructive effects. We are moving towards a 'fatherless society' and the 'son' is not yet born, i.e., realized consciously in our psyches. This inner birth could only take place with the help of the feminine principle. That is why the collective attention has turned now to the latter."[28]

Jung said that the birth of Christ was a unique historical event that happened only once but is an eternal process that is always happening in the *pleroma*, the Gnostic equivalent of the Dream. In the Gnostic writings (circa 100–300 C.E.) Yahweh has a feminine counterpart, Sophia, who falls to earth, becomes enamored of matter, and has to be rescued from its embrace. This is the process of a spiritual content undergoing embodiment, the alchemical *coagulatio,* the movement from *nagual* (the Dream or fifth dimension) to the *tonal* (the physical world or third dimension). So at the same time as Yahweh considered himself the only god and on high, the feminine principle was consigned to matter, downward to earth, and became lost. Job's effect on Yahweh was to make him conscious of the feminine principle of relatedness, Eros, the relationship of subject to object.

This is what happens in therapy: once the unconscious is seen and recognized for what it is, it becomes related to, and that in itself constellates a process of change. God needed Job to become conscious of part of himself. So, the process of witnessing the unconscious is, to a greater or lesser degree, participating in the divine drama and the transformation of the collective unconscious. An endeavor, fraught with the potential for inflation, which requires deep humility.

The outcome of Job's world-changing encounter was the New Testament God. Yahweh became the loving, benevolent God who has no darkness in him, and incarnated in matter through Christ. God's guilt, when he realized how inhuman he was, led to his dramatic conversion to extreme goodness, overcompensating by becoming more human than humans. Job was the fulcrum of this transformation through his human consciousness and his own values.

In a letter of November 16, 1951, in answer to a criticism of his sarcasm in *Answer to Job*, Jung wrote that sarcasm, while not an attractive quality, was the only way to deliver himself from the Father. He would have preferred to "remain in the Father's protection and shun the problem of the opposites. It is probably even more difficult to deliver oneself from good than from evil. But without sin there is no breaking away from the good Father."[29]

The hero, whether ordinary or extraordinary, is always born of two fathers, human and divine. The earth father teaches him the cultural traditions and values. The divine father frees his spirit from traditions and conventions and brings him knowledge of new horizons. But the hero must then free himself from both fathers to live his own life. In 1912, in the Little Southwest Moon of the Big South, Jung had broken away from the professional father, Freud. Now at age 75, across the Wheel in the Little Northeast Moon of the Big North, thirty-nine years (double Death and Change) later, he broke away from the archetypal father, God.

JOB AND KLEIN

Jung's association to the dream that gave birth to *Answer to Job* was one of early maternal experiences with the maid who looked after him. To further understand the importance of *Answer to Job* and its relationship to the Moon Cycles, we must go back and look at what happens in the nine months before and after birth. There is a small Moon (not shown in figure 2, p. 18) in the Center of the Little Center

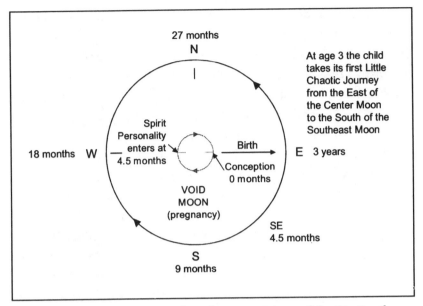

Fig 8. The Void Moon and Little Center Moon of the Big South

Moon of the Big South. It is the Void, or Womb, Moon that we travel around during the nine months of pregnancy (see figure 8). We are conceived in the East of this Void Moon in the light of Spirit, and by the time we reach the West (the place of the body and earth), after four and a half months *in utero*, the Spirit Personality is fully present in the fetus.[30] The fetus then continues clockwise around to the East again and during birth it travels from the East of the Void Moon to the East of the Little Center Moon of the Big South, where it is born. Birth is the first Big Chaotic Journey. Death is the last Big Chaotic Journey.

Only ten percent of abortions are performed after thirteen weeks of pregnancy and, more significantly, only one percent after 20 weeks, the usual obstetrical limit for abortions. If we adjust this twenty weeks, which is the norm calculated from the beginning of the last menstrual period, by subtracting the roughly fourteen days into the menstrual cycle when conception takes place, then this upper limit of abortion is eighteen weeks, or four and a half months, after conception. Put another way, ninety-nine percent of abortions are done before the Spirit Personality comes into the fetus.

All the Chaotic Journeys during the Moon Cycles are internal journeys. The only time we cross the Southeast externally is during the first Little Moon after we are born. After the infant is born into the East of the Little Center Moon it travels clockwise through the Southeast at 4 1/2 months, into the South at 9 months, the West at 18 months, the North at 27 months and arrives in the East again at age 3. The first nine months of life are critically important as a prototype for later experiences during the remaining Chaotic Journeys in our lives (how we cope with chaos, dependence, trauma, not knowing) and in all the Little Southeast Moons (how we see ourselves, our self-image, our "self-esteem"). The reason for this is that although the baby is physically born in the East of the Little Center Moon, it is not psychologically born until it is in the South of that Moon, and the first nine months of life is the journey in the outside womb after nine months in the inside womb. During this time of what Ashley Montagu calls "exterogestation," touch is the first language and the skin is an external nervous system.[31]

The age of four and a half months, in the Southeast, is significant, and modern psychoanalytic thinking and infant research substantiates this. The baby is capable of a wide range of emotional and cognitive responses, but the ideas most relevant to us here about the infant's inner emotional life are those of Melanie Klein.

Freud proposed that the oedipal phase of development between the ages four and six occupied a central place in psychic development. However, in her work with children beginning in the 1920s, Klein observed that the roots of psychic life began much earlier with what she called the paranoid-schizoid position, characterized by splitting and projection.

Klein said, "It is splitting which allows the ego to emerge out of chaos and to order its experiences."[32] Although the infant is capable of a range of emotions, it does not yet have the ability to alleviate states of unpleasure, or maintain states of pleasure. In the early months of life, experiences are felt as all-good and all-bad, and all-outside and all-inside. The defense mechanism of projection is necessary when an infant cannot tolerate the anxiety created by frightening impulses and feelings. The anxiety-producing impulses are split-off and projected onto the mother who, under ordinary circumstances, is able to accept them and hold them until the baby is more mature. In other words, a mother feels what her baby feels (or the baby "makes" her feel what it feels) and she is closely attuned to her baby's feeling states. With "good enough" mothering, the mother can know what the baby needs without becoming emotionally overwhelmed by the baby's pain, distress, anger, need, or dependence. The mother acts as a container for these feelings, which Wilfred Bion refers to as the mother's "reverie," her willingness and ability to think about and know her baby and its impulses, needs, and feelings.[33]

The mother's capacity to attune to the feeling states of the baby during its early infancy allows it to experience an outer object that has the power to alleviate its distress, contain its feelings, and not be destroyed (as Yahweh experienced Job). This allows the baby to move from the paranoid-schizoid position to the depressive position. Klein proposed that in approximately the first year of life, the internal world of the infant is split and fragmented (schizoid) and it sees pleasure and danger as coming from the outside (paranoid). Destructive impulses and persecutory anxieties are strongest in the paranoid-schizoid position and it is easily observed that infants experience terror, fright, and pleasure. As experiences become less fragmented the ego becomes more able to see objects as related wholes. The infant then begins to experience a kind of sorrow or guilt concerning the harm that its needs and demands have made on the loved object. Klein calls this "depressive anxiety," and it is expressed unconsciously in the omnipotent fantasy: "Did I destroy the loved object?" or "Am I too much for mommy?" The guilt and fear that arises from the anxiety that the good object has been harmed constitutes the depressive position. If these new anxieties cannot be contained within the mother-baby relationship, there may be a return to the paranoid-schizoid position.

Significantly, it is around four or five months that the baby begins to distinguish between itself and the external world and begins to move toward the depressive position. In the depressive position, the ego begins to perceive that love, as well as anger, come from the same caring parent, and that the person who is hated is the same as the one who is loved. Jealousy, an emotion rooted in earlier envy, also makes its appearance at about the same age.[34] In other words, the Image of Self begins to form in the Southeast at the age of four and a half months, or as Donald Kalsched puts it, "the omnipotent God-identified ego cannot come into life until its love and hate can be experienced toward the same human person."[35]

As these emotions are integrated, the primary anxiety shifts from being harmed, or not being taken care of, to a kind of guilt for having harmed (in fantasy) the nurturing object. In response to this the infant begins to show concern for the mother and her needs. At this point, mothers often talk about the sudden change in their babies' response to them, "Now I know my baby loves me." What emerges out of the depressive position is the capacity for gratitude and reparation and this becomes more observable when the baby is about six to eight months of age.

At first glance, Kleinian notions have some of the arcane nature of alchemical language, with talk of containment, the breast, projecting into, introjection, splitting, devouring, and part-objects. However, when experienced in the context of actual work with infants and children they immediately reveal their utility, much like Jung's use of the alchemical *Rosarium Philosophorum* to understand transference and counter-transference. The early psychic dynamics that Klein has described can apply to any stage of life, not only as a re-working of the residues of earlier experience but also because the Kleinian processes of projection, introjection, identification, and projective identification are archetypal processes, and as such they can emerge at any time during the life cycle.

Klein adhered to Freud's drive concepts of Eros, the life instinct, and *thanatos*, the death instinct, but gave more importance to the death instinct than Freud had, particularly in relation to the destructive envy and aggression that infants and young children feel. Although Klein thought about the death instinct as a biological force, we might also think about it, in Jungian terms, as an aspect of the

Self. The wholeness of the Self is present at birth. It contains all the opposites in raw, chaotic, rudimentary form; thus, the infant's psychic life is made up of as yet unconnected fragments of satisfaction, pleasure, anxiety, and terrifying abandonment. The best and the worst, life and death, lie side by side. In ancient Greece, *thanatos* was often referred to as *thymoraistes,* or "he who strikes down the *thymos.*" *Thymos* is the courage to face life, or the life impulse.[36] The shadow side of the Self—which annihilates, takes apart, and threatens to destroy not only the ego but also the mother—is what Klein refers to as the death instinct.

As the infant experiences good-enough parenting, the destructive shadow side of the Self is civilized, so to speak. However, if there is severe abuse, trauma, or overwhelming neglect at a young age, then the shadow side of the Self remains in archaic form. Donald Kalsched proposes that in these cases this shadow side of the Self paradoxically preserves the "personal spirit," or the Spirit Personality of the infant, by severing thinking and feeling and dissociating experience into fragments in a primitive, last-ditch attempt to protect the child from further psychological pain. The outcome of this process is dissociative and borderline personality states characterized by inner persecutory objects symbolized in dream images of rape, cutting, shooting, concentration camps, torture, or decapitation. Thus the inner trauma continues long after the outer trauma has stopped.

JOB'S BABY

So how are *Answer to Job* and Melanie Klein's work related? They describe the same process from different vantage points: one developmental or "instinctual" and the other archetypal or "spiritual." In our Chaotic Journeys, as we move from the East of one Little Moon to the South of the next and cross the Southeast, we come face-to-face with both the light and the shadow side of the Self, or the God-image within. In the Little Southeast Moons and in the Chaotic Journeys, we are participating in the alchemy of, on the one hand, the reworking of our early experiences in the first nine months of life, and on the other hand, re-enacting the spiritual encounter of Job with Yahweh in the continuing incarnation of the Self.

So we could think about the infant, in the paranoid-schizoid position, as the embodiment of Yahweh; and the mother as Job. In the infant, the "uncivilized" Self is incarnated in the raw, light and dark, and neither light nor dark knows the existence of the other as they are split and projected. If the child is deprived of the maternal container and the mother's reverie, then it will be forced to deal with its intolerable feelings by denial, splitting, and projection, by becoming omniscient. It will be unable, as it matures, to think about feelings (as these are the first facts of psychic life) and later may have learning difficulties.[37]

This describes Yahweh in his unutterable longing to be seen. When he is not seen, he cannot learn; he cannot objectively "think" about himself or other objects in a discriminative act of consciousness. We know that some learning difficulties in children are related to their inability to take in the goodness of what is offered (information or knowledge) because of their unconscious fantasy that their bad internal objects will destroy it. When Job is able to "think" about Yahweh as a phenomenon and not be destroyed, then both are transformed.

In the early stages of the depressive position, manic defenses are used to defend against the anxiety that aggressive impulses will get the better of the good inner and outer objects, as well as against the realization of the dependence on a separate object. These defenses are Yahweh-like denial and omnipotence—I am in control, I cannot harm and I cannot be harmed. In normal development, the mother acts like Job to the baby's Yahweh. In her humanity she witnesses and contains the shadow side of the Self and the baby moves through the paranoid-schizoid position. In its awareness of dependence, the baby's omnipotence is moderated, which leads to reparation of the fantasized attacks on the mother. Reparation is the interaction with others, in reality or in fantasy, which permits the child to feel that goodness has been restored to the damaged person and that the internal object, destroyed or damaged in fantasy, has been re-created or restored. So the baby, like Yahweh, realizes the effect of its own destructiveness, the Self protects against the Self, and it begins to move into the depressive position. In the drama of Job, Yahweh incarnates Christ in reparation. In the mother-infant drama the Self incarnates the healthy ego, gratitude, and relatedness.

The story of Job and the early vicissitudes of the paranoid-schizoid and depressive positions are the macrocosmic and microcosmic ends of the same stick, and this is why the Southeast and the Chaotic Journeys are so important. In the first nine months of life, the divine drama is re-enacted in every infant, in a personal encounter between two Humans where each touches the other with intimacy, and which is full of emotions and feeling for both. For the rest of our lives, for the nine months of our Chaotic Journey every three years, we are engaged in the same process, but internally, between the ego and the Self.

The same archetypal process applies on a cultural level. When Europeans came to Turtle Island, the first thing they did was take inventory. The land (mother) was a part-object to be used and devoured in an omnipotent way. In the last 500 years, Western culture has developed manic defenses against the depressive position and the ensuing awareness of its own destructiveness, and oscillates between this and the warring paranoid-schizoid position. It is unable to render gratitude and reparation to the mother on whom we depend.

Much of the current interest in indigenous spirituality, as well as ecological preservation, animal rights activism, and similar movements, is partly motivated by the sentimentalities of *puer* or *puella* psychology. But this should not blind us to the fact that these movements also represent a differentiation, and a return to, feeling values toward the planet that we live on. Indigenous cultures have stood with their integrity, like Job, through 500 years of the ruthless European Yahweh. Their integrity in the face of this may lead, and perhaps is leading, to an enlargement of consciousness for non-indigenous cultures—the beginning of a different relationship with All Our Relations, and the reparation of the effects of our own destructiveness.

SYNCHRONICITY

Jung wrote about synchronicity in 1951 after completing *Answer to Job*. He gave a short lecture on the topic at Eranos in the summer of 1951 and revised it immediately afterward for publication as *Synchronicity: An Acausal Connecting Principle*. Jung defined a synchronistic event as the coincidence in time of two or more causally unrelated events that have the same meaning. In other words, it is the coincidence between an inner image or hunch, and an outer event that has the same meaning. It is the meaning for the individual that differentiates synchronicity and mere coincidence.

Jung felt that synchronistic events were acts of creation in time: "It is only the ingrained belief in the sovereign power of causality that creates intellectual difficulties and makes it appear unthinkable that causeless events exist or could ever occur. But if they do, then we must regard them as *creative acts*, as the continuous creation of pattern that exists from all eternity, repeats itself sporadically, and is not derivable from any known antecedents."[38] He also said, "Synchronism is the prejudice of the East, causality is the modern prejudice of the West."[39] This notion of acausality has been difficult for Western science to grasp. Synchronicity is the principle underlying games of chance and divinatory oracles. The Elders say it is the play of the Great Spirit—its sense of humor, and its desire to continually create and recreate new forms of itself—that we experience as chance. Eighty percent of all movement of energy is patterned, that is, to some extent predictable, but twenty percent is chaotic and unpredictable; the latter is the Free Will of the Great Spirit and so cannot be known. So all divinatory oracles, prophecies, or clairvoyance can only predict with a maximum accuracy of eighty percent.

> [Scientific] experiments eliminate chance, the oracle makes chance the center.... Very accurate thinkers get irritated with oracle techniques because they are so indefinite. Naturally anything can be read into them, and because it is all so

vague, foolish superstitious people always see a connection and after the event say that it was in the oracle. One might say it is all so vague that practically anything could happen, but that is just not true, that is an emotional argument born of prejudice. It is true, however, in so far as an oracle technique is never quite accurate and cannot predict exactly. . . . But it can give an "expectation list," which can cast an image of a certain area or qualitative field of events and predict that something is going to happen with that field. There is a certain psychological probability because of what Jung calls the collective unconscious. . . . one sees that actual events are never predicted, but only the quality of possible events.[40]

Synchronicities are often associated with liminal, or boundary, periods where there is a transition from one state to another accompanied by a significant charge of psychic energy (for example, biological or developmental rites of passage such as adolescence, birth, death, or marriage; as well as more personal events such as falling in love, creative work, or Chaotic Journeys). These are psychic capacitors, so to speak, or ceremonial containers, where libido and emotion accumulate for discharge and transformation when the event occurs.

Keeping in mind that Jung was in the Little Northeast Moon of the Big North (the Wisdom and Knowledge of the Design of Energy) when he wrote *Synchronicity,* let us look at the relationship of the Northeast-Southwest axis to synchronicity. In the Southwest is the Dream, and Needs, Wants and Desires, in other words, differentiated libido or Intent that has emerged from the pool of undifferentiated libido in the South. This sings with the Design of Energy, and Choices and Decisions, in the Northeast. This Southwest-Northeast axis is associated with what the Elders call the *connecting link with intent.* In order for something to happen, for an energy to move in the world, the *nagual* (the unconscious) and *tonal* (the conscious) need to come into proximity. In turn, for this to occur there has to be Choice, a Design of Energy, that links with our Needs, Wants, and Desires, or our Intent. This is the basis for all ceremony, magic, and healing.

When this proximity occurs, then time (the fourth dimension) is changed, spirit and matter touch, and synchronistic events occur.

Von Franz refers to this when she writes of the double mandala that is created when time-bound reality touches the eternal order, and how dreams with double motifs often refer to synchronicity. As the unconscious content approaches the threshold of consciousness, it splits into two. At the moment of a synchronistic event there is a *coniunctio* of psyche and matter; psyche behaves as if it were matter and matter as if it were psyche. An exchange takes place between the *hieros gamos* (the Dream), and the phenomenal world.[41] In ceremony, magic, dreams, prayer, or creative work, the veil between the seen and the unseen becomes thinner, the fifth dimension and the third dimension touch, and an infinity loop is created between the two and a doubling takes place (5 + 3 = 8) when something is about to emerge from the fifth into the third dimension.

While Jung was writing his paper on synchronicity, he also carved the face of a trickster—the archetype of synchronicity—on the West wall of the original Tower.[42] He said, "The so-called civilized man has forgotten the trickster. He remembers him only figuratively and metaphorically, when, irritated by his own ineptitude, he speaks of fate playing tricks on him or of things being bewitched."[43]

Another of Jung's carvings was the Bollingen Stone. In 1950, some months before Jung carved the trickster, he received a large block of stone for a wall he was building, but it was the wrong size and shape. Jung knew that it was *his* stone, however, and that he needed it for an as yet unknown purpose. During the following year he first carved a verse referring to the *lapis*, the alchemist's stone, on one of the side faces. Then on the front—facing the lake—he chiseled a little man, or Telesphoros, with an inscription in Greek. On the third face he carved a Latin inscription about the orphan as *Mercurius*.[44] Then, underneath the first verse, he carved a thanksoffering in remembrance of his 75th birthday. While carving the stone, Jung had begun his Chaotic Journey into the Little Northeast Moon. So the first manikin he carved, when he was in the South of the Little Southwest Moon at age 9, returned to him as the stone carving of the Telesphoros, across the Wheel in the Northeast.[45]

Looking at the Pattern of Jung's carvings we can see, as near as we can date them, that he did six of his nine carvings in the South of the Little Moon he was in at the time. Whenever he came up against a blank wall, he painted or worked in stone and each time this led him to new ideas.[46] The Rocks and Stones are the Keepers of Memory and when his creative energy (South) was blocked he was able to free it up, to create a new Dream (Southwest) by working in stone and fixing it in physical form (West). The exceptions to this internal process were the last three carvings he did. Two of them were carved in memory of Emma, and the third was a series of images of things to come, that were hidden in the future.

Notes

1   Job 6:7.
2   *Letters* 2, p. 155.
3   *Letters* 2, p. 116.
4   A medical doctor and colleague of Jung's since the 1920s who pioneered, with Eleanor Bertine and Kristine Mann, the development of analytical psychology in the USA, and is the author of *Women's Mysteries*.
5   The term used by the Christian theologian Origen (c. 185–254 C.E.) to refer to the first five books of the Bible that the Jews of the time called the "five-fifths" of the Torah.
6   *Letters* 1, p. 491.
7   Carl Jung, "The letters of C. G. Jung to Sabina Spielrein," in *Journal of Analytical Psychology* 46 (2001): 177.
8   *MDR*, pp. 8–9.
9   As far as we know, Jung reports only three dreams relating to his father—the one shortly after his death in 1896, the one in 1922 shortly before his mother's death, and this one in 1948.
10   In the dream Jung's mother was to turn 70 in 1948 and he had the dream in January of that year.
11   *CW* 14, § 272.
12   Akbar (1542–1605) was the third Mughal Emperor of India who established an empire from Afghanistan to the Bay of Bengal.

13 *Letters* 1, pp. 490–493.

14 *MDR*, p. 220.

15 *CW* 11, § 561.

16 *CW* 11, § 568 *ff.*

17 Donald Kalsched, *The Inner World of Trauma: Archetypal Defenses of the Personal Spirit* (London: Routledge, 1996), pp. 39–40.

18 *CW* 11, § 578, 587, 591.

19 Edward Edinger, *The Bible and the Psyche: Individuation Symbolism in the Old Testament* (Toronto: Inner City, 1986), pp. 35, 40, 49.

20 Job 27:5.

21 Job 40:4.

22 Job 42:4.

23 *CW* 11, § 661, 689.

24 Edward Edinger, *Transformation of the God-image: An Elucidation of Jung's Answer to Job* (Toronto: Inner City, 1992), pp. 71, 95, 130–132.

25 John Beebe, *Integrity in Depth* (New York: Fromm, 1995), pp. 15, 19.

26 Edinger, *Transformation of the God-image*, pp. 36–37.

27 Edinger, *Transformation of the God-image*, pp. 40–41.

28 Marie-Louise von Franz, *Alchemy: An Introduction to the Symbolism and the Psychology* (Toronto: Inner City, 1980), pp. 291–292.

29 *Letters* 2, p. 29.

30 The Spirit Personality is the "soul" or Image of Self that retains continuity of Memory from life to life. William Wordsworth said, "Not in entire forgetfulness. . . . But trailing clouds of glory do we come." This Memory is not normally available to the conscious ego, and it is the function of ceremony (particularly initiation ceremonies at puberty) to re-awaken this Memory. In this sense, most of the learning of wisdom or knowledge (as opposed to the gathering of information) is a remembering of what has been forgotten.

31 Ashley Montagu, *Touching: The Human Significance of the Skin* (3rd ed.), (San Francisco: HarperCollins, 1986).

32 Hannah Segal, *Introduction to the Work of Melanie Klein* (London: Hogarth, 1973), p. 35.

33 Wilfred Bion, *Learning from Experience* (Northvale, NJ: Jason Aronson, 1962), p. 36.

34 Otto Weininger, *Melanie Klein: From Theory to Reality* (London: Karnac, 1992), pp. 33, 37; Otto Weininger, *View from the Cradle: Children's Emotions in Everyday Life* (London: Karnac, 1993), p. 98.

35 Kalsched, *The Inner World of Trauma*, p. 98.

36 Marie-Louise von Franz, *On Dreams and Death: A Jungian Interpretation* (La Salle: Open Court, 1998), p. 62.

37 Weininger, *View from the Cradle: Children's Emotions in Everyday Life*, pp. 93, 149.

38 *CW* 8, § 967.

39 From a 1929 seminar, quoted in David Peat, *Synchronicity: The Bridge between Matter and Mind* (New York: Bantam, 1987), p. 22.

40 Marie-Louise von Franz, *On Divination and Synchronicity: The Psychology of Meaningful Chance* (Toronto: Inner City, 1980), pp. 50, 55–56, 101.

41 Von Franz, *On Divination and Synchronicity*, p. 116.

42 Barbara Hannah, *Jung: His Life and Work* (New York: Putnam, 1976), p. 308. Tricksters are common figures in mythology who are practical jokers. They flout convention and cause mischief and mayhem. They are associated with chance, chaos, and the unexpected, but also with creative and magical powers. For example: Coyote in North American mythologies and Loki in Nordic mythology.

43 *CW* 9i, § 478.

44 *MDR*, p. 227.

45 Hannah, *Jung: His Life and Work*, p. 309.

46 *MDR*, p. 175.

LITTLE EAST MOON
OF THE BIG NORTH —
ILLUMINATION OF
WISDOM AND KNOWLEDGE

Women grow to know the man they fell in love with;
men grow to love the woman they got to know.
(ANON.)

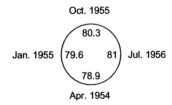

Oct. 1955

Jan. 1955 · 80.3 / 79.6 · 81 · Jul. 1956 · 78.9

Apr. 1954

T his Little East Moon saw the birth of Jung's major work on alchemy, *Mysterium Coniunctionis,* and the death of the two women who had walked his road with him throughout his life. After Jung had written *Aion, Answer to Job,* and the paper on synchronicity, the way was clear for him to devote himself to finishing *Mysterium Coniunctionis,* his goal ever since finishing *Psychology and Alchemy.* He had written the bulk of the first five sections before his illness in 1944, but it was only after he completed the other works that he wrote the sixth and last part on the *coniunctio* itself which contained the essence of the book—the union of the opposites.[1] He had begun writing the final chapter by the end of 1951, but in the autumn of 1952 Marie-Jeanne Schmid, his secretary for over twenty years, left in order to get married, which "delayed" the work; perhaps it was not yet ready to be born. If we can judge from the foreword, it was not finished until October 1954. It was Jung's *magnum opus* and fitting that it was born in this Little Moon—the Illumination and Enlightenment of Wisdom and Knowledge.

Again, we can see the Pattern of a 27-year cycle in the life of this creative child of Jung's. *Mysterium Coniunctionis* was completed in 1954, 27 years after its birth when Jung had the dream of the "other library" in an annex to his house, which contained books from the 16th century that were full of strange symbols. After that dream, he began collecting books related to alchemy. The editors of the *Collected Works* note that he was engaged in writing *Mysterium Coniunctionis* from 1941 to 1954.[2] When he began writing it in 1941 the book was 13 or 14 years old, an adolescent in the Little West Moon of the Big South, and Jung himself was in the Little West Moon of the Big North. The work entered the world as an adult at age 27, in the Little East Moon of the Big South, in 1954, when Jung was in the Little East Moon of the Big North.

TWO DEATHS

On March 21, 1953 Toni Wolff, Jung's *soror mystica*, died unexpectedly at age 65. Jung's tachycardia returned for several weeks and he was unable to attend the funeral. In October 1952, he had had a dream of a black elephant uprooting a tree, and felt this to be a warning of a death. At the time, he had assumed it was his own but later saw it as a harbinger of Toni's death.[3] As with the dream that foreshadowed his mother's death, this dream occurred five to six months beforehand. After Toni's death, he saw her again in a dream on the eve of Good Friday.[4]

Just two years later, in the spring of 1955, Emma fell ill with cancer and made a temporary recovery, but died on November 27, 1955 at age 73. These two deaths pierced Jung to the core, for now he had to live without Emma, his "Queen" and "foundation" of his house, and Toni, "the fragrance of the house."[5]

Again we can see Pattern if we look at Jung and Emma's relationship. Jung had first met Emma in 1896 when she was 14. We do not know when they met again as adults, but we do know that Emma turned down Jung's first proposal of marriage, and then they became engaged in July 1902 and were married in February 1903. If they had met again around November 1901, then Emma's death would have been on the 54th anniversary of their meeting—the beginning of the second Big Chaotic Journey of their relationship.

Jung had dreams of his parents, Toni, and Emma, either before they died or shortly after they died. Their deaths occurred when the energy of the North was strongly constellated for Jung. As we have seen, his father died when Jung was in the North of the Little North Moon of the Big South and his mother died when he was in the North of the Little North Moon of the Big West. Now in the Big North, Toni died when he was in the Northeast of the Little Northeast Moon, and Emma died when he was in the North of the Little East Moon. The veil drawn by time obscures our insight into what inner meaning this might have held for Jung, and so we can only notice the external Form and Pattern.

Shortly after Emma's death, in a letter to Erich Neumann on December 15, 1955, when Jung was standing in the place of the double Wisdom and Knowledge of Illumination and Enlightenment, he described an Illumination he experienced shortly before her death. "I had what one can only call a great illumination which, like a flash of lightning, lit up a centuries-old secret that was embodied in her and had exerted an unfathomable influence on my life."[6] After her death, in a vision-like dream, he saw Emma as she had been in her prime, with an objectively wise and understanding expression, unclouded by emotion.

During the following weeks, Jung said that what helped him most was not to dwell on the past, but to focus on why he had to be a survivor, and to give his whole energy to finding the purpose he still had to fulfill.[7] Franz Jung (Jung's only son) said his father was deeply depressed for over five months after Emma's death.[8] During the winter of 1955–1956 he carved the names of his paternal ancestors on three stone tablets and placed them in the courtyard of the Tower. This contact with stone helped Jung regain himself, and his writing in 1956–1957 grew out of the stone sculptures he carved.[9]

BOLLINGEN

In 1935 Jung had made another addition to Bollingen, adding a court-yard and loggia open to the lake that formed a fourth element to the trinity of the house.[10] He made no further changes to Bollingen until the spring of 1956, when he began making plans for a second storey to the low section of the 1927 annex that added the quintessence to the four existing elements. After Emma's death, he had felt an inner obligation to become himself *in toto*. He realized that he was the low, hidden section, and that he could no longer hide behind the maternal and spiritual towers, so he added the second storey which represent-ed his ego-personality. If Jung had built it at a younger age, it would have been a presumptuous grandiosity, but now it represented his life-time of hard-won wisdom and consciousness.[11]

Bollingen was built from 1923 to 1956, beginning two months after his mother's death and the last part built some months after Emma's death in 1955.[12] If we date it from its conception in the Dream—a gradual process, but let us say from the summer of 1922 when he purchased the land, or 1923 when he started to build—we can see the Moon Cycles of Jung's retreat.

The first building in 1923, the original Tower, was the home of the Self. In 1927, Jung added another tower "off to the side," con-nected to the original Tower by an annex. In his flowering tree dream of 1927 Jung had realized that we lived in a replica of the Self "off to the side." At the time of this first addition, Bollingen was four years old, and in the Little Southeast Moon of the Big South. The Southeast is the place of the Image of Self, a replica of the Self at the center of the Wheel.

In 1931, the building of the retiring room extended the second tower. At age 9, Bollingen was in the Little Southwest Moon of the Big South, the childhood of the Sacred Dream. In the seclusion of this retiring room, Jung began to do much of his writing and

Dreaming. In 1935, Bollingen was thirteen years old in the West of the Little West Moon of the Big South, and entering adolescence. Up until now, it had not been possible to sit outside without being in full view of passing boats. In the spirit of the shy extroversion of early adolescence, Jung built a walled courtyard and a loggia, a raised cooking area, where there was a full view of the lake and mountains, but with privacy from the lake. Now in 1956, Bollingen was 33 years old, in the Little Southeast Moon of the Big West, the place of the Illumination of Self-Image and Jung had built the addition as a symbol of his ego-personality. In 1961, when Jung died, Bollingen was 39 years old, in the Little West Moon of the Big West—the place of double Death and Change.

Notes

1 Barbara Hannah, *Jung: His Life and Work* (New York: Putnam, 1976), p. 311.

2 *CW* 14, p. v.

3 *Letters* 2, pp. 117–118, letter to James Kirsch, 28 May 1953.

4 Hannah, *Jung: His Life and Work*, p. 313.

5 Laurens van der Post, *Jung and the Story of Our Time*, p. 178.

6 *Letters* 2, p. 284.

7 Hannah, *Jung: His Life and Work*, p. 326.

8 David Rosen, *The Tao of Jung: The Way of Integrity* (London: Penguin Arkana, 1997), p. 151.

9 *MDR*, p. 175.

10 *MDR*, p. 224.

11 *MDR*, p. 225.

12 Hannah, *Jung: His Life and Work*, p. 156.

BIG EAST MOON—
ILLUMINATION AND
ENLIGHTENMENT

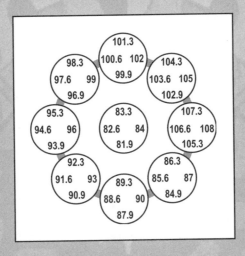

"Some energy you can thrust out into the sacred rounds of life and it will return to you like a boomerang."

"What kind of energy is that, Agnes?"

"The energy of creativity."

"What kind of creativity?" Agnes stuck the end of her awl into the pinkish sand and drew a circle.

"You remember the medicine wheel?" She winked at me. "Energy always returns to its source when it is born of creativity." She pointed the bone awl to the North position on the wheel. "In the North, your spirit is inspired with the Wisdom of an idea. You take it to the South, to Trust and Innocence and you dress that inspiration with a physical presence—you manifest your spirit, say, into a book. Then you travel North again for recognition and the fullness of your spirit becomes an exchange of energy with the world. There's a circle and new energy is born…"

—LYNN ANDREWS, *Crystal Woman*, p. 38.

LITTLE CENTER MOON
OF THE BIG EAST—
CATALYST OF ILLUMINATION
AND ENLIGHTENMENT

The spark becomes active at the moment of intuitive perception when the truth that we have heard a hundred times awakens a creative response and becomes alive in us. Then it, in turn, creates sparks from its own radiant center. And through this radiant quality man gives testimony not only to the wholeness of the Self but to the essence of the man's being, so enabling him to manifest that which was given him to bring forth.[1]

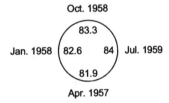

Oct. 1958

Jan. 1958   83.3

82.6   84   Jul. 1959

81.9

Apr. 1957

As our lives draw to a close, the light of Grandfather Sun begins to dawn in the Big East. On our eighty-first birthday we stand in the place of double Illumination and Enlightenment of Wisdom and Knowledge and we have the opportunity to review in the light of the consciousness we have gained, *deo concedente*, the Self-Images, Innocences, Dreams, Deaths, Patterns, Wisdoms, Decisions, and Illuminations of all the other Moon Cycles we have walked. It is also a time of looking forward to our journey around the Big East Moon from 81 to 108, and the Big Center Moon from age 108 to 135, either in substance or spirit.

At age 81, the significance of the number 9 becomes more apparent. The Elders say that all configurations and movements of energy in this universe can be expressed by the numbers 0 to 20. The number 9 sits in the Northeast of the Wheel and is the number of the

Design and Choreography of Energy. It is the last number before the return to unity (10); all energy moves in nine movements; the World Tree had nine roots plunging into nine springs, and the nine branches reached toward the nine heavens; Odin hung from the World Tree for nine days and nine nights pierced by a spear; there are nine planets; nine months of pregnancy; nine months in a Chaotic Journey; nine Little Moons in a Big Moon; and the 27 years in a Big Moon equal nine (2 + 7 = 9). So 9 is the number of becoming, a movement into a new cycle. Eighty-one years represents consciousness of Pattern (Pattern 8 + 1 Consciousness = 9 Movement), and is nine cycles of nine (9 x 9 = 81). Jung said, "Unless the conscious mind intervened, the unconscious would go on sending out wave after wave without result, like the treasure that is said to take nine years, nine months, and nine nights [3 x 9 = 27] to come to the surface and, if not found on the last night, sinks back to start all over again from the beginning."[2]

THE THIRD BIG CHAOTIC JOURNEY

A Big Chaotic Journey is different from a Little Chaotic Journey in that it is followed by a Little Center Moon—the Moon of the Catalyst energy—where our Free Will has the most "leverage," so to speak, and can change the form and expression of the rest of the Big Moon Cycle. In the Little Center Moons everything that is a lesser *coniunctio*, a projection, a ghost not laid to rest, re-emerges. Like the smelting of metal, the dross comes to the surface to be removed and further distill the Catalyst of our lives. As well, anything that has future potential comes closer to the horizon of consciousness. Everything, past and future, is thrown into the pot, to be stirred and combined in a new way, prior to moving into the Little Southeast Moons where the projections can be withdrawn. The Little Center Moon is both the *katalysis* and the *katabasis*, the taking apart and the bringing together.

So the Big Chaotic Journey involves a greater shift in archetypal energy than with a Little Chaotic Journey, and the Little Center Moon immediately following it is where we have the opportunity to redirect the movement of our life. The additive difference in the Big East Moon is that this is the Big Moon of consciousness, where all the processes are potentiated and amplified by the consciousness that has been won, or lost, in our journey around the Moon Cycles.

The Little Center Moon is the time of the light or shadow *coniunctio*. In alchemy, the lesser *coniunctio* is when the mixture is still impure and contaminated, and needs to be subjected to further procedures. The greater *coniunctio* is the goal of the *opus*, the supreme accomplishment, the Philosopher's Stone, the union of the opposites. Edward Edinger says of the greater *coniunctio*, "That which goes by the name of love is fundamental to the phenomenology of the *coniunctio*. Love is both cause and effect . . . object love is *objective* love, a love purged of personal desirousness, not one side of the pair of opposites, but rather beyond the opposites. This transpersonal love is at the root of all group and social loyalties such as the allegiance to family, party, nation, church and humanity itself. The extroverted aspect of the *coniunctio* promotes social interest and the unity of the human race; the introverted aspect promotes connection with the Self and the unity of the individual psyche."[3]

We see Pattern in Jung's relationship to love and the *coniunctio*. Shortly before his Little Center Moon in the Big West, he touched the light side of the lesser *coniunctio*—he and Emma were married in 1903 when Jung was 27. At age 54, in the Little Center Moon of the Big North, the shadow aspect of the lesser *coniunctio* began, leading up to the Nazi controversies in the 1930s. Now, at age 81 in the Little Center Moon of the Big East, Jung approached the greater *coniunctio*, the synthesis of his life's work.

As in the previous Big Chaotic Journey into the Big North, the biographical record is mute compared to other periods of his life. It was the first winter after Emma's death, and in the following summer, we find him beginning to carve a stone in her memory, and painting and mending at Bollingen. If we look to his letters there was nothing that distinguished his correspondence from the tenor or content of letters at other times—with one exception. The Medicine of the Little Center Moons is that all things unfinished return for the purpose of

resolution (the "return of the repressed"). Here, Jung wrote one letter, harking back to the past, that stands out like an incongruous
image in a dream, and as such, it leads to a web of associations.

Shortly before the end of his Big Chaotic Journey, on March 28,
1957, Jung received a long letter from Walter Cimbal about developments in psychiatry to which he replied briefly. Cimbal had been the
managing editor of the *Zentralblatt* journal during the storm of
protest in 1934 and, as far as we know, had been responsible for the
publishing of the Nazi supplement in the international edition of the
journal. There had been a flurry of letters between them in 1934, but
this was the only time Jung and Cimbal had corresponded in the
intervening years and they never corresponded again. Was Jung
being reminded of his dealings with Göring and the Nazis?

If we follow this web further to see if there were any other references to the 1930s in Jung's correspondence during his 1956–1957
Chaotic Journey, we find only one other letter. On February 23,
1957, he replied to a request to publish a letter he had written to
James Joyce in 1932. We shall see later that this link to Joyce will
connect us to another singular, atypical letter that referred to both
Joyce and Picasso, and was connected to Jung's death.

One other letter of note during Jung's Big Chaotic Journey contains one of his most quoted aphorisms. But, as background to this
letter, let us see what Aniela Jaffé said about her first day, in mid-1955,
of her new role as Jung's secretary. "Because of his wife's severe illness
the atmosphere in the house was muted.... Then we went upstairs to
the library. Pulling a little key from his pocket, he opened a narrow
safe let into the wall, which he called his 'cache,' and took out the four
fragments of the bread knife that had exploded with a loud bang
when he was experimenting with occultism as a student. He asked me
to mount the four pieces as one, with that I was dismissed."[4]

The letter was from a man in his early 70s who had written to
Jung about his three marriages to talented women. Since the death of
his second wife, he had heard tapping and doors opening in his bed-
room. In his reply of August 1956, Jung wrote that the man's choice
of wives were expressions of his anima and, regrettably for him, his

wives were competent enough to do what he should have done in an incompetent way. "In practice it means that the woman of your choice represents your own task you did not understand."[5]

This letter was written nine months after Emma's death and in it, Jung captures the essence of anima projection more succinctly than anywhere in his writings. We have seen that he had a "great illumination" before her death, and from his letters we know that in July 1956 Jung was carving a stone in her memory. The knife that had shattered into pieces on a summer's day in 1896 had been kept for fifty-nine years in the safe, and as Emma lay dying, Jung had the pieces re-united. On its Moon Cycles, the event was in the North of the Little Southeast Moon of the Big North—the double Wisdom and Knowledge of Self-Images. In re-uniting the broken knife that had been split, and during this Big Chaotic Journey, was Jung coming to a new consciousness of what Emma had carried for him all these years?

LATE WRITINGS

One notices in Jung's writing after *Mysterium Coniunctionis* a hopeful despair, or a despairing hope, about the world. He was slightly optimistic that good might win out over evil.[6] The "Sage of Kusnacht," as others had come to see him, was beset with increasing calls for his views on the state of the world—the Korean War, the suppression of the Hungarian uprising by Russia in 1956, the Suez Crisis, the occupation of Tibet by China, and the ever-present threat of nuclear war. As Jung had done before, in the Little Center and Little Southeast Moons from 1902–1908 and 1929–1935, he turned his attention to the affairs of the world-at-large. In the Little Center Moon in the Big South, Jung's concern for the world had been the treatment of the mentally ill at Burghölzli; in the Big West it was Nazi Germany; now it was Russia, the Cold War, and the nuclear arms race.

He seemed, however, to find his own ground more quickly than in the 1930s: "The world situation has reached the stage where even the most stirring words no longer mean anything. What matters more now, it seems to me, is for each of us to be sure of his own attitude. . . . Talk has become much too cheap. Being is harder, and therefore easily replaced by words."[7]

In the spring of 1956 he wrote *The Undiscovered Self (Present and Future)*, which was published in March 1957. It was written as a response to the many questions that had been asked of him about the future of the world. He expressed anxious concern about what the end of the millennium might hold and for the future of the individual ("the makeweight that tips the scales") in mass culture: "If the individual is not truly regenerated in spirit, society cannot be either, for society is the sum total of individuals in need of redemption."[8] "Resistance to the organized mass can be effected only by the man who is as well organized in his individuality as the mass itself."[9]

Shortly after finishing *The Undiscovered Self*, he turned to writing his paper on UFO's, *Flying Saucers: A Modern Myth*, a subject he had been interested in since after the war. Just as his undergraduate investigations into spiritualism had led him to explore subjects off the beaten track, he now explored the psychic aspect of UFO's as a fascination with, and projection of, the archetype of the Self.

In 1958 Jung was in the Northwest of the Little Center Moon of the Big East, the place of the Illumination of the Catalyst of Laws and Patterns, and he wrote *A Psychological View of Conscience*. This is an essay about the distinction between civil, social, and religious law, and Sacred Law, between conscience and the moral code—all concerns of the Northwest. If our conscience is allowed to make every decision according to the moral standards of right and wrong, we include only one opposite and are deaf to the *vox Dei*, whether that be called voice of God or voice of the Self. Jung had known since he was 12, with his experience in the cathedral square, that God asks more of us than obedience to the moral code.[10]

> Distinct from this [conscience in its ordinary usage] is the ethical form of conscience, which appears when two decisions or ways of acting, both affirmed to be moral and therefore regarded as "duties," collide with one another. In these cases, not foreseen by the moral code because they are mostly

very individual, a judgment is required which cannot properly be called "moral" or in accord with custom. . . . The decid-
ing factor appears to be something else: it proceeds not from
the traditional moral code but from the unconscious foundation of the personality.... It is true that these conflicts of duty
are solved very often and very conveniently by a decision in
accordance with custom, that is, by suppressing one of the
opposites. . . . If one is sufficiently conscientious the conflict
is endured to the end and a creative solution emerges which
is produced by the constellated archetype and possesses that
compelling authority not unjustly characterized as the voice
of God . . . it embraces conscious and unconscious and therefore transcends the ego.[11]

SEEING THE DREAM

Jung entered this Big East Moon on his own. Emma, his earth, his
foundation, and Toni, his medial Salome, had both passed away, and
he had learned the limits and potentials of his prophetic, Cassandra
anima of the 1930s. Cassandra was the daughter of Priam and
Hecuba, the king and queen of Troy. Apollo appeared to her and
offered her the gift of prophecy if she would lie with him. She accepted the gift but did not keep her part of the bargain. Apollo, unable to
take back a gift already given, begged her to give him one kiss and
he breathed into her mouth (like Care with Faust) insuring no one
would believe her prophecies. Cassandra could see the Dream of the
People, both light and shadow, and what was hidden in the future,
but she was not believed.

Jung suffered the anguish of Cassandra, "O woe, O woe, O woe!
The torment of seeing sweeps me away again." Laurie Layton
Schapira writes of her: "Just as the dream belongs to the collective,
so does medial knowledge. We no longer have institutions to honor
and utilize mediality, as did the ancients. Therefore we must, as individuals, be open to the collective value of the messages that come
through ourselves and others. . . . Because of their source in the

collective shadow, her prophecies are seditious; they threaten the conservative order. Thus she speaks treason. Until the intrinsic value of mediality can be accepted, we shall continue to attack her for bearing bad tidings."[12]

Jung saw what was at work in the Dream, the archetypal realm, and in May 1956 he wrote that for a long time he had been misunderstood, despite careful, reasoned argument, and "I have resigned myself to being posthumous."[13] Neither he, nor Western culture, had any traditions or structures that could protect him against the impact of seeing the collective Dream, or give legitimacy to what he saw. He had to create his own myth, his own container. Jung consistently presented himself, and indeed was in part, the Apollonian, empirical scientist who was concerned with demonstrable facts, and what could be proven by the senses and consciousness. But he was also a Cassandra and struggled to clothe his intuition in respectable garments that could be seen by others. Laurens van der Post said: "Already in his first years as a medical student at Basel he was reprimanding himself, 'I must stop talking to others out of my intuition. I must talk more out of facts. Somehow, somewhere, I must find the facts to match my intuition.'"[14] On Jung's 60th birthday, Albert Oeri, an old friend from his student days, said that in those early days Jung underwent a test of personal courage when he studied spiritualist literature but stood by his convictions unless they were modified by further evidence.[15]

Jung was a pioneer in trying to hold these Apollonian-Cassandran polarities in proximity, for which he paid a price. There is much between the lines in Jung's writing. He spoke of the "double floor" of meaning in his books (which was sometimes lost in the translation to English) and it is obvious that he knew more than he wrote. He was interested in what the collective would have considered in his time, and still does, as irrational, fringe, or marginal subjects, not fit for legitimate inquiry other than as objects of distant scholastic interest—Mithraism, Gnosticism, alchemy, parapsychology, UFOs, synchronicity—the list is long. Sherry Salman said that Jung was reluctant to acknowledge these esoteric roots and this has resulted in the occult background to Jung's thinking falling into the Jungian collective shadow, and thereby breeding many misconceptions. But the ancient tools of magic and imagination, which Jung understood, have been reborn in many post-modern ideas about the nature of mind and psyche.[16]

Jung perhaps knew the guns too well and was more circumscribed in later years as to what he revealed about his esoteric interests and what he saw. This would have been prudent; what he did write elicited more than enough censure and attack. But as he withdrew externally to shield himself from criticism, did he also shrink internally from his own visionary capacities? Did he wish, understandably, to disbelieve himself, to censor his own Cassandran vision? In his 1929 seminars, he spoke of the fateful events to come as the Age of Pisces drew to a close. Did all this lead to the curious *tabula rasa* around the time of the Big Chaotic Journey and Little Center Moon from 1929–1932, and the curious reminder of those times, in the letter from Cimbal, during his Big Chaotic Journey in 1957?

Living close to the Dream takes a toll on the physical body and surrounding matter, and all of this, perhaps, exacted its due. Between 1959 and up to a month before his death, Jung and Miguel Serrano, the writer and poet who had been Chilean ambassador to India, struck up a friendship. Serrano noticed "what had also struck others who had compared the mature man with pictures from his youth, namely the dissimilarity between then and now in the face of this man who had had to go through a drastic transformation, which was visible even in his physiognomy and clearly could not be explained as merely the result of age. This could be noted as early as Jung's fifties and sixties."[17]

In 1958, Jung carved the figure of a woman milking a mare, with a female bear rolling a round sphere toward the woman's back, on the West outer wall of the original Tower. Above the woman, he chiseled the words: "May the light I carried in my womb arise. 1958." Above the horse: "Pegasus, living spring, the water poured out by the water carrier." Above the bear: "The bear who moves the mass."[18] The bear is the symbol of the savage strength and energy of

Artemis; the ball is being brought to the woman as a symbol of individuation; the primitive woman is milking Pegasus (Greek, meaning "fount horse"), and the constellation Pegasus stands above the second fish in Pisces, which precedes Aquarius in the precession of the equinoxes. Jung carved these figures when he was in the Northwest of the Little Center Moon of the Big East—the Illumination of the Laws and Patterns of the Catalyst energy. He said they expressed future events still concealed in the archetypal realm. In the latter half of the 20th century the feminine has begun to emerge from its banishment and oppression to become a potent archetypal force in the collective consciousness.

MEMORIES

From 1956 onward, a great deal of pressure was brought to bear on Jung to give his attention to an autobiography, but if he had followed his own inclination he would likely have written something on the archetypes of numbers.[19] He was skeptical of autobiography and the perils of self-portrayal, and dreaded the reaction to its publication. With the memory of the hostility aroused by *Answer to Job* still fresh, and after much doubt and hesitation, he agreed to do it.[20] Although he was active in its authorship he always spoke of it as Aniela Jaffé's project to which he had made contributions. At his specific request, it was not included in the *Collected Works*.

In the spring of 1957, when he was in the South of the Little Center Moon of the Big East—the Illumination of the Catalyst of Mythology—he began work on *Memories* with Aniela Jaffé, who said that she often asked Jung for specific details of events but it seemed that only the spiritual distillate of his life was worth the effort of telling. And so Jung began to write his own story, his Mythology, the Story-That-Gives-Life. The objective truth of this story was irrelevant, the only question was whether it was his truth or not.[21]

He soon warmed to the task and he and Jaffé worked on it one afternoon a week, he talking and she taking notes. By the end of 1957, images of his childhood began to emerge and he told Jaffé that he wished to write his recollections down directly. After he had made that decision, the unconscious was not going to let him off the hook, and he remarked to Jaffé that the autobiography was taking quite a different direction from what he had imagined. If he neglected to write, disagreeable physical symptoms followed, and as soon as he set to writing, they vanished.

By April 1958 he had finished the first three chapters on childhood, school days, and university, up to the completion of his medical studies in 1900. And so, by the end of his third Big Chaotic Journey, he had recapitulated his life up to his first Big Chaotic Journey. Jung wrote the penultimate chapter "Late Thoughts," perhaps the most personal chapter in the book, in January 1959, when he told Jaffé that he felt compelled to write again.[22] This chapter is in three sections; first, the relationship to the creator, light and dark; second, the individual and the ego; and the third, Eros or love—a fitting trinity with which to end the book.

We know, from Miguel Serrano's conversation with Jung on May 5, 1959, that around this time Jung had been reflecting on love, as he said to Serrano, in a reverie: "Once there was a flower, a stone, a crystal, a queen, a king, a place, a lover and his beloved, somewhere, a long, long, time ago, on an island in the middle of the ocean, five thousand years ago. . . . Such a thing is love, the mystical flower of the soul. That is the center of the Self . . ."[23]

Love is the Catalyst energy that turns the Wheels, it is the Breath of Life that moves through all things. Jung wrote "Late Thoughts," and made his comments to Serrano, when he was in the North of the Little Center Moon of the Big East—the Illumination of the Wisdom and Knowledge of the Catalyst energy.

Jung finished his direct contributions to *Memories* by writing about his 1925 trip to Kenya, where the cosmic meaning of consciousness had become clear to him for the first time. He completed this by the summer of 1959, in the East of the Little Center Moon of the Big East, the place of double Illumination and Enlightenment of the Catalyst energy.

Notes

1   Frances Wickes, *The Inner World of Choice* (Englewood Cliffs, NJ: Prentice-Hall, 1963), p. 279.
2   *CW* 12, § 111.
3   Edward Edinger, *Anatomy of the Psyche: Alchemical Symbolism in Psychotherapy* (La Salle, IL: Open Court, 1985), p. 223.
4   Aniela Jaffé, *From the Life and Work of C. G. Jung* (New York: Harper, 1971), p. 123.
5   *Letters* 2, p. 321. We might also add "Hanging and wiving go by destiny." (George Farquahar).
6   *MDR*, p. 359.
7   Quoted in Gerhard Wehr, *Jung: A Biography* (Boston: Shambhala, 1987), p. 432.
8   *CW* 10, § 536.
9   *CW* 10, § 540.
10 Hannah, *Jung: His Life and Work* (New York: Putnam, 1976), p. 339.
11 *CW* 10, § 856.
12 Laurie Layton Schapira, *The Cassandra Complex: Living with Disbelief, A Modern Perspective on Hysteria* (Toronto: Inner City, 1988), pp. 147–148.
13 *Letters* 2, p. 299.
14 Laurens van der Post, *Jung and the Story of Our Time* (London: Penguin, 1976), p. 104.
15 Jaffé, *From the Life and Work of C. G. Jung*, p. 3.
16 Sherry Salman, "Dissociation and the Self in the Magical Pre-Oedipal Field," in *Journal of Analytical Psychology* 44 (1999): 78.
17 Wehr, *Jung: A Biography*, p. 448.
18 Aniela Jaffé, ed., *C. G. Jung: Word and Image* (Princeton: Princeton University Press, 1979).
19 Barbara Hannah, *Jung: His Life and Work*, p. 339.
20 *MDR*, p. viii.
21 *MDR*, p. 3.
22 *MDR*, p. vii.
23 Miguel Serrano, *C. G. Jung and Herman Hesse: A Record of Two Friendships* (New York: Schocken, 1966), p. 60.

LITTLE SOUTHEAST MOON
OF THE BIG EAST—ILLUMINATION
AND ENLIGHTENMENT
OF IMAGES OF SELF

It is time to be old, to take in sail.[1]

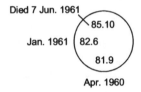

B efore we look at Jung's last Little Chaotic Journey, let us look back at the events during all his Chaotic Journeys, or within four to five months on either side (see Table 1, pp. 256–257). Without some form of qualitative or quantitative analysis, we do not know whether the incidence of events was more frequent, or of more emotional gravity, than during any other nine-month period in Jung's life. To know the answer to that, we would have to consult the feeling function of Jung himself.

By 1959, Jung felt his writing days were over. On January 23, 1960 he had another slight embolism, and afterward was confined to bed for a month. "Retrospect" is the last chapter of *Memories*, and was probably written in late 1959, when he was on his last Chaotic Journey, into the Little Southeast Moon of the Big East, the place of the Illumination of Images of Self. He opens the chapter by declining

Table 1. *Jung's Chaotic Journeys.*
Bold entries indicate Big Chaotic Journeys.

Year	Age	Events
1875	0–0.9	No recorded events
1878	3.0–3.9	Eczema; Phallus dream
1881	6.0–6.9	No recorded events
1884	9.0–9.9	Carves manikin
1887	12.0–12.9	Fainting spells; cathedral and turd vision
1890	15.0–15.9	Mother recommends *Faust*
1893	18.0–18.9	Dream of the "little light" of consciousness
1896	21.0–21.9	Father dies; radiolarian dream; meets Emma
1899	24.0–24.9	No recorded events
1902	**27.0–27.9**	Becomes engaged to and marries Emma; re-reads Freud's *Interpretation of Dreams*
1905	30.0–30.9	Publishes dissertation; writes first letter to Freud
1908	33.0–33.9	Height of Sabina Spielrein affair; visits Freud—"reports" in the bookshelf; Freud faints
1911	36.0–36.9	Begins relationship with Toni Wolff; dream of assemblage of distinguished spirits; dream of 12th-century knight; beginning of break with Freud
1914	39.0–39.9	Repetitive dream of catastrophe; beginning of descent into the unconscious; beginning of WWI

Table 1. Jung's Chaotic Journeys (cont.)
Bold entries indicate Big Chaotic Journeys.

Year	Age	Events
1917	42.0–42.9	End of descent; end of WWI
1920	45.0–45.9	Journey to North Africa; Kasbah dream; Buckinghamshire hauntings
1923	48.0–48.9	No recorded events
1926	51.0–51.9	Begins Bollingen; flowering tree dream; alchemy dream of being caught in the 17th century; sandfly fever
1929	**54.0–54.9**	Writes Stages of Life; Great Depression
1932	57.0–57.9	Paper on Picasso; accepts Presidency of IGMSP
1935	60.0–60.9	Addition to Bollingen
1938	63.0–63.9	Freud dies; dysentery; Nazis annex Austria, WWII begins
1941	66.0–66.9	Exhaustion and recurrent heart problems
1944	69.0–69.9	Near-fatal heart attack
1947	72.0–72.9	Begins writing Aion; forms Jung Institute; Uriah dream
1950	75.0–75.9	Writes Answer to Job; carves Bollingen Stone; hepatitis
1953	78.0–78.9	Toni Wolff dies
1956	**81.0–81.9**	Letter from Walter Cimbal; disclosure to Billinsky; begins work on Memories
1959	84.0–84.9	Finishes Memories; wolverine dream; letter to Read re: Picasso

to accept others' description of him as a sage or a wise man. During the last decade of life, Jung vowed not to identify with any archetype, especially that of the wise old man, the archetype of meaning, and held the tension between meaning and meaninglessness.[2] He goes on to say that the unconscious itself and his early dreams determined the course of his life from the outset. The first dream that Jung had at the age of 3, when he was also on a Chaotic Journey into the Southeast, anticipated the creative principle that suffused his life—his fate that stood in the Northwest. The phallus represented the creative principle of Nature that was striving toward light and consciousness.

In "Retrospect," he also speaks of the fated creativity that was his, and sums up his Self-Image, the ego's view of itself, in the light of that fate. He had to obey a law that was imposed on him from inside and paradoxically left him without free will: "The daimon of creativity has ruthlessly had its way with me." But he did not always obey it for life cannot be without inconsistency. He felt unable to judge himself or his life and had come to a place where he was without convictions other than the feeling that something outside his ken had carried him along through his life.[3]

In the final passage in *Memories* he comes full circle, and perhaps gives words to the Self's view of the ego, which has carried the Self in the world for a lifetime: "The more uncertain I have felt about myself, the more there has grown up in me a feeling of kinship with all things. In fact it seems to me as if that alienation which so long separated me from the world has become transferred to my own inner world, and has revealed to me an unexpected unfamiliarity with myself."[4]

THE MEDICINE OF THE WOLVERINE

Not long after his 85th birthday on July 25, 1960, Jung dreamed of the "other Bollingen," which he had dreamed of before in various stages of construction. This time, he saw the other Bollingen suffused in a glow of light, and a voice told him that it was now complete and ready for habitation. Then, far below in a stretch of water, he saw a mother wolverine teaching her children to dive and swim.[5]

We don't know the date of the dream, but Jung had become quite seriously ill the night of his 85th birthday, so that his doctor had to be called to the hotel where Jung was staying in Onnens, in western Switzerland. When he was well enough to travel, he returned, by ambulance, to Kusnacht to convalesce, and he had the dream "not long" after his return. So we might place the dream some time in August 1960. Was his death conceived in the Dream some nine months before he died?

The dream image of the polarity of spirit (Bollingen) and instinct (the wolverine) was much of what Jung's life was about—uniting these opposites in the wholeness of being human. The Circle of Law gathers to ensure that the laws of the People remain aligned with the Laws of the Creator. Each of the eight directions on the Circle of Law has a medicine animal that is the Keeper of the power of that direction. The Center is the place of the Children's Fire and the medicine animal of the Center is the wolverine. The wolverine is the Keeper of Personal Medicine Power and it is the guardian of the Children's Fire just as Jung was the guardian of the *principium individuationis*, the "little light" of consciousness.

The wolverine is a mostly carnivorous mammal that inhabits the northern regions of North America, Asia, and Europe; it is nocturnal, does not hibernate, and usually travels alone except during the breeding season. It can be fiercely aggressive, can sense at some distance when its territory is invaded, and will stand its ground if intruded upon. In the dream, we see the maternal aspect of the wolverine image teaching its young to adapt to a new element, as Jung's spirit was preparing to do. The Dream Teachers teach through the medicine animals. For Jung, the spiritual work (Bollingen) was complete but it was under the tutelage of the animals, far below, where the instinctual teaching would be continued.

SHADOW DREAMING

If we look for other events that occurred nine months before Jung's death, we find nothing of note in the published record other than a letter Jung wrote about Picasso, that, like the Cimbal letter, recalls the past and leads us into a web of associations. To help us understand the issues that this letter raises we need to digress and look at the light and dark sides of death.

The Elders say Cosmic Law teaches that Birth gives Life, Life gives Movement, Movement gives Change, Change gives Chaos, Chaos gives Death, and Death gives Birth—in each moment. As Bob Dylan said, "He who is not busy being born is busy dying." So Death is the Benevolent Death, the Death-That-Gives-Life. However, Humans are Determiners and have been given the Gift of Free Will with which to make Choices and Decisions, and so Humans can choose either for Life, or choose against Life and dream the Shadow Dream. If the Mother Law (All Things are Born of the Feminine) and the Child Law (Nothing Shall be Done to Harm the Children) are crossed, then what is born is Death-Death, not the Death-That-Gives-Life where destruction is in the service of creation.

Over millennia, the Shadow Dream has grown, particularly in the last two thousand years where there has been an idealization of spirit and a debasing of matter. When we identify too much with spirit, nature itself becomes demonic.[6] The Elders say that around the beginning of the 1300s, like a cloud saturated with moisture that precipitates rain, this accumulation of Choices against Life, the crossing of the Child Law, reached sufficient quantity and intensity that it precipitated out Stalking Death, an entity that had Form and Intent in the Dream. In Christian theology, this is called "Satan" or "Evil." Over the centuries, the Shadow Dreaming of the People had become alive.

If we use the Moon Cycles to view the last 2000 years we can see this process of Shadow Dreaming from another perspective. As an archetypal patterning of time, the Moon Cycles are applicable to any humanly created division of time that has had attention and focus over millennia, sufficient for it to have weight and meaning in the collective unconscious. The Christian measurement of time has been in years and centuries since the birth of Christ. So, like a human life, the history of Christianity (and Europe as the cradle of Christianity) can be put on the Moon Cycles with the "units" being centuries instead of years as with the human lifespan (i.e. one century is equal to one year of human life). If we do this then we can see that Western culture is about "twenty years" old. In the year 2000, we stand just past the Northwest of the Little North Moon of the Big South.

If we now look to the 13th century we see that 1350 C.E. (13 ½ centuries equals 13.6 human years) was the West of the Little West Moon of the Big South, the time of early adolescence and the place of double Death and Change. The 1300s were a momentous time in European history, encompassing the rise of nationalism and state power against the Church that had held sway for centuries, great social turmoil, the explosion of intellectual and artistic creativity in the Renaissance, and a sharp increase in the persecution of Jews across Europe. Beginning in China in 1333, the Black Death spread across the Middle East to Europe and between 1345 and 1350, the population of Europe was reduced from 75 million to 50 million, with over 50 percent mortality in some places. The bubonic plague killed more people worldwide than any other war or natural event in history.

Edinger refers to a similar idea when he writes about the "nodal points" of the last two thousand years. He says the year 1000 C.E. was the end of the age of the first fish (Christ) and the beginning of the age of the second fish (the Antichrist). About 1500 C.E., the anti-Christian aspect of the aeon came into its own and at that time, "an absolute explosion in the collective psyche took place."[7]

In the year 1500, Europe and Christianity stood in the East of the Little West Moon of the Big South—the place of the Death and Change of the Illusion of Trust and Innocence—and on October 12, 1492, Christopher Columbus "discovered" Turtle Island. Christianity's Chaotic Journey from 1500–1575 from the Little West Moon into the Little Northwest Moon of the Big South (from Death and Change to Laws and Patterns) was the beginning of the incursion of Christian laws and European customs into the Americas, and their eventual colonization. World War II occurred just prior to the West of the Little North Moon of the Big South (1950)—the place of the Death and Change of Wisdom and

Knowledge of Trust and Innocence. Between 2020 and 2025 (depending which date is used for the birth of Christ—0 C.E. or the more historically accurate 4–8 B.C.E.) Western culture will be in the North of the Little North Moon of the Big South—the double Wisdom and Knowledge of Trust and Innocence.

So from the 1300s onward, Stalking Death has had Form and Intent in the Dream and this Intent is to unwind the Circle of Creation. It was this dark side of the Great Mystery that Jung dealt with at length in *Answer to Job*. From that time on, those who chose to use their Free Will for personal ends, and not within Sacred Law, could Dream the Shadow Dream and decide with full consciousness to work on the dark side. Von Franz elaborates:

> Primitive peoples distinguish with great accuracy between a man who is possessed by a "spirit," that is, by an archetypal content, and is therefore in need of treatment, and a shaman or medicine man who knows how to control spirits and can give them free rein to work their powers through him without becoming possessed himself. . . . The symbolic inner experiences which the shaman lives through during his period of initiation are identical with the symbolic experiences the man of today lives through during the individuation process. One may therefore say that the shaman or the medicine man was the most individuated, that is, the most conscious, person of the group to which he belonged. From the very beginning, however, even in this early stage, the shaman's shadow appeared, namely the psychopathic black magician, who misused his inner experience (the experience of the spirit-world) for personal power aims. The real shaman has an unintended power in that the spirits, especially the archetype of the Self, stand behind him, but the black magician claims collective power with his ego and consequently is psychically ill.[8]

In using their Free Will to choose, Humans are always birthing twins—the road we take and the road we do not take. The choice may be highly conflicted (and indeed, if there is no conflict, then there has not really been a choice) and with great attachment to the road not taken. The letting go may be a wrenching loss. We have regrets, nostalgia, and melancholy, and think "if only." Sometimes thinking of it at all is too painful. One twin is taken home, the other is left to die; a light twin and a shadow twin. Unless we make the perilous choice consciously, knowing that either way we'll get it wrong, unless we mourn, then the shadow twin sinks into the unconscious or, we might say, unconsciously becomes part of the Shadow Dream.

In every decision and the contemplation of a decision there are two forces. One is the Desire or Intent (the spirit) that stands behind the decision, the other is the manifestation (the body or form) the Desire takes on. The ego may, by way of protecting itself against disappointment or hurt, insist on a particular form to the Desire. And in its insistence it may miss a thousand other possible forms of the same Desire. If the Desire is not met in the particular form in which it has been imagined, the ego, feeling betrayed, disappointed, and hurt by Life, attacks and banishes both the Desire and the form. The form dissolves, and was of no consequence in the first place, but the disowned Desire is set loose in the Dream, like a lost spirit still looking for the body that has not had a proper burial. It becomes a psychic free radical, so to speak. If we can unlink Desire and form, and not have them yoked and lashed together by the ego, then we allow Life to give form to our Desire in its own way. We can sacrifice the form (and this may be half a life's work), but can retain the Intent; we bury the body and recycle the Desire.

Once Stalking Death had been constellated, individuals who worked with the Shadow Dream were no longer isolated. They could now align their individual Will with the Will of this shadow side of the Self. They could now harvest the lost, disowned, or unconscious Desires let loose in the Dream, and work to manifest the Shadow Dream in the third dimension for their own ends. Such is the basis of all black magic. Jung said that the best protection against evil is knowledge of one's own shadow—that is, knowing where the bodies of Desire are buried and mourning them consciously.

The Elders say that when we die, when Benevolent Death comes, our Shields—the Self-Images that we have created during a lifetime—are dispersed, and Benevolent Death, the Death-that-gives-Life, takes our Spirit Personality back to the Great Round. At the moment of death and shortly after, as the Spirit Personality makes its journey back to the Ancestors, it is also vulnerable to being taken by Stalking Death, in its desire to destroy the birth that comes at the moment of death. If this happens, death becomes Death-Death, the Death-that-gives-Death, and a page is removed from the Book of Life. Hollywood, which dreams for the collective, produces many archetypal images, and in the movie *Ghost* there are several scenes where, as people die, dark forms come out of the shadows and take the departing spirit away. All cultures have specific ceremonies and knowledge to assist the dead in the journey back to the "other side."[9]

PICASSO AND THE BIRTH OF DEATH

With the notion of the shadow side of death in mind let us return to Jung's letter. On September 2, 1960 he wrote a letter to Sir Herbert Read concerning modern art and Picasso.[10] Read (1893–1968) was a British poet, art critic, and later one of the editors of the *Collected Works*.

The letter was written four and a half months after Jung had finished his Chaotic Journey from the Little Center into the Little Southeast Moon. The only other time we find Jung writing about Picasso is the November 1932 article that I discussed previously (see pp. 153–155). Jung wrote that article when he was on a Chaotic Journey from the Little Center to the Little Southeast Moon in the Big North, and nine months before a death, as we shall see. What can we make of this mention of Picasso, after 27 years of silence, at almost the same place on the Moon Cycles? We shall see that for Jung, Picasso may have symbolized the dark side of his own death.

Is this letter to Read also similar to the other ghost from the past in the letter from Cimbal in 1957, one Little Moon Cycle earlier, that harkened back to the ill-fated year of 1934? In that year Jung was continuing to give his weekly seminars and in March 1934, his class voted to move on from the Visions of Christiana Morgan to the subject of Nietzsche's Zarathustra. In the summer of 1934 they reached the episode on the fate of the rope dancer. Jung had mentioned this in his 1932 article and in reference to the possible catastrophe that might befall Picasso.

In the letter to Read, Jung writes of James Joyce and Picasso as "masters of the fragmentation of aesthetic contents and the accumulators of ingenious shards," and of Joyce's *Ulysses* where "a world comes down in an almost endless, breathless stream of debris." He also clarified his earlier position on Picasso saying that he was not diagnosing him a schizophrenic but only emphasizing the analogy to the schizophrenic process. However, he was still of the same view of Picasso's work as too much of decay and siding with the forces of disorder, but also felt that Picasso knew and understood the depths of the psyche. In a reply to a letter in September 1952 about the "magical" and "daemonic" with regard to artistic creation, Jung linked modern art with black magic. He said that the chaotic forces embodied in modern art are antithetical to the orderliness of consciousness, although this fertile chaos of new ideas is needed. However such disorder needs symbolic or religious containers, to allow the separation of the constructive elements from the destructive elements in the chaos. This containment has a magical effect that binds the destructive forces and in ancient times this was called white magic. Black magic, however, amplifies the destructive forces. "In so far as modern art uses such means as ends in themselves and thereby increases the state of disorder it can be described outright as black magic."[11] Jung lived close to the unconscious and was both familiar with its creative potential and, rightly, afraid of its destructive potential. Is it possible that in Picasso, this other immensely creative man, was a shadow brother who represented not only strength but also the forces of dissolution and decay that Jung had fought so much of his life against?

To take us further, let us look at what Jung writes in *Memories*. In the chapter "On Life after Death," he relates a terrifying dream he had the night before his mother's death, while he was staying at Tessin. In the dream he was in a dense, gloomy forest and heard an earsplitting whistle and an enormous wolfhound burst from the bushes. He knew that the Wild Huntsman had commanded the hound to take a human soul. Jung woke in terror and the following morning received news of his mother's death. She had been taken to her ancestors—"negatively to the 'wild horde,' but positively to the . . . blessed folk."[12] On his way home from Tessin, he alternated between hearing dance music and laughter, as though a wedding were being celebrated, and the devastating impression the dream had made on him—between warmth and joy, terror and grief. He said that "death is indeed a fearful piece of brutality" and all that is left is its icy stillness.[13]

Jung was no stranger to evil, as we can see from what he wrote in *Aion* about the shadow: "With a little self-criticism one can see through the shadow—so far as its nature is personal. But when it appears as an archetype, one encounters the same difficulties as with anima and animus. In other words, it is quite within the bounds of possibility for a man to recognize the relative evil of his nature, but it is a rare and shattering experience for him to gaze into the face of absolute evil."[14]

We would consider Jung less than human if we did not grant him a human shadow—the horror, all the keener for such as he, of absolute evil. This is the empty terror of the extinguishing of the light of consciousness in the darkness of non-being, the Death-Death. It is the shadow of Jung's realization that, "As far as we can discern, the sole purpose of human existence is to kindle a light in the darkness of mere being,"[15] and the dark twin to the Illumination of the meaning of consciousness that he experienced when he looked out over the Athi Plains in 1926.

This is Stalking Death. It is the shadow of the *coniunctio*, the mystical marriage, or the Death-that-gives-Life, which Jung had experienced in the garden of pomegranates. It is the *disconiunctio*, so to speak, the shattering into shards, where all human births, in spirit and in substance, disappear without evidence of existence, and the Sacred Hoop of Creation is broken.

So was the act of writing a letter about Picasso at this point in the Moon Cycles, an expression of Jung's very human fears of dissolution into nothing, and his concerns about the other face of his own death? Not the light side of death that the wolverine dream had shown, but the shadow side of death, the archetypal shadow of Stalking Death. We should recall that he was all the more exposed as a man who had the courage not to take refuge in faith or belief, and who had the audacity to confront God in his unconsciousness. In a letter to Erich Neumann on January 5, 1952 he wrote, "Not in my livery, but 'naked and bare I must go down to the grave,' fully aware of the outrage my nakedness will provoke. But what is that compared with the arrogance I had to summon up in order to be able to insult God?"[16]

To not go beyond the evidence, perhaps all we can do is note that Jung's only two writings about Picasso occurred nine months before a death. His November 1932 paper on Picasso was about nine months before the "death" of Europe[17] and the death of the old Jung in the controversies of 1933-1934. His letter to Read about Picasso was nine months before his own death.

THE FRUIT OF THE MOON LODGE TREE

Jung's acceptance of the wolverine dream gave him a new lease on life; there was still more to be done. In the spring of 1959, the BBC TV program, *Face to Face*, filmed an interview of Jung with John Freeman. After seeing the interview, a London publisher wanted to publish a book that would make Jung's work accessible to the general public, so Freeman traveled to Zurich to broach the idea. Sitting in his garden at Kusnacht, Jung listened to Freeman for two hours without interruption, and then said "No," with great firmness. He had never tried to popularize his work and he wasn't sure that he could successfully do it now. Furthermore, he was old and rather tired and did not want take on such a long commitment about which he had many reservations. However, after the interview broadcast, Jung received volumes of mail and then dreamed that he was standing in a public place and addressing a multitude of people who were listening to him with rapt attention and understanding what he said.[18] This was the work that still remained—his last paper, "Approaching the Unconscious" for *Man and His Symbols*, which he began after he recovered his health in the late summer of 1960.[19] Jung was well all winter and gave himself to writing the rest of the paper, which he completed only ten days before his death.

On May 6, 1961, exactly a month before his death, while on one of his once-frequent drives in the countryside with Barbara Hannah, Jung met three wedding processions—he called them his "death wedding." He was just past the West of the Little Southeast Moon of the Big East—the Illumination and Enlightenment of the Death and Change of Images of Self. On May 17, he had another embolism that impaired his speech slightly. Ruth Bailey, an old family friend who had been on the Kenya journey with Jung, and who Jung had asked to "see him out," cared for him in the last years after Emma died. His last recorded dream, which Ruth wrote down for him a few nights before he died, was "1) He saw a big, round block of stone in a high bare place and on it was inscribed 'This shall be sign unto you of wholeness and oneness.' 2) A lot of vessels, pottery vases, on the right side of a square place. 3) A square of trees, all fibrous roots, coming up from the ground and surrounding him. There were gold threads gleaming among the roots."[20]

So it was here, in the Little Southeast Moon of the Big East, that the fear-inspiring, underground phallus in his dream at age 3 in the Little Southeast Moon of the Big South had been liberated from the unconscious, rounded out, brought into the light, and placed on high, in memory of a life's work. The block of stone is a repository of strength, and was in a place symbolizing the isolation that knowledge of the unconscious brings. The stone is the *lapis*, the Philosopher's Stone. It symbolizes endurance, like the gravestone, a symbol of what lives on after death, something that survives the outside storms and collective influences, and is the resurrected, incorruptible body.

The stone that is "set apart" is the masculine stone, and the vessel is the feminine container, or maternal womb, in which the god-man is transformed and reborn. The vessels and vases also remind us of the Egyptian canopic jars that were prepared for the souls of the dead, and in medieval mysticism, the vessel (the Grail) was seen as an image of the soul which receives divine grace. In Wolfram von Eschenbach's *Parsifal*, the Grail is replaced by a stone that has fallen from heaven, the *lapis exilis*. According to Gnostic tradition, the creator sent down a mixing vessel, or *krater*, in which those who sought spiritual transformation could be immersed. The vessel also takes us back to India in 1938 where Jung had the dream of fetching the Grail.

The legend of Merlin is also intimately associated with the Grail legend, and there are links between Jung and Merlin. It was not until 20 years after the Grail dream that Jung became acquainted with the Merlin legend, and he was astounded to learn that like Merlin, at Bollingen he had a house in the forest and a spring nearby. For Jung, Bollingen was a place of retreat and transformation, and Merlin's retreat was called an *esplumoir* (French for a place where falcons molted, and so a place of transformation).

The story of Merlin tells us that he was born of the devil and a virgin. He inherited the gift of prophecy from his mother and, from the devil, the knowledge of the past. We know that Merlin possesses traits that link him with Elijah, Jung's first personification of the wisdom of the unconscious. Merlin's legend grew in the Middle Ages as a healing of the collective split between Christ and the Antichrist, and seems to represent an intuition that reaches beyond this polarity and softens "the conflict between an absolute good and evil," by promoting the "creative act of individual ethical decision,"[21] or, we might say, integrity. Merlin is the essence of the Grail, the Catalyst at the Center that is never depleted, that heals all wounds and unites all opposites.

The legend tells that Merlin's cry could be heard in the forests after his death.[22] In 1950 and 1951 Jung carved the Bollingen Stone when he was in the Little Northeast Moon of the Big North (the place of Wisdom and Knowledge of Choices and Decisions), but he left one face bare. At the time it occurred to him to carve the words *le cri de Merlin* on the virgin face, but he never carried this out.

The alchemists from Zosimos onward have repeatedly empha-
sized, "One the procedure, one the vessel, one the stone." Reading
this backward, we can see Jung's dream as a circle. The three
images—the stone, the vessels, and the gold—stand as the three
stages of alchemical transformation. The stone is the beginning and
end of the work; the *prima materia* or the Philosopher's Stone that is
found everywhere. It is cheap and lies within the reach of all; it
unites the warring elements and contains all the opposites in a state
of undivided nature. The vessels symbolize the *albedo* (Latin, meaning "the whitening"), the integration of the anima/animus through
containment of water and emotions in the South, balancing the
extremes of becoming too cool (physical: West) or too hot (spiritual: East) so that the King and Queen, who lie in the vessel, do not get
scorched. The *albedo*, however, is not the end product of the work
because in the state of "whiteness"—a sort of abstract, ideal state—
life is not lived fully and in order to make it come alive it must have
"blood" or what the alchemists call the *rubedo*, the "redness" of life.[23]
The gold threads are the *rubedo* or *citrinitas* (Latin, meaning "the yel-
lowing"), the final procedure. The Stone has transformed itself
through the vessels into the gold of highest value.[24]

This last dream image of the gold threads intertwined with the
roots of the tree reminds us of two of Jung's experiences. First, in
the Big South Moon when he was in his mid-teens in the Little
Northwest Moon directly across the Wheel from where he had this
final dream, is Jung's alchemical fantasy where his tree of life was
inverted. He imagined an apparatus making gold from a mysterious
substance that copper roots drew from the air. Copper is the central
element of hemoglobin, the carrier of life to the cells. It is also associated with the color green, in combination with oxygen it produces
verdigris, the "blessed greenness" of the alchemists, and is the prime
metallic conductor of energy and libido. Second, is the vision in
1939, of the greenish-gold Christ at the foot of his bed that was a
symbol of the union of spiritually alive and physically dead matter.
In alchemy, the *lapis,* or Philosopher's Stone—the goal of the
work—is described as the fruit of the Sun tree and the Moon tree.

Now Jung, as the sum of the procedure, the vessel, and the stone at the beginning and the stone at the end, had transformed the experiences of his life into gold in the earth. Jung's Tree of Life had borne fruit above and below ground. The teacher Sweet Medicine says of this Tree:

"The human being is the earthly symbol of the sacred tree in animal form. This tree is called the Tree of The Shaman And Shamaness, or the Animal Tree.

"The Animal Tree represents human growth and learning. There is as much tree above the ground as there is below. The tree we see above the ground is called the Sun Lodge Tree. It represents the half of the mind we understand as being awake. The tree below the ground, which we know as the roots, is called the Moon Lodge Tree. This represents the half of the mind we experience when we are dreaming, our sleep dreams and also our daydreams."

Estchimah listened raptly. Sweet Medicine continued . . . "The Sun Lodge Tree is our conscious mind, and the Moon Lodge Tree is our subconscious mind—the shadow mind.

"The medicine people tell us we are the principal person in each of these two lodges. However one of us is male and the other is female. These twins are one principal person but have two kinds.

"In the beginning, the chiefs tell us, when we are seedlings, we are completely dependent upon the roots of the sacred tree. All of our power comes from the roots. The roots are the eyes, ears, voice and mind of the young seedling. But when the tree is adult this is reversed, and the roots are completely dependent upon that part of the tree within the sunlight.

"That portion of the tree that is below ground remembers all. Its memory goes beyond itself, its roots, into the total of the earth. But that portion of the tree that is above ground remembers only those things that it needs to grow.

"If the roots do not nourish and provide for the tree above the ground, the tree will die. And if the tree above the ground does not nourish and provide for its roots, again the tree will die."

Sweet Medicine smiled a mischievous smile and began again.

"A shaman named Buffalo Teachers told me that the Sacred Tree Above The Ground had to have a model, an image, to learn. But he went on to say that the Tree Below The Ground always transforms every model or image into the power of the earth."[25]

In *Memories* Jung writes: "Life has always seemed to me like a plant that lives on its rhizome. Its true life is invisible, hidden in the rhizome. The part that appears above the ground lasts only a single summer. Then it withers away—an ephemeral apparition. . . . Yet I have never lost a sense of something that lives and endures underneath the eternal flux. What we see is the blossom, which passes. The rhizome remains."[26]

Jung's visions in the last week before his death were largely concerned with the future of the world after his death. But Ruth Bailey said that, "During the last two days he lived in a faraway world and saw wonderful and magnificent things there, of that I am sure. He smiled often and was happy. When we sat on the terrace for the last time, he spoke of an enchanting dream he had had, he said, 'Now I know the truth down to a very little bit that is still missing. When I know this too, then I will have died.'"[27]

DROPPING THE ROBE

Jung died in the late afternoon on June 6, 1961, at the age of eighty-five years and ten months. He Dropped his Robe, walked out of his Earth Lodge, and journeyed back to the Great Round.

It remains for us to weave together the final strands of Jung's life, to see the web and hear the song. To do so we must look at Jung's death place—the Northwest of the Little Southeast Moon, and his life place, the mirror of where he died—the Southeast of the Little Northwest Moon (see figure 9, below).

If we look at what sung with his death place on previous Moon Cycles we see this: in the Big South Moon, Jung was in his death place in the Northwest of the Little Southeast Moon in June 1880 at age 4.10. Between "three and four years old" he had the dream of the underground "man-eater." In the Big West Moon, his death place was in June 1907 at age 31.10, and his first meeting with Freud was in March 1907. In the Big North Moon, on June 7, 1934, at age 58.10, he wrote the fateful letter to Göring.

If we look at his life place, in the Southeast of the Little Northwest Moons, we see that he is in the middle of his Chaotic Journeys, in early December of the particular years. In the Big South Moon, in early December 1890 when he was 15.4, it was close in time to his fantasy of the roots that made gold out of the air. In the Big West Moon, in early December 1917 at age 42.4, he was coming out of his descent into the unconscious. In the Big North Moon, in early December 1944 at age 69.4, he was ending his convalescence ten months after his heart attack.

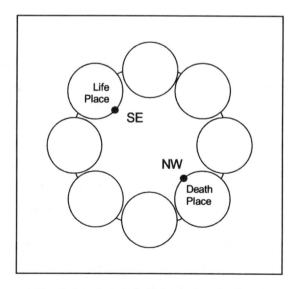

Fig 9. Jung's Death Place and Life Place

And so, Jung died in the Northwest of the Little Southeast Moon of the Big East Moon—the place of the Illumination and Enlightenment of the Laws, Cycles and Patterns of the Ancestors and Images of Self. He was looking across the Wheel toward the Southeast, facing the puzzle that had occupied his life—the Self, the Image of the Self, the mystery of his own Ancestors, and the Ancestors of us all—the collective unconscious.

Jung left behind incalculable gifts, many yet to come into collective consciousness. Edward Edinger said of Jung's Gift to the People: "Jung is the new Aion, he is the harbinger of the new aeon—what I call and what I think will in the future be called the Jungian aeon. Jung could not have perceived and summarized the content of the aeon of Pisces unless he was already outside it. . . . Jung was already in the next aeon, so to speak. Just as Christ was the first person to enter the aeon of Pisces, so Jung is the first to inaugurate the aeon of Aquarius. . . . [which] will generate individual water carriers. The numinous reality of the psyche will no longer be carried by religious communities—the church, the synagogue, or the mosque—but instead it will be carried by conscious individuals. This is the idea Jung puts forward in his notion of a continuing incarnation, the idea that individuals are to become incarnating vessels of the Holy Spirit on an ongoing basis."[28]

Laurens van der Post, who knew Jung during the last sixteen years of his life said, "I have known, perhaps, an unusual number of those who the world considered great, but Carl Gustav Jung . . . through whom the universe dreamt a dream, giving him the capacity and courage to live it . . . is almost the only one of whose greatness I am certain."[29]

With every death, there is a birth—that is Law and Pattern. Every archetypal event sends out ripples in the pool of time. Jung's life has been the subject of much biography, but the biography of Jung's death is the unseen story that endures. In 1989, when his death was on its first Big Chaotic Journey at 27 years old, the conference on the Jewish question was held. In June 2000, when his death was 39 years old and entering the Little Moon of double Death and Change, the

Red Book was released for publication. On December 6, 2001 Jung's death was 40.6 years old, in the place of triple Death and Change, and, in the West, to give birth in the place of physical form, Introspection and Intuition, and the place of Woman. But to what? That is the Mystery.

Notes

1   Ralph Waldo Emerson, "Terminus."
2   Personal communication to David Rosen from Marie-Louise von Franz, in David Rosen, *The Tao of Jung: The Way of Integrity* (London: Penguin Arkana, 1997), p. 156.
3   *MDR*, pp. 356–358.
4   *MDR*, p. 359.
5   Hannah, *Jung: His Life and Work* (New York: Putnam, 1976), p. 344.
6   Edward Edinger, *The Bible and the Psyche: Individuation Symbolism in the Old Testament* (Toronto: Inner City, 1986), p. 97.
7   Edward Edinger, *The Aion Lectures* (Toronto: Inner City, 1996), p. 78.
8   Marie-Louise von Franz, *C. G. Jung: His Myth in Our Time* (London: Hodder & Stoughton, 1975), pp. 99, 137, 263.
9   For example, the Egyptian and Tibetan Books of the Dead and the Medieval European *Ars Moriendi*.
10 *Letters* 2, p. 589.
11 *Letters* 2, p. 82.
12 *MDR*, p. 313.
13 *MDR*, p. 313.
14 *CW* 9ii, § 19.
15 *CW* 11, § 256.
16 *Letters* 2, p. 32.
17 Hitler was appointed Chancellor in January 1933, granted dictatorial powers in March 1933, and in December 1933 the National Socialist Party was "indissolubly joined to the state." In August 1934 he became Führer.
18 C. G. Jung, *Man and His Symbols* (London: Aldus, 1964), p. vi.
19 Hannah, *Jung: His Life and Work*, p. 342.
20 Hannah, *Jung: His Life and Work*, p. 347.
21 Marie-Louise von Franz, "Antichrist or Merlin?: A Problem Inherited from the Middle Ages," in *Archetypal Dimensions of the Psyche* (Boston: Shambhala, 1997), p. 29.

22 Von Franz, *C. G. Jung: His Myth in Our Time* (London: Holder & Stoughton, 1975) p. 272.

23 C. G. Jung, *C. G. Jung Speaking*, R. Hull, ed. (Princeton: Princeton University Press, 1977), pp. 228 *ff.*

24 Von Franz, *C. G. Jung: His Myth in Our Time*, p. 222 *ff.*

25 Hyemeyohsts Storm, *Song of Heyoehkah* (New York: Ballantine, 1981), pp. 76–77.

26 MDR, p. 4.

27 Gerhard Wehr, *Jung: A Biography* (Boston: Shambhala, 1987), p. 453.

28 Edward Edinger, *The Aion Lectures* (Toronto: Inner City, 1996), pp. 192–193.

29 Laurens van der Post, *Jung and the Story of Our Time*, (London: Penguin, 1976), pp. ix and 275.

CHARTING YOUR OWN
MOON CYCLES

CHARTING YOUR OWN
MOON CYCLES

R eaders may wish to chart their own Moon Cycles, using the table on pages 280–293. I would suggest that it become an ongoing project—to see the Pattern of a life takes a lifetime. Start by writing down the events, inner and outer, that correspond to the particular dates in your life, without initially bothering too much about the Medicine, or influence, of the place or the Moon. If you rephrase the Medicine of the particular Moon it may resonate better with the events you record (see pages 23–24). Keep adding to the table and over time a Pattern will appear. The Moon Cycles are useful not only in seeing what unique Pattern emerges as you look back on your engagements with life (Jung's Pattern was particularly visible around the North, and the Northwest-Southeast axis, but yours will be different), but also as a map and compass to navigate your future. The Moon Cycles are an *aide-mémoire* to the business of the soul and a reminder that "to every thing there is a season."

Age	Place	Little Moon	Big Moon	Influence	Dates	Events
0	E	C	S	Catalyst of Illumination and Enlightenment of Trust and Innocence		
0.9	S	C	S	Catalyst of double Trust and Innocence		
1.6	W	C	S	Catalyst of Death and Change of Trust and Innocence		
2.3	N	C	S	Catalyst of Wisdom and Knowledge of Trust and Innocence		
3.0	E	C	S	Illumination and Enlightenment of the Catalyst of Trust and Innocence **Little Chaotic Journey**		
3.9	S	SE	S	Double Trust and Innocence of Self-Images		
4.6	W	SE	S	Death and Change of Self-Images of Trust and Innocence		
5.3	N	SE	S	Wisdom and Knowledge of Self-Images of Trust and Innocence		
6.0	E	SE	S	Illumination and Enlightenment of Self-Images of Trust and Innocence **Little Chaotic Journey**		
6.9	S	S	S	Triple Trust and Innocence		

Age	Place	Little Moon	Big Moon	Influence	Dates	Events
7.6	W	S	S	Death and Change of double Trust and Innocence		
8.3	N	S	S	Wisdom and Knowledge of double Trust and Innocence		
9.0	E	S	S	Illumination and Enlightenment of double Trust and Innocence **Little Chaotic Journey**		
9.9	S	SW	S	Dream of double Trust and Innocence		
10.6	W	SW	S	Death and Change of the Dream of Trust and Innocence		
11.3	N	SW	S	Wisdom and Knowledge of the Dream of Trust and Innocence		
12.0	E	SW	S	Illumination and Enlightenment of the Dream of Trust and Innocence **Little Chaotic Journey**		
12.9	S	W	S	Death and Change of double Trust and Innocence		
13.6	W	W	S	Double Death and Change of Trust and Innocence		

Age	Place	Little Moon	Big Moon	Influence	Dates	Events
14.3	N	W	S	Wisdom and Knowledge of Death and Change of Trust and Innocence		
15.0	E	W	S	Illumination and Enlightenment of Death and Change of Trust and Innocence **Little Chaotic Journey**		
15.9	S	NW	S	Double Trust and Innocence of Laws and Patterns		
16.6	W	NW	S	Death and Change of Trust and Innocence of Laws and Patterns		
17.3	N	NW	S	Wisdom and Knowledge of Laws and Patterns of Trust and Innocence		
18.0	E	NW	S	Illumination and Enlightenment of Laws and Patterns of Trust and Innocence **Little Chaotic Journey**		
18.9	S	N	S	Double Trust and Innocence of Wisdom and Knowledge		
19.6	W	N	S	Death and Change of Wisdom and Knowledge of Trust and Innocence		
20.3	N	N	S	Double Wisdom and Knowledge of Trust and Innocence		

Age	Place	Little Moon	Big Moon	Influence	Dates	Events
21.0	E	N	S	Illumination and Enlightenment of Wisdom and Knowledge of Trust and Innocence **Little Chaotic Journey**		
21.9	S	NE	S	Double Trust and Innocence of Choices and Decisions		
22.6	W	NE	S	Death and Change of Trust and Innocence of Choices and Decisions		
23.3	N	NE	S	Wisdom and Knowledge of Trust and Innocence of Choices and Decisions		
24.0	E	NE	S	Illumination and Enlightenment of Choices and Decisions of Trust and Innocence **Little Chaotic Journey**		
24.9	S	E	S	Double Trust and Innocence of Illumination and Enlightenment		
25.6	W	E	S	Death and Change of Illumination and Enlightenment of Trust and Innocence		
26.3	N	E	S	Wisdom and Knowledge of the Illumination and Enlightenment of Trust and Innocence		

Age	Place	Little Moon	Big Moon	Influence	Dates	Events
27.0	E	E	S	Double Illumination and Enlightenment of Trust and Innocence **BIG CHAOTIC JOURNEY**		
27.9	S	C	W	Catalyst of Trust and Innocence of Death and Change		
28.6	W	C	W	Catalyst of double Death and Change		
29.3	N	C	W	Wisdom and Knowledge of the Catalyst of Death and Change		
30.0	E	C	W	Illumination and Enlightenment of the Catalyst of Death and Change **Little Chaotic Journey**		
30.9	S	SE	W	Trust and Innocence of the Death and Change of Self-Images		
31.6	W	SE	W	Double Death and Change of Self-Images		
32.3	N	SE	W	Wisdom and Knowledge of the Death and Change of Self-Images		
33.0	E	SE	W	Illumination and Enlightenment of the Death and Change of Self-Images **Little Chaotic Journey**		

Age	Place	Little Moon	Big Moon	Influence	Dates	Events
33.9	S	S	W	Double Trust and Innocence of Death and Change		
34.6	W	S	W	Double Death and Change of Trust and Innocence		
35.3	N	S	W	Wisdom and Knowledge of Trust and Innocence of Death and Change		
36.0	E	S	W	Illumination and Enlightenment of Trust and Innocence of Death and Change **Little Chaotic Journey**		
36.9	S	SW	W	Trust and Innocence of Death and Change of the Dream		
37.6	W	SW	W	Double Death and Change of the Dream		
38.3	N	SW	W	Wisdom and Knowledge of Death and Change of the Dream		
39.0	E	SW	W	Illumination and Enlightenment of Death and Change of the Dream **Little Chaotic Journey**		
39.9	S	W	W	Trust and Innocence of double Death and Change		

Age	Place	Little Moon	Big Moon	Influence	Dates	Events
40.6	W	W	W	Triple Death and Change		
41.3	N	W	W	Wisdom and Knowledge of double Death and Change		
42.0	E	W	W	Illumination and Enlightenment of double Death and Change **Little Chaotic Journey**		
42.9	S	NW	W	Trust and Innocence of Laws and Patterns of Death and Change		
43.6	W	NW	W	Double Death and Change of Laws and Patterns		
44.3	N	NW	W	Wisdom and Knowledge of Laws and Patterns of Death and Change		
45.0	E	NW	W	Illumination and Enlightenment of Laws and Patterns of Death and Change **Little Chaotic Journey**		
45.9	S	N	W	Trust and Innocence of Wisdom and Knowledge of Death and Change		
46.6	W	N	W	Double Death and Change of Wisdom and Knowledge		

Age	Place	Little Moon	Big Moon	Influence	Dates	Events
47.3	N	N	W	Double Wisdom and Knowledge of Death and Change		
48.0	E	N	W	Illumination and Enlightenment of Wisdom and Knowledge of Death and Change **Little Chaotic Journey**		
48.9	S	NE	W	Trust and Innocence of Choices and Decisions of Death and Change		
49.6	W	NE	W	Double Death and Change of Choices and Decisions		
50.3	N	NE	W	Wisdom and Knowledge of Choices and Decisions of Death and Change		
51.0	E	NE	W	Illumination and Enlightenment of Choices and Decisions of Death and Change **Little Chaotic Journey**		
51.9	S	E	W	Trust and Innocence of Illumination and Enlightenment of Death and Change		
52.6	W	E	W	Double Death and Change of Illumination and Enlightenment		

Age	Place	Little Moon	Big Moon	Influence	Dates	Events
53.3	N	E	W	Wisdom and Knowledge of Illumination and Enlightenment of Death and Change		
54.0	E	E	W	Double Illumination and Enlightenment of Death and Change **BIG CHAOTIC JOURNEY**		
54.9	S	C	N	Catalyst of Trust and Innocence of Wisdom and Knowledge		
55.6	W	C	N	Death and Change of the Catalyst of Wisdom and Knowledge		
56.3	N	C	N	Double Wisdom and Knowledge of the Catalyst		
57.0	E	C	N	Catalyst of Illumination and Enlightenment of Wisdom and Knowledge **Little Chaotic Journey**		
57.9	S	SE	N	Trust and Innocence of Self-Images of Wisdom and Knowledge		
58.6	W	SE	N	Death and Change of Self-Images of Wisdom and Knowledge		
59.3	N	SE	N	Double Wisdom and Knowledge of Self-Images		

Age	Place	Little Moon	Big Moon	Influence	Dates	Events
60.0	E	SE	N	Illumination and Enlightenment of Self-Images of Wisdom and Knowledge **Little Chaotic Journey**		
60.9	S	S	N	Double Trust and Innocence of Wisdom and Knowledge		
61.6	W	S	N	Death and Change of Trust and Innocence of Wisdom and Knowledge		
62.3	N	S	N	Double Wisdom and Knowledge of Trust and Innocence		
63.0	E	S	N	Illumination and Enlightenment of Trust and Innocence of Wisdom and Knowledge **Little Chaotic Journey**		
63.9	S	SW	N	Trust and Innocence of the Dream of Wisdom and Knowledge		
64.6	W	SW	N	Death and Change of the Dream of Wisdom and Knowledge		
65.3	N	SW	N	Double Wisdom and Knowledge of the Dream		

Age	Place	Little Moon	Big Moon	Influence	Dates	Events
66.0	E	SW	N	Illumination and Enlightenment of the Dream of Wisdom and Knowledge **Little Chaotic Journey**		
66.9	S	W	N	Trust and Innocence of Death and Change of Wisdom and Knowledge		
67.6	W	W	N	Double Death and Change of Wisdom and Knowledge		
68.3	N	W	N	Double Wisdom and Knowledge of Death and Change		
69.0	E	W	N	Illumination and Enlightenment of Death and Change of Wisdom and Knowledge **Little Chaotic Journey**		
69.9	S	NW	N	Trust and Innocence of Laws and Patterns of Wisdom and Knowledge		
70.6	W	NW	N	Death and Change of Laws and Patterns of Wisdom and Knowledge		
71.3	N	NW	N	Double Wisdom and Knowledge of Laws and Patterns		

Age	Place	Little Moon	Big Moon	Influence	Dates	Events
72.0	E	NW	N	Illumination and Enlightenment of Laws and Patterns of Wisdom and Knowledge **Little Chaotic Journey**		
72.9	S	N	N	Trust and Innocence of double Wisdom and Knowledge		
73.6	W	N	N	Death and Change of double Wisdom and Knowledge		
74.3	N	N	N	Triple Wisdom and Knowledge		
75.0	E	N	N	Illumination and Enlightenment of double Wisdom and Knowledge **Little Chaotic Journey**		
75.9	S	NE	N	Trust and Innocence of Choices and Decisions of Wisdom and Knowledge		
76.6	W	NE	N	Death and Change of Choices and Decisions of Wisdom and Knowledge		
77.3	N	NE	N	Choices and Decisions of double Wisdom and Knowledge		
78.0	E	NE	N	Illumination and Enlightenment of Choices and Decisions of Wisdom and Knowledge **Little Chaotic Journey**		

Age	Place	Little Moon	Big Moon	Influence	Dates	Events
78.9	S	E	N	Trust and Innocence of Illumination and Enlightenment of Wisdom and Knowledge		
79.6	W	E	N	Death and Change of Illumination and Enlightenment of Wisdom and Knowledge		
80.3	N	E	N	Illumination and Enlightenment of double Wisdom and Knowledge		
81.0	E	E	N	Double Illumination and Enlightenment of Wisdom and Knowledge **BIG CHAOTIC JOURNEY**		
81.9	S	C	E	Trust and Innocence of the Catalyst of Illumination and Enlightenment		
82.6	W	C	E	Death and Change of the Catalyst of Illumination and Enlightenment		
83.3	N	C	E	Wisdom and Knowledge of the Catalyst of Illumination and Enlightenment		
84.0	E	C	E	Illumination and Enlightenment of Choices and Decisions of Wisdom and Knowledge **Little Chaotic Journey**		
84.9	S	SE	E	Trust and Innocence of Self-Images of Illumination and Enlightenment		

Age	Place	Little Moon	Big Moon	Influence	Dates	Events
85.6	W	SE	E	Death and Change of Self-Images of Illumination and Enlightenment		
86.3	N	SE	E	Wisdom and Knowledge of Self-Images of Illumination and Enlightenment		
87.0	E	SE	E	Double Illumination and Enlightenment of Self-Images **Little Chaotic Journey**		
87.9	S	S	E	Double Trust and Innocence of Illumination and Enlightenment		
88.6	W	S	E	Death and Change of Trust and Innocence of Illumination and Enlightenment		
89.3	N	S	E	Wisdom and Knowledge of Trust and Innocence of Illumination and Enlightenment		
90.0	E	S	E	Trust and Innocence of double Illumination and Enlightenment **Little Chaotic Journey**		

BIBLIOGRAPHY

Andrews, Lynn. *Flight of the Seventh Moon: The Teaching of the Shields.* San Francisco: HarperSanFrancisco, 1984.

————. *Crystal Woman: Sisters of the Dreamtime.* New York: Warner, 1988.

Balin, Peter. *The Flight of Feathered Serpent.* Wilmot, WI: Arcana. 1978.

Beebe, John, *Integrity in Depth.* New York: Fromm, 1995.

Berry, Patricia, ed. *Fathers and Mothers.* Dallas, TX: Spring, 1990.

Billinsky, John. "Jung and Freud." *Andover Newton Quarterly* 10, 1969.

Bly, Robert. *Iron John: A Book about Men.* New York: Addison-Wesley, 1990.

Brome, Vincent. *Jung: Man and Myth.* London: Macmillan, 1978.

Carotenuto, Aldo. *A Secret Symmetry: Sabina Spielrein Between Jung and Freud.* New York: Pantheon, 1982.

————. *Eros and Pathos: Shades of Love and Suffering.* Toronto, Inner City, 1989.

Castaneda, Carlos. *Tales of Power.* New York: Simon & Schuster, 1972.

————. *The Fire From Within.* New York: Simon & Schuster, 1984.

————. *The Power of Silence.* New York: Simon & Schuster, 1987.

Charet, Francis. "Understanding Jung: Recent Biographies and Scholarship," in *Journal of Analytical Psychology,* 2000, vol. 45.

Corneau, Guy. *Absent Fathers, Lost Sons: The Search for Masculine Identity.* Boston: Shambhala, 1991.

Dodd, Dale. "Reflections on the Analytic Mirror." *Forum: Journal of the New Zealand Association of Psychotherapists* 6, 2000.

Drob, Sanford. "Jung and the Kabbalah." *History of Psychology* 2, 1999.

Edinger, Edward. *Ego and Archetype*. Boston: Shambhala, 1972.

————. *Anatomy of the Psyche: Alchemical Symbolism in Psychotherapy*. La Salle, IL: Open Court, 1985.

————. *The Bible and the Psyche: Individuation Symbolism in the Old Testament*. Toronto: Inner City, 1986.

————. *Goethe's Faust: Notes for a Jungian Commentary*. Toronto: Inner City, 1990.

————. *Transformation of the God-Image: An Elucidation of Jung's Answer to Job*. Toronto: Inner City, 1992.

————. *The Mysterium Lectures*. Toronto: Inner City, 1995.

————. *The Aion Lectures*. Toronto: Inner City, 1996.

Eliade, Mircea. *Shamanism: Archaic Techniques of Ecstasy*. Princeton: Princeton University Press, 1972.

Freud, Sigmund and Carl Jung, William McGuire, ed. *The Freud/Jung Letters*. Princeton: Princeton University Press, 1974.

Gay, Peter. *Freud: A Life for Our Time*. New York: W. W. Norton, 1988.

Grivet-Shillito, Marie-Laure. "Carl Gustav Before He Became Jung." *Journal of Analytical Psychology* 44, 1999.

Halligan, Fredrica and John Shea, eds. *The Fires of Desire: Erotic Energies and the Spiritual Quest*. New York: Crossroad, 1992.

Hannah, Barbara. *Jung: His Life and Work*. New York: Putnam, 1976.

Harms, Valerie. "As Within, So Without. Book review of Nancy Ryley, *The Forsaken Garden: Four Conversations on the Deep Meaning of Environmental Illness*." http://www.cgjungpage.org/articles/harmsreview.html.

Hartman, Gary. *History and Development of Jung's Psychology: The Early Years, 1900 to 1935*. http://www.cgjung.com/articles/hdself3.html, 1995.

Heuer, Gottfried. "Jung's Twin Brother: Otto Gross and Carl Gustav Jung." *Journal of Analytical Psychology*, 2001, vol. 46.

Hillman, James. *Insearch: Psychology and Religion*. Dallas, TX: Spring, 1967.

————. *Loose Ends*. Dallas, TX: Spring, 1975.

————. *The Myth of Analysis*. New York: Harper, 1978.

————. "Salt: A Chapter in Alchemical Psychology," in Joanne Stroud and Gail Thomas, eds. *Images of the Untouched: Virginity in Psyche, Myth and Community*. Dallas, TX: Spring, 1982.

————. *Puer Papers*. Dallas, TX: Spring, 1987.

————. "The Great Mother, Her Son, Her Hero, and the Puer," in Patricia Berry, ed. *Fathers and Mothers*. Dallas, TX: Spring, 1990.

Jaffé, Aniela. *From the Life and Work of C. G. Jung*. New York: Harper, 1971.

Jaffé, Aniela, ed. *C. G. Jung: Word and Image*. Bollingen Series XCVII, Princeton: Princeton University Press, 1979.

Jung, C. G. *The Collected Works*. Herbert Read, Michael Fordham and Gerhard Adler, eds. Princeton: Princeton University Press, 1953-1979.

————. *Man and His Symbols*. London: Aldus, 1964.

————. *Letters, Vol. 1, 1906-1950*. Gerhard Adler and Aniela Jaffé, eds. Princeton: Princeton University Press, 1973.

————. *Letters, Vol. 2, 1951-1961*. Gerhard Adler and Aniela Jaffé, eds. Princeton: Princeton University Press, 1975.

————. *C. G. Jung Speaking*. R. Hull, ed. Princeton: Princeton University Press, 1977.

————. *Dream Analysis: Notes of the Seminar Given in 1928-1930*. William McGuire, ed. Princeton: Princeton University Press, 1984.

————. *Nietzsche's Zarathustra: Notes of the Seminar Given in 1934-1939*. James Jarrett, ed. Princeton: Princeton University Press, 1988.

————. *Analytical Psychology: Notes of the Seminar Given in 1925*. William McGuire, ed. Princeton: Princeton University Press, 1989.

————. *Memories, Dreams, Reflections.* Aniela Jaffé, ed. Vintage: New York, 1989.

————. *Visions: Notes of the Seminar Given in 1930-1934.* Claire Douglas, ed. Princeton: Princeton University Press, 1997.

————. "The Letters of C. G. Jung to Sabina Spielrein." *Journal of Analytical Psychology* 46, 2001.

Kalsched, Donald. *The Inner World of Trauma: Archetypal Defenses of the Personal Spirit.* London: Routledge, 1996.

Kerr, John. *A Most Dangerous Method: The Story of Jung, Freud, & Sabina Spielrein.* London: Sinclair Stevenson, 1994.

Kirsch, James. "Jung's Transference on Freud: The Jewish Element." *American Imago* 41, no. 77, 1984.

————. "Carl Gustav Jung and the Jews: The Real Story," in Aryeh Maidenbaum and Stephen Martin, eds. *Lingering Shadows: Jungians, Freudians, and Anti-Semitism.* Boston: Shambhala, 1991.

Kirsch, Thomas. *The Jungians: A Comparative and Historical Perspective.* London: Routledge, 2000.

Klein, Melanie. *Envy and Gratitude and Other Works.* London: Hogarth, 1975.

Lothane, Zvi. "Tender love and transference: unpublished letters of C. G. Jung and Sabina Spielrein." *International Journal of Psychoanalysis,* 1999, vol. 80.

Luke, Helen. *The Voice Within: Love and Virtue in the Age of the Spirit.* New York: Crossroad, 1988.

Maidenbaum, Aryeh and Stephen Martin, eds. *Lingering Shadows: Jungians, Freudians, and Anti-Semitism.* Boston: Shambhala, 1991.

McGuire, William, ed. *The Freud/Jung Letters.* Princeton: Princeton University Press, 1974.

McLynn, Frank. *Carl Gustav Jung: A Biography.* London: Bantam, 1996.

Montagu, Ashley. *Touching: The Human Significance of the Skin* (3rd ed.). San Francisco: HarperCollins, 1986.

Moore, Robert. "Decoding the Diamond Body," in Fredrica Halligan and John Shea, eds. *The Fires of Desire: Erotic Energies and the Spiritual Quest*. New York: Crossroad, 1992.

Moore, Robert and Douglas Gillette. *King, Warrior, Magician, Lover: Rediscovering the Archetypes of the Mature Masculine*. San Francisco: HarperCollins, 1990.

Mountain Dreamer, Oriah. *Confessions of a Spiritual Thrillseeker: Medicine Teachings from the Grandmother*. Toronto: Moonfox Press, 1991.

Nietzsche, Friedrich. *Human, All Too Human: A Book for Free Spirits*. Cambridge: Cambridge University Press, 1996.

Noll, Richard. *The Jung Cult*. Princeton: Princeton University Press, 1994.

———. *The Aryan Christ: The Secret Life of Carl Jung*. New York: Random House, 1997.

Peat, David. *Synchronicity: The Bridge Between Matter and Mind*. New York: Bantam, 1987.

Rosen, David. *The Tao of Jung: The Way of Integrity*. London: Penguin Arkana, 1997.

Salman, Sherry. "Dissociation and the Self in the Magical Pre-Oedipal Field." *Journal of Analytical Psychology*, 1999, vol. 44.

Sandner, Donald. and Steven Wong. *The Sacred Heritage: The Influence of Shamanism on Analytical Psychology*. London: Routledge, 1997.

Schapira, Laurie Layton. *The Cassandra Complex: Living with Disbelief, A Modern Perspective on Hysteria*. Toronto: Inner City, 1988.

Segal, Hannah. *Introduction to the Work of Melanie Klein*. London: Hogarth, 1973.

Serrano, Miguel. *C. G. Jung and Herman Hesse: A Record of Two Friendships*. New York, Schocken, 1968.

Shamdasani, Sonu. "Why Are Jung Biographies so Bad? Review of Frank McLynn's *Carl Gustav Jung: A Biograph*.," London, *The Guardian*, 12 July 2000.

Sharp, Daryl, *C. G. Jung Lexicon*. Toronto: Inner City, 1991.

Stein, Richard. "Jung's 'Mana Personality' and the Nazi Era," in Aryeh Maidenbaum and Stephen Martin, eds. *Lingering Shadows: Jungians, Freudians, and Anti-Semitism*. Boston: Shambhala, 1991.

Stern, Paul. *C. G. Jung: The Haunted Prophet*. New York, Dell, 1976.

Storm, Hyemeyohsts. *Seven Arrows*. New York: Ballantine, 1972.

———. *Song of Heyoehkah*. New York: Ballantine, 1981.

Stroud, Joanne and Gail Thomas, eds. *Images of the Untouched: Virginity in Psyche, Myth and Community*. Dallas, TX: Spring, 1982.

Sun Bear. *The Medicine Wheel: Earth Astrology*. New York: Prentice-Hall, 1986.

Ulanov, Ann Belford. "Scapegoating: The Double Cross," in Aryeh Maidenbaum and Stephen Martin, eds. *Lingering Shadows: Jungians, Freudians, and Anti-Semitism*. Boston: Shambhala, 1991.

Ulansey, David. *The Origins of the Mithraic Mysteries*. New York: Oxford, 1989.

Van der Post, Laurens. *Jung and the Story of Our Time*. London: Penguin, 1976.

Vida, Judith. "Book review of Thomas Kirsch, *The Jungians: A Comparative and Historical Perspective*." *Journal of Analytical Psychology*, 2001, vol. 46.

Von Franz, Marie-Louise. *The Interpretation of Fairytales*. Boston: Shambhala, 1996.

———. *Patterns of Creativity Mirrored in Creation Myths*. Dallas, TX: Spring, 1972.

———. *C. G. Jung: His Myth in Our Time*. London: Hodder & Stoughton, 1975.

———. *Time: Rhythm and Repose*. London: Thames and Hudson, 1978.

———. *Alchemy: An Introduction to the Symbolism and the Psychology*. Toronto: Inner City, 1980.

———. *On Divination and Synchronicity: The Psychology of Meaningful Chance*. Toronto: Inner City, 1980.

———. *Projection and Recollection in Jungian Psychology: Reflections of the Soul*. La Salle, IL: Open Court, 1980.

———. *Puer Aeternus: A Psychological Study of the Adult Struggle with the Paradise of Childhood*. Santa Monica, CA: Sigo, 1981.

———. *Archetypal Dimensions of the Psyche*. Boston: Shambhala, 1997.

———. *On Dreams and Death: A Jungian Interpretation*. La Salle, IL: Open Court, 1998.

Von Franz, Marie-Louise and James Hillman. *Lectures on Jung's Typology*. Dallas: TX, Spring, 1971.

Wehr, Gerhard. *Jung: A Biography*. Boston: Shambhala, 1987.

———. *An Illustrated Biography of C. G. Jung*. Boston: Shambhala, 1989.

Weininger, Otto. *Melanie Klein: From Theory to Reality*. London: Karnac, 1992.

———. *View from the Cradle: Children's Emotions in Everyday Life*. London: Karnac, 1993.

———. *Being and Not Being: Clinical Applications of the Death Instinct*. London: Karnac, 1996.

Wickes, Frances. *The Inner World of Choice*. Englewood Cliffs, NJ: Prentice-Hall, 1963.

Wilson, Colin. *C. G. Jung: Lord of the Underworld*. London: Aquarian, 1984.

Winnicott, Donald. "Review of *Memories, Dreams, Reflections*." *International Journal of Psychoanalysis*, 1964, vol. 45.

Wyly, James. "Jung and Picasso." *Quadrant*, 1987, vol. 20, no. 2.

Zabriskie, Philip. "Shadows and Light: Closing Reflections on Jung and Jungian Psychology," in Aryeh Maidenbaum and Stephen Martin, eds. *Lingering Shadows: Jungians, Freudians, and Anti-Semitism*. Boston: Shambhala, 1991.

Zoja, Luigi. *Growth and Guilt: Psychology and the Limits of Development*. London: Routledge, 1995.

INDEX